Margaret Helliwell

unter Mitarbeit von
Philipp Fehrenbach
Petra Lehmann
Petra Veit
Marco Zimmermann
und der Verlagsredaktion

5th edition

crossover

1

Ausgabe Baden-Württemberg
Ein Lehrwerk für berufliche Gymnasien

KLASSE 11

Cornelsen

Verfasserin:	Margaret Helliwell
Berater/Beraterinnen:	Philipp Fehrenbach, Nürtingen
	Petra Lehmann, Neuried
	Petra Veit, Stuttgart
	Marco Zimmermann, Geislingen
Redakteur:	Chris Caridia
Wortverzeichnisse:	Oliver Busch
Redaktionelle Mitarbeit:	Oliver Busch, Megan Hadgraft, Valentin Olbrich
Projektleitung:	Shaunessy Ashdown
Bildredaktion:	Simone Conrad, Gertha Maly
Gesamtgestaltung und Coverbild:	Klein & Halm Grafikdesign, Berlin
Illustrationen:	Oxford Designers & Illustrators

Zum Band 1 von Ausgabe Baden-Württemberg sind ebenfalls erhältlich:

Workbook	ISBN 978-3-06-451131-6
Interaktives Workbook für mobile Endgeräte	ISBN 978-3-06-451470-6 (erhältlich auf cornelsen.de zur Nutzung in der Scook-App)
Handreichungen für den Unterricht mit Unterrichtsmanager (UM) und zwei Audio-CDs	ISBN 978-3-06-451136-1
Unterrichtsmanager (UM) als Download	ISBN 978-3-06-451140-8
Vokabeltrainer-App für Android, Apple und Windows	In dem jeweiligen App-Store

Soweit in diesem Lehrwerk Personen fotografisch abgebildet sind und ihnen von der Redaktion fiktive Namen, Berufe, Dialoge und Ähnliches zugeordnet oder diese Personen in bestimmte Kontexte gesetzt werden, dienen diese Zuordnungen und Darstellungen ausschließlich der Veranschaulichung und dem besseren Verständnis des Inhalts.

www.cornelsen.de

Die Webseiten Dritter, deren Internetadressen in diesem Lehrwerk angegeben sind, wurden vor Drucklegung sorgfältig geprüft. Der Verlag übernimmt keine Gewähr für die Aktualität und den Inhalt dieser Seiten oder solcher, die mit ihnen verlinkt sind.

1. Auflage, 3. Druck 2018

Alle Drucke dieser Auflage sind inhaltlich unverändert und können im Unterricht nebeneinander verwendet werden.

© 2016 Cornelsen Schulverlage GmbH, Berlin
© 2017 Cornelsen Verlag GmbH, Berlin

Druck: Firmengruppe APPL, aprinta Druck, Wemding

ISBN 978-3-06-451129-3
ISBN 978-3-06-451181-1 (E-Book)

PEFC zertifiziert
Dieses Produkt stammt aus nachhaltig bewirtschafteten Wäldern und kontrollierten Quellen.
www.pefc.de
PEFC/04-32-0928

Vorwort

Crossover 1 – 5th edition, Ausgabe Baden-Württemberg ist ein Lehrwerk für Klasse 11 an beruflichen Gymnasien. Voraussetzung für die Arbeit mit dem Buch ist der Mittlere Schulabschluss. Das Lehrwerk deckt die grundlegenden Anforderungen der Stufe B1/B1+ des Europäischen Referenzrahmens ab; Band 2 führt zu Stufe B2 und teilweise C1.

Crossover 1 bietet eine Fülle von Materialien, die es den Lernenden ermöglichen, ihre Kenntnisse aus der Mittelstufe zu festigen und zu erweitern. Die authentischen Texte verschiedener Herkunft, denen *Warm-up activities* als Einstieg vorangestellt sind, behandeln aktuelle und relevante Themen. Die Erarbeitung geschieht über vielfältige Textverständnisaufgaben, die unter der Rubrik *Working with the text* zusammengefasst sind.

Bei den Textverständnisaufgaben wurde darauf geachtet, bereits in Stufe 11 methodisch auf die Anforderungen der Abiturprüfung vorzubereiten. Zahlreiche mit dem Verweis **EXAM PREPARATION** gekennzeichnete Aufgabenstellungen, unterstützt durch zwei schriftliche **Musterprüfungen**, eine Kommunikationsprüfung, sowie einen kurzen Leitfaden im Anhang, gewöhnen die Lernenden so schon an die relevanten Aufgabenformen.

Ebenso wurde auch vorbereitendes Material für die übrigen Teile der Abiturprüfung wie Textproduktion, Kommunikationsprüfung, Präsentationsprüfung sowie die zentrale Klassenarbeit Hörverstehen, jeweils ergänzt durch Querverweise zum Anhang, in den Band eingearbeitet. So sind die Lernenden gleich zu Beginn der Qualifikationsphase mit den Anforderungen vertraut und wissen mit den Prüfungsaufgaben umzugehen.

Andere Rubriken sind dem Aufbau des Wortschatzes (*Working with words*), der Festigung grammatischer Strukturen (*Looking at language*), der Entwicklung mündlicher Sprachkenntnisse (*Class debate*, *Role-play*), der Sprachmittlung (*Mediation*) und anderen Schlüsselfertigkeiten gewidmet.

Neu in der 5th edition ist die Hervorhebung von Kompetenzen in der Rubrik **COMPETENCE TRAINING**, in der sowohl prüfungsrelevante Fertigkeiten als auch Lerntechniken ausführlich beschrieben und intensiv trainiert werden.

Ebenfalls neu in der 5th edition sind die mit **Challenge!** gekennzeichneten Übungen für leistungsstarke bzw. schnelle Lerner.

In der Randspalte des Buches finden sich durchgehend Querverweise zum Anhang:
- Der Buchstabe **L** verweist auf den Teil **Lernstrategien**, der einen handlichen Leitfaden mit Lernhilfen zu allen wichtigen Fertigkeiten enthält.
- Der Buchstabe **G** verweist auf die **Grammar summary**, in der die wesentlichen Bereiche der Grammatik übersichtlich zusammengefasst sind.
- Die Kästchen **EXAM PREPARATION** bzw. **ZENTRALE KLASSENARBEIT** kennzeichnen Aufgaben, die auf die Anforderungen der neuen Abiturprüfung vorbereiten, und verweisen auf die Übersicht zur Abiturprüfung im Anhang.

Ebenso in der Randspalte finden sich Übersetzungen anspruchsvoller **Vokabeln**. Es empfiehlt sich, die fett gedruckten Wörter in den aktiven Wortschatz aufzunehmen. Die nicht fett gedruckten Wörter dienen lediglich zum Verständnis des jeweiligen Textes.
Zum Nachschlagen stehen umfangreiche Wörterverzeichnisse zur Verfügung. Die **Unit word list** enthält ausschließlich Wörter für den aktiven Wortschatz und bietet den Lernenden die Wahl zwischen Definitionen und Übersetzungen, um sich diese Vokabeln möglichst effektiv einzuprägen.

Nicht zu vergessen: die hintere Umschlagklappe. Im Unterricht lässt sie sich für den mündlichen Gebrauch ausklappen, die eingeklappte Seite hilft bei den Hausaufgaben.

Das Crossover-Team hofft, dass die Arbeit mit dem Buch Freude bereitet und in motivierender und herausfordernder Weise auf Begegnungen mit der englischsprachigen Welt vorbereitet.

INHALT

TOPIC 3 The media today

TOPIC 4 The state we're in – USA and UK

ANHANG

Young people in Britain and America

TEXT 1   What teens worry about

WARM UP . . . .

L ▶ Lesen schwieriger Texte
Grobverständnis (p. 134)

1 Work in small groups. List eight things that teenagers might worry about. Compare your list with another group. Then skim the article below to see if any of your ideas are in it.

1.02

¹ **adolescent** *Jugendliche/r, Heranwachsende/r*
³ **support** *ernähren, versorgen*
⁵ **adolescence** *Pubertät*
⁶ **anxious** *verunsichert, sorgenvoll*
⁷ **demand** *Anforderung*
¹⁵ **bullying** *Mobbing*
¹⁶ **play truant** *die Schule schwänzen*
¹⁶ **tormentor** *Peiniger*
²² **issue** *Problem, Streitfrage, Thema*
²³ **assert** *geltend machen, durchsetzen*
²⁵ **nag** *meckern, nörgeln*
³¹ **break up with sb** *sich von jdm trennen*

Stress factors for teens

Many adults think that adolescents have relatively carefree lives because they don't have to work and support a family. But they are wrong! Adolescence can be an uncomfortable and anxious phase. Most teens have many demands on their time and energy – school, family, friends, hobbies and part-time jobs. Here are some of the main stress factors that teenagers have.   5 ... 10

School
Teens worry about how to manage all their coursework and prepare for exams. They may become depressed because they can't do as well as they'd like to, or their parents or teachers expect them to. Bullying can also be a problem and may lead to a young person playing truant to avoid his or her tormentors.   15

Identity
Adolescence is a time when teenagers are searching for their own identity. They ask themselves: Who am I? What are my strengths and weaknesses? What kind of person do I want to be? How can I plan my future? At the same time, teenagers want to identify with a group and friendships are extremely important to them.   20

Family issues
Conflicts may arise at home as adolescents begin to assert their independence. Teenagers often feel completely misunderstood by their parents and other family members. They may feel that parents are always nagging them about their clothes or friends at a time when they want to experiment and be free to make their own choices – and their own mistakes.   25

Friends
During teenage years friendships often become more important than family. With friends, teens can not only have fun, they can talk about things they can't discuss with their parents. Not having friends or breaking up with a friend can be traumatic for a teenager.   30

Peer pressure

Adolescents are often worried about how they measure up to their peers in terms
of looks, academic achievement and popularity. The pressure to conform may lead
to them doing things that they don't really want to do simply to be accepted. They
may, for example, start drinking alcohol, taking drugs or bullying. Saying no to
peer pressure is difficult.

Body image

The media have a powerful influence on young people and many teens have
unrealistic expectations of themselves, based on the actors and singers they see in
TV shows and advertising. Both boys and girls feel the pressure to live up to ideals
of beauty that can only make them feel inadequate. Dissatisfaction with their own
appearance can lead, among other things, to unhealthy eating habits and even to
serious eating disorders.

Romantic relationships

Love is an especially big concern for teenagers. Dealing with the drama of deep
emotions can be highly stressful for both girls and boys. Many teens who are
looking for a partner worry about being attractive enough to find a boyfriend or
girlfriend. Teens who have partners may have problems within the relationship.

Money

Teens want to buy things and have fun. They may feel frustrated at being totally
dependent on their parents for pocket money, and want to get a part-time job. But
fitting in work with classes and homework may be an additional stress factor.

(512 words)

[33] **peer** *Gleichaltrige/r*
[34] **measure up to sb** *jdm gewachsen sein, mit jdm mithalten (können)*
[34] **in terms of** *hinsichtlich, bezüglich*
[35] **achievement** *Leistung(en)*
[35] **conform** *sich anpassen*
[42] **live up to sth** *einer Sache gerecht werden*
[43] **inadequate** *unzulänglich*
[43] **dissatisfaction** *Unzufriedenheit*
[45] **eating disorder** *Essstörung*
[47] **deal with sth** *mit etw umgehen*
[54] **additional** *zusätzlich*

WORKING WITH THE TEXT

2 Answer the following questions about the text using your own words as far as
possible.

1 Why do some teenagers become depressed about school?
2 Why might a teenager play truant?
3 Which choices that teenagers make may lead to family conflict?
4 Why are friendships often more important than family?
5 What negative results can peer pressure have?
6 How do TV shows and advertising make young people feel inadequate?
7 How can a part-time job be an additional stress factor for a teenager?

3 Decide if the statements about the text are true or false. Give reasons for your
decisions in complete German sentences.

1 Finding their own identity is more important to teenagers than finding friends.
2 Teenagers should listen more to their parents if they want to avoid making
mistakes.
3 Unachievable ideals can lead teenagers to unhealthy behaviour.
4 Once teenagers find a partner, they have fewer problems.

CHALLENGE!

EXAM PREPARATION
Leseverstehen (p.149)

WORKING WITH WORDS

4 **a** Find words in the text with these prefixes:

dis- | in- | mis- | un-

b Find words in the text with these suffixes:

-al | -ation | -ful | - ment | -ness | -ship

c Form ten words by adding a prefix from column A and a suffix from column C to the words in column B. Use each word in column B only once.

Example: *dis + agree + ment = disagreement*

A	B	C
dis-	agree	-al
in-	appoint	-ful
mis-	corrupt	-ible
un-	courage	-ing
	emotion	-ment
	faith	
	employ	
	music	
	spell	
	understand	

d Use words you found in 4a–c to complete the sentences.

1 It is totally ... to want to look like a TV star.
2 There was a ... and I got the wrong date.
3 Passing your exam was a great ...
4 My girlfriend and I had a terrible ... and now we aren't speaking.
5 Our teacher gave us some ... exercises to do for homework.
6 What are your strengths and ...?
7 You can avoid ... if your ... are not too high.

CHALLENGE!

e Write sentences using one of these words in each of them.

discouragement | incorruptible | misspelling

5 Fill in the missing prepositions. Then scan the text to check your answers.

1 Teens don't like being totally dependent ... their parents.
2 Sandy was depressed after she broke ... ... her boyfriend.
3 My mother is always nagging me ... my untidy room.
4 Teens have just as many demands ... their time as adults do.
5 I hope I can live ... ... my parents' expectations.
6 Advertising has a big influence ... many people.
7 Our school is one of the best ... terms ... academic achievement.
8 Dissatisfaction ... your body image can lead ... serious problems.

LOOKING AT LANGUAGE

6 Complete the text with the simple present tense of the verb in brackets and the adverbs in the correct order.

G ▶ The simple present (p. 152)

G ▶ Adjectives and adverbs (pp. 163–164)

Young people … ¹(suffer) from a lot more stress than adults … ² (realize usually). One of the main sources of stress … ³ (be) school. Teens … ⁴ (worry often) about their coursework and their exams, and they … ⁵ (be sometimes) afraid that they … ⁶ (not come) up to their parents' expectations. Young people … ⁷ (report also) that their parents … ⁸ (not understand always) that they … ⁹ (want) to make their own choices. It … ¹⁰ (not be always) helpful when parents … ¹¹ (criticize) their kid's clothes or friends. Teens … ¹² (not want) to be like their parents. They … ¹³ (prefer usually) to be like their peers. Unfortunately, a peer group … ¹⁴ (not have always) have a positive influence. Peer pressure … ¹⁵ (lead sometimes) to teens doing things that … ¹⁶ (be clearly) wrong.

COMPETENCE TRAINING: TAKING NOTES WHILE LISTENING

TIP
It is important to take notes while listening. You usually need to write fast, so you should concentrate on the main information and write key words and phrases. Don't write whole sentences. Develop your own shorthand. Here are some examples:

Signs:	+ *and*	£ *pound*	= *the same as*
	< *less than*	→ *becomes, will be*	♂ *man*
Abbreviations:	e. g. *for example*	cm *centimetres*	mph *miles per hour*
	a. m. *morning*	etc. *et cetera*	w *with* w/o *without*
Short forms	sch *school*	hw *homework*	Jan *January* mins *minutes*

7 What do these abbreviations and symbols stand for?

anon | asap | ATM | def | hrs | Tues | p.m. | ≠ | ♀ | >

LISTENING

 1.03

8 **a** Listen to eight young people talking about things that concern them and decide which of the headings in the text they refer to.

    b Listen again and make notes in English about their problems, then write up your notes about each person in German.

L ▶ Das Hörverständnis üben (pp. 137–138)

SPEAKING

9 Work with a partner or in a small group. What advice would you give to a friend who has problems 1–8 below? Use a different phrase from the box for each piece of advice.

Giving advice

If I were you, I'd …
If I were in that situation, I'd …
If had that problem, I would …
My suggestion / advice / recommendation is …
In my experience … works really well.
… is worth a try.

The sooner you … the better.
I can't recommend … strongly enough.
Have you thought about …?
You have no choice but to …
One thing you could do is …
You'd better …

1 I'm being bullied at school.
2 My mother is always nagging me about my clothes.
3 I find it hard to get up in the mornings and I'm often late for school.
4 I think my girlfriend/boyfriend is seeing another guy/girl.
5 My parents don't like my friends.
6 My parents don't respect my privacy and look into my computer when I'm not at home.
7 My best friend has started smoking and wants me to start, too.
8 I'm addicted to computer games.

DESCRIBING A CARTOON

L ▶ Interpretation von Bildern und Karikaturen (pp. 145–146)

 EXAM PREPARATION
Kommunikationsprüfung (p. 150)

10 Work with a partner.
Produce an uninterrupted one-minute discourse (in monologue) based on the cartoon below.

Today's youth and their challenges

ROLE PLAY

11 Work in pairs. Student A takes the role of a parent who does not like the behaviour of her teenage son/daughter. Student B takes the role of the teenage son/daughter who feels misunderstood.

L ▶ Interaktion (pp. 147–148)

Student A: Study the role card below.
Student B: Study the role card on page 133.

Then role-play the discussion. Try to find a solution to your problems.

Student A

- You don't like your son's/daughter's hair/clothes/friends.

- You worry about the impression your son/daughter makes on his/her teachers.

- You buy your son's/daughter's clothes and school books and pay for any large expenses. Therefore you think his/her pocket money is adequate.

- You don't think your son/daughter does enough school work.

Useful language:

Look, there's something we need to talk about.

I'm a bit worried about …

I don't want to tell you what to wear / who to be friends with, but …

I only want the best for you.

Can we discuss this calmly?

Listen, how about this for an idea/ a compromise/deal?

Couldn't you …? Why don't you …?

WRITING

12 Work in groups. You are going to write a leaflet giving teenagers tips on how to survive their teenage years.

**HANDS-ON
TASK**

1 Decide what information you want to include in the leaflet. Look at the headings in the article *Stress factors for teens* to help you with some ideas.
2 Write your leaflet. When you have finished, choose a group speaker to present your leaflet to the class.

TEXT 2   Education today in the USA

WARM UP

1 Work with a partner. In three minutes pick out as many words as possible from the word cloud. Make a list and add the German equivalents. Use a dictionary if necessary.

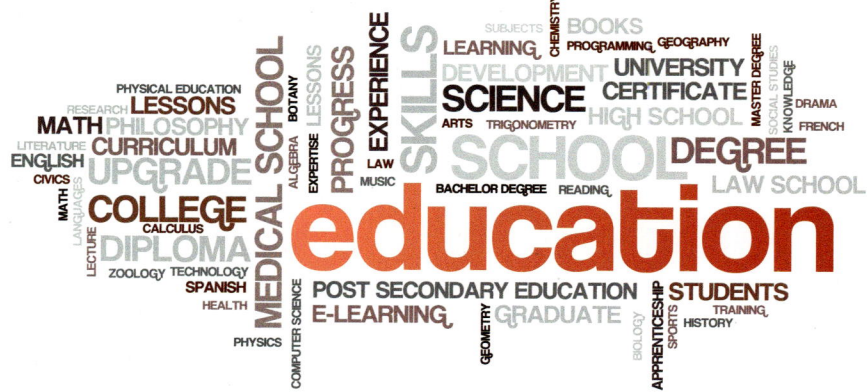

2 Before you read the text below, read the Info box and explain in your own words how schools in the USA are funded.

0 funding *Finanzierung*

1 **public school** *staatliche Schule (US)*

1 federal *Bundes-*

2 **property** *Grund und Boden, Eigentum*

5 **be available** *zur Verfügung stehen*

8 **hire sb** *jdn einstellen*

9 **sophisticated** *modern, technisch ausgereift*

INFO

School funding in the USA

Public school funding in the United States comes from federal, state and local sources. Nearly half the funding comes from property taxes. Property tax is a tax paid to the local government and is based on the value of the property (house, land, etc.) you own. This means that wealthy neighbourhoods pay higher taxes and there is more money available for schools – about $15,000 per student per year. In poorer neighbourhoods where property is less expensive, taxes are much lower, so funding for schools in those districts is lower – often less than $4,000 per student per year. Better funded schools can afford to hire better qualified teachers and have smaller classes. They can make more books and sophisticated equipment available to pupils. Thus, students in poorer districts do not receive the same quality of education as those from wealthier neighbourhoods. 10

1 apply *gelten*

8 **drop** *sinken, (zurück)fallen*

1.04

What has gone wrong with our schools?

The best way to get on in life is through education. Yet although that applies in the USA as much as anywhere else, something is going badly wrong, according to a recent survey by the Organisation for Economic Cooperation and Development (OECD).

The survey shows that Russia now has a higher percentage of people with a university education than any other industrialized country. This position was once held by the US. Until a few years ago, the US took second place in terms of the percentage of the whole population with a college degree. Now we have dropped to fifth place. With a figure of 42 per cent among 25- to 34-year-olds we rank only 12th. – South Korea is top of the league with 65 per cent. 10

Parents all over the world are usually anxious to give their kids a better education than they had themselves, yet about one third of young Americans today have had less education than their parents. Only five per cent of young people whose parents didn't graduate from high school make it through college, far fewer than in other wealthy countries, where the average is 23 per cent.

America has always had a fine record for mass education. By the mid-1880s the majority of white children had access to free elementary education, and by the 1930s the majority of children were attending high school. By contrast, Britain excelled at providing first-rate education only for an elite, and as late as 1957 only nine per cent of 17-year-olds were in school.

So what has gone wrong with our schools? Education has been a victim of the global financial crisis, and the OECD findings seem to be further evidence of the growing gap between rich and poor in our country. Education budgets have been drastically cut, and since the system is, to a large extent, dependent on local property taxes, rich kids in the suburbs, who need the least help, have well-equipped schools with smaller classes, while poor inner-city kids, who desperately need a decent education in order to achieve social mobility and move up and out, have to make do with large classes in broken-down schools that lack resources.

Educationally the US is letting its young people down. American industry is crying out for skilled workers, and young people must be prepared for the future and equipped with the skills that will take them from the classroom to the workplace. This isn't happening.   (409 words)

11 **anxious to do sth** *darauf erpicht sein, etw zu tun*
14 **graduate** *einen Schlulabschluss machen*
17 **access** *Zugang*
21 **victim** *Opfer*
22 findings *Ergebnisse*
22 **evidence** *Beweis(e), Nachweis(e)*
24 to a large extent *weitgehend*
26 **equipped** *ausgestattet*
26 inner-city *in der Innenstadt*
26 desperately *dringend*
27 decent *ordentlich*
28 lack sth *etw nicht haben*
28 **resource** *Ressource, Geldmittel*
30 **skilled worker** *Facharbeiter/in*
31 **skill** *Fertigkeit, Fähigkeit*

WORKING WITH THE TEXT

3 **Read the text and choose the most suitable phrase to complete the sentences.**

1 The writer tells us that the US education system ...
   a is one of the best in the world.
   b has improved compared to the 19th century.
   c does not offer the same opportunities to everyone.

2 The number of people with a university education is highest in ...
   a South Korea.
   b Russia.
   c Britain.

3 ... of young Americans are not as well educated as their parents.
   a Five per cent
   b 23 per cent
   c 30 per cent

4 The OECD education report shows that ...
   a the US used to have a better ranking in education.
   b South Korea has the best education system in the world.
   c the rich are getting richer and the poor are getting poorer.

5 The writer strongly criticizes ...
   a the quality of elitist education in the Britain.
   b the decline of mass education in the US.
   c the way the US education system is financed.

L ▶ Lesen schwieriger Texte
Suche nach Einzelinformationen
(pp. 134–135)

LOOKING AT LANGUAGE

G ▶ Adjectives and adverbs
(pp. 163–164)

4 a Complete the box with adjectives or adverbs from the text.

Adjective	bad	desperate	drastic	educational	...	...
Adverb	...	...	...	...	locally	recently

b Use the correct word from 4a to complete the sentences.

1 We have a subscription for a(n) ... magazine for our children.
2 Some inner-city children are... disadvantaged and ... need better schools.
3 Society has changed ... over the last fifty years.
4 The shop sells only ... grown fruit and vegetables.
5 I think I was ... advised by my bank.
6 The US education system has suffered ... cuts in the budget.
7 ... I have sent off twenty job applications and I'm ... to find a job.

5 a Find the correct words in the text to complete the sentences.

1 Until ... years ago, the US took second place.
2 About one third of young Americans today have had ... education than their parents.
3 ... young people make it through college than in other wealthy countries.
4 Rich kids in the suburbs need ... help.

b Complete the table.

	Comparative	Superlative
(a) little	less	...
(a) few	...	...

c Complete the sentences with words from the table.

1 Our teacher gave us very ... homework this week. It was a lot ... than last week.
2 ... students graduated this year than last year. The school had the ... graduates ever.
3 We get so much homework, I have ... time for other things.
4 I don't like living in New York because I have ... friends there.
5 Mark speaks very ... English, Joe speaks even ... and I speak ...
6 The ESC song I liked best got the ... votes.
7 To make a good salad dressing you need ... vinegar, ... spoonfuls of olive oil and ... salt and pepper.

WORKING WITH WORDS

6 Find phrasal verbs in the text for the underlined German words and then translate the sentences into English.

1 Ich muss leider mit sehr wenig Taschengeld <u>auskommen</u>.
2 Ich war enttäuscht, weil meine Freunde mich <u>im Stich gelassen haben</u>.
3 Um im Leben <u>weiterzukommen</u>, braucht man Energie und Ehrgeiz.
4 Menschen brauchen Bildung, um in der Gesellschaft <u>aufzusteigen</u>.

CHALLENGE!   5 Unsere Firma <u>braucht dringend</u> neue Mitarbeiter.

7 Use a dictionary to find out the meanings of these words from the US education system. Explain their meanings in English.

CHALLENGE!

1 freshman   4 senior   6 valedictorian
2 sophomore   5 major (n.)   7 Ivy League
3 junior

INTERNET RESEARCH

8 Read the Info box then research on the internet and find the answers to the questions below.

HANDS-ON
TASK

INFO

The Organisation for Economic Cooperation and Development (OECD) aims to improve the economic and social well-being of people around the world. Within the organisation, governments can work together to share experience, look for solutions to common
5 problems and coordinate international policies in economic, environmental and social issues. The organisation looks at and reports on issues that directly affect people's daily lives, like how much tax they pay, how much leisure time they have, and how different countries' school systems prepare their young people for modern life. Every three years the OECD publishes the Programme for International Student Assessment (PISA), a
10 worldwide study of 15-year-old pupils' performance in maths, science and reading.

² **well-being** *Wohl, Wohlergehen*
⁹ **assessment** *Beurteilung*

1 How many countries are members of the OECD?
2 When was the OECD founded?
3 Name two European and two other countries which were founder members.
4 Where are the OECD's headquarters?
5 What are the official languages of the OECD?
6 When was the PISA study first carried out?

PROJECT

Education in the USA

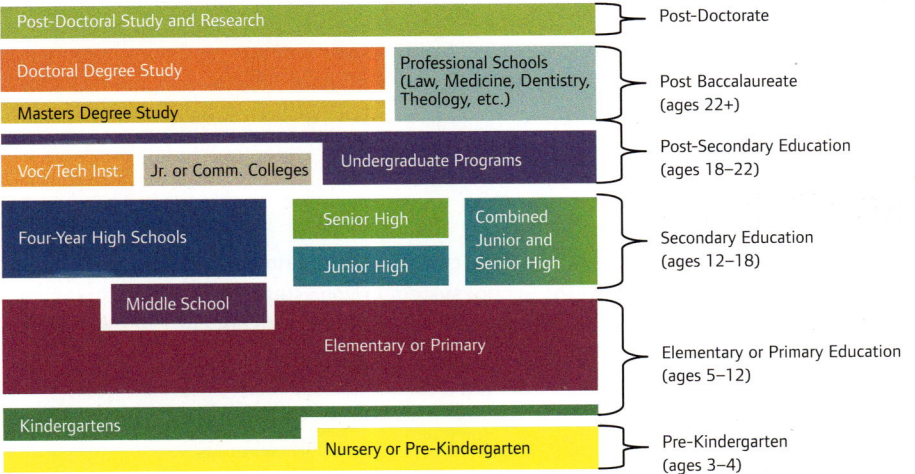

Source: http://www.isss.umn.edu/publications/USEducation/2.pdf

HANDS-ON
TASK

9 a Look at the chart on page 15 showing the school system for primary, secondary and post-secondary education in the United States. Make a similar chart in English showing the German school system in your state. Use vocabulary from the Info box below to help you.

INFO

It is difficult to find direct translations for school types and qualifications because the systems in the USA, the UK and Germany are different. However, here are some of the nearest equivalents.

Allgemeine Hochschulreife (Abitur)	*German university entrance qualification*
Berufliches Gymnasium	*vocational grammar school (BE)*
Berufsschule, berufsbildende Schule	*vocational college (BE), vocational school (AE)*
Fachhochschulreife	*German higher education entrance qualification*
Gesamtschule	*comprehensive school (BE), high school (AE)*
Grundschule	*primary school (BE and AE), elementary school (AE)*
Gymnasium	*grammar school (BE)*
Hauptschule	*No equivalent in UK and USA – it could be described as a general level secondary school (BE) or general level high school (AE)*
Werkrealschule	*secondary technical school*
Mittlere Reife, Realschulabschluss	*General Certificate of Secondary Education (BE) 10th grade school leaving certificate (AE)*
Realschule	*secondary modern school (BE – but almost non-existent today – it could be described as a higher level secondary school.)*
Sekundarstufe	*secondary education (BE), high school (AE)*

b Give a two-minute talk about your education so far, your plans for the future and the qualifications you hope to achieve.

COMPETENCE TRAINING: THE WRITING PROCESS

L ▶ Einen Text sinnvoll gliedern (pp. 142–143)

TIP
Before you write, make a three-part outline of your text:
Introduction: State your topic and your opinion.
Development: Main ideas with examples.
Conclusion: Restate your opinion with a summary of reasons.

After you have written, check your draft for:
Ideas: Are they logical? Can you add any more?
Language: Carefully check and correct vocabulary, grammar and spelling.

C ▶ Proofreading (p. 120)

Finally, write a clean copy of your final version.

10 Write an article for the school magazine comparing the primary and secondary school system in the US with the school system in your state. In your opinion, what are the advantages and disadvantages of each system? Use some of the following words and phrases:

both … and | compared to | in contrast to | different from | one of the main differences | on the one hand …, on the other … | unlike | whereas

TEXT 3   Teens and sleep

L ▶ Interpretation von Bildern und Karikaturen (pp. 145–146)

WARM UP

1 Work with a partner. Describe the photograph. What do you think will happen next? What will the teacher and the student say?

2 Ask and answer the questions:

1 What time do you usually go to bed?
2 What time do you have to get up for school?
3 How many hours sleep do you get on average? Is that enough for you? Why / Why not?
4 Have you ever fallen asleep in the classroom or in a bus or train on your way to school? What happened?

The teen who woke up her school

1.05

On a typical school night, Jilly Dos Santos was lucky if she got four to six hours of sleep. Even when she finished her homework early, she often didn't feel tired enough to fall asleep. So when her school board proposed switching her Columbia, Missouri, high school's start time from 7.50 a.m. to 7.20 a.m., she was outraged.
5 "I thought it was the worst idea I'd ever heard," she says.

Fired up, Jilly used social media to encourage other students to join her in speaking up at the next school board meeting, and she started an online petition. Then, with the help of another student, she plastered more than 100 posters on school walls and emailed teachers to spread the word. The fight was on!

10 Jilly wasn't alone – once she started her fight, she became part of a growing movement to start school later. Currently, about 43 percent of public high schools in the U.S. start before 8 a.m., which is earlier than at most workplaces. But now, hundreds of middle schools, high schools, and school districts in 41 different states have pushed back their start times, and the issue has made headlines in
15 national newspapers and magazines.

[3] school board *Schulbehörde*
[3] **propose** *vorhaben, vorschlagen*
[4] **outraged** *empört*
[6] fired up *aufgebracht*
[6] **encourage** *ermutigen*
[8] plaster *kleben, kleistern*
[11] **currently** *derzeit*
[14] push back *(nach hinten) verschieben*

¹⁷ **hardwired** *programmiert, veranlagt*

²⁰ **growth** *Wachstum*

²¹ **tissue** *Gewebe*

²³ **course** *strömen*

²⁶ **kick in** *anfangen zu wirken*

²⁷ **drowsy** *schläfrig*

²⁸ **schedule** *Zeitplan*

³⁰ **squeeze in** *einschieben, hineinzwängen*

³⁰ **on average** *im Durchschnitt*

³¹ **dig into sth** *sich intensiv mit etw beschäftigen, sich auf etw stürzen*

³² **confidence** *Selbstvertrauen, Zuversicht*

³⁶ **rest** *Ruhe*

³⁶ **alert** *aufmerksam*

³⁷ **process** *verarbeiten*

³⁸ **exhausted** *erschöpft*

³⁹ **boost** *heben, erhöhen*

³⁹ **mood** *Stimmung*

³⁹ **lower** *senken, reduzieren*

³⁹ **anxiety** *Ängste, Angst*

⁴⁰ **snap at sb** *jdn anschnauzen*

⁴¹ **armed** *bewaffnet*

⁴² **convincingly** *überzeugend*

⁴² **pay off** *sich lohnen*

The problem is, as a teen you are actually hardwired to fall asleep later at night and wake up later in the morning. It all has to do with something called growth hormone, which helps your bones and tissues grow during puberty. When this hormone starts coursing through your system around midnight, it also blocks melatonin, the hormone that's meant to kick in and make you drowsy.   20

25

Your body isn't just on a later schedule though – your brain also needs more total hours of sleep (about 9.25 a night) to function at its best. Sadly, most teens are able to squeeze in only about 7.1 hours, on average.   30

While Jilly knew she often felt like a zombie, digging into the research on teens and sleep gave her the confidence and motivation to continue her campaign. "I realized that there wasn't something wrong with me and my time management skills," she says. "The way I was feeling was physical and biological."

As she prepared for the school board meeting, Jilly learned all of the ways that   35
more sleep makes for better students. After a good night's rest, you're more alert, and it's easier to solve problems, process and remember information, and be creative. Plus, when you're not exhausted 24/7, you feel better emotionally. Sleep boosts your mood and lowers anxiety, meaning you're less likely to stress about exams, snap at your parents, or fight with friends.   40

At the school board meeting, Jilly shared what she had learned. Armed with facts, Jilly explained her case calmly and convincingly. All of that hard work paid off. The school board decided that instead of making Jilly's high school's start time earlier, they would make the start time even later, at 8.55 a.m.

The new, later schedule has been a positive change for Jilly and her classmates.   45
"I'm late a lot less," she says, "plus I feel more refreshed and alert."   (514 words)

Adapted from *Huffington Post*

WORKING WITH THE TEXT ....

L ▸ Lesen schwieriger Texte: Detailverständnis (p. 135)

3 Read the text and do the following tasks.

1 Explain why Jilly was fired up enough to start a campaign.
2 Describe Jilly's campaign.
3 How did Jilly's campaign affect other schools?
4 Summarize the facts about teenagers and sleep that Jilly discovered.
5 Give your opinion of Jilly's campaign and its results.

CHALLENGE!

EXAM PREPARATION
Leserverstehen (p. 149)

4 What are the positive psychological effects of sleep? Make a list in German with five items. Write complete sentences. You will find the answers in paragraph 7 "*As she prepared …*".

5 Use suitable words from the text to complete the gaps.

Jilly Dos Santos was … ¹ when she heard that her school wanted to put back its 7.50 a.m.
start time to 7.20 a.m. She was often … ² for school and sometimes felt like a … ³.
Yet her … ⁴ showed that she was just a normal teenager and there were … ⁵ reasons
for her sleep patterns. Teenagers are actually …⁶ to fall asleep late because of a … ⁷
hormone that … ⁸ melatonin, the hormone that makes you feel … ⁹. Jilly spoke up at
the school board meeting and argued so … ¹⁰ that the board pushed back the start
time to 8.55 a.m.

LOOKING AT LANGUAGE

6 a **Complete the conditional sentences with information from the text.**

G ▶ Conditionals (pp. 161 – 162)

1 Even if she went to bed earlier, Jilly …
2 Jilly wouldn't have felt like a zombie if …
3 If the school board hadn't proposed switching the school's start time
   to 7.20 a.m., Jilly …
4 If Jilly hadn't been fired up, she …
5 Jilly couldn't have reached so many students if …
6 If it weren't for growth hormone in their system, teenagers …
7 If teenagers got more sleep, they …
8 If Jilly hadn't been so convincing, the school board …

b **Complete these sentences about yourself.**

1 My life would be better if …
2 Life in my town would be better if …
3 If you had forgotten my birthday, …
4 If I had more pocket money, …

5 I wouldn't have come to school today
   if …
6 If I didn't have to work so hard at
   school, …
7 If I had had the chance, …

CHALLENGE!

READING

7 Read the extract from the book *Teen Angst? Naaah* by Ned Vizzini. In the book, Vizzini
writes about some strange and funny things that he experienced in his teenage years.

The Grind

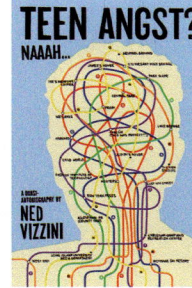

After a week at Stuy*, I started hearing about how hard it
was to get up in the morning and how "the daily grind is
getting to me, man."

5

10

The workload *was* hard. Freshman year, we had up to three
hours of homework each night, and that worsened as time
went on. A biology teacher once put it to me this way:
"Getting through Stuy is easy. You have three options: good
grades, social success, and sleep. You can only have two out
of three." I chose grades and sleep. The people who chose
grades and social success (getting drunk on the weekends
when they should've been studying) ended up with some problems. They'd come
to school bleary-eyed and sleep in the hallways. But missing sleep was cool – it
gave them something to brag about. They'd meet each other and say, "Man, I am
so tired. I got, like, twenty hours of sleep this whole week, and I partied all weekend."

² grind *Plackerei*
³ get to sb *jdm an die Nieren gehen*
⁴ **freshman** *Student/in im ersten
   Studienjahr*
¹² bleary-eyed *übernächtigt*
¹³ brag *angeben, prahlen*

[15] kid *scherzen*
[18] buzz *brummen*
[20] rush *Rausch*

Response: "Yeah … I'm not kidding, man, I have three tests today. I was up studying for bio until four."   15

Some days, I went to school on no sleep, but adrenaline got me through. When I took tests, I always got high – my brain buzzed with endorphins as I stared at those questions. Stuyvesant was a big, exciting place and just being in the building   20 was a rush for me.

*Stuyvesant High School   (233 words)

Abridged from: *Teen angst? Naaah* by Ned Vizzini

WORKING WITH THE TEXT

8   Which statement about Ned Vizzini do you think is true?

   a   He didn't enjoy school because it was such hard work.
   b   He was probably a good student.
   c   He didn't listen to the advice of his biology teacher.

WORKING WITH WORDS

9   Find words and phrases in the text that mean the same as the underlined words.

   1   My school mates socialized a lot and <u>eventually had</u> a lot of problems.
   2   I didn't have many <u>choices</u>.
   3   We had to wait outside the classroom in the <u>corridor</u>.
   4   This dull weather is really <u>depressing me</u>.
   5   The way he <u>looked directly</u> at me made me feel uncomfortable.
   6   He always <u>tells everyone</u> about his good grades.
   7   I'm tired because I <u>was at a party</u> all night.

10   The German words below are used in English. Look on the internet and find five more words. Then write five sample sentences using the words.

angst | kaput | kitschy | rucksack | schnitzel

DESCRIBING A PICTURE

L ▶ Interpretation von Bildern und Karikaturen (pp. 145 – 146)

11   Look at picture and at the sample description opposite. Improve the answer by following the steps and using the tips for improvement.

COMPETENCE TRAINING: WORKING WITH CARTOONS AND PICTURES

Step 1: **Look** carefully to see what the main theme of the picture is.
The picture/photo/cartoon is about … / shows …

Step 2: **Describe** the picture material systematically, e.g. from left to right.
In the foreground/background you can see … / there is/are …
At the top/bottom …   On the left/right …   In the middle …
In front of …   Behind …

Step 3: **Analyze** the picture. What is the artist/photographer trying to tell us?
The artist/photographer wants us to … / is trying to show … / is trying to capture. In my opinion, the artist's/photographer's aim is to …

Step 4: **Comment** on the picture material.
I think the picture/photo/cartoon …
gets / fails to get the message across successfully because …
is/isn't very convincing because …
would have been more/less effective if …

Important: Verbs that interpret a picture are in the present simple, e.g. *The picture shows …* Use the present progressive to describe actions in a picture unless you are using a verb that does not usually appear in the progressive form, e.g. *The boy is sitting in the classroom. He seems to be bored.*

Average answer	Tips for improvement
	Begin with an introductory statement stating the general theme of the picture.
Here there is a dark-haired teenage boy. He is sitting in the classroom.	Use the language for describing pictures. Here *In the foreground* could be used.
	Try to connect ideas using a participle. Here the present participle could be used.
He looks bored and tired and he doesn't listen to the lesson.	Use the present progressive to describe what is happening, but be careful with the verbs that are not used in the progressive form.
At the desk in front of him there is a blonde girl. She seems to be interested in the lesson.	Use connecting words such as relative pronouns to link simple sentences. See the back flap for other connecting words.
Behind the boy we can see the teacher. He is wearing a white coat. I think it is probably a science lesson.	Use the language for describing pictures. Here *in the background, in the middle* could be used.
	Participles or connecting words.
A girl is writing on the blackboard.	Use the language for describing pictures: *In the background, behind the teacher …*
I think the photographer wants to show the boredom that students sometimes feel in their lessons.	Use a different phrase for giving an opinion.
	Finish with a closing comment on the picture, e.g. *I (don't) think the photographer gets his message across because …*

TEXT 4   Is one language enough?

WARM UP

L ▶ Interaktion (pp. 147–148)

1 How important is it to speak another language? Decide which opinions you agree with. Then compare and discuss your opinions in small groups.

1 It is more important than ever for young people to learn other languages.
2 You don't need to learn foreign languages as you can rely on machine translations.
3 One day the whole world will speak only one major language and that will be English.
4 It doesn't matter if unimportant languages die out.
5 You can't understand another culture if you don't speak the language.
6 Unless you are planning to move to another country, it is not worth all the cost and effort to learn another language.
7 People who want to live in our country should learn our language.
8 You can't learn a foreign language in a classroom.

INFO

Ninety per cent of German pupils learn English at school. About 25 per cent learn French. Italian and Spanish are also popular choices. In Britain learning a foreign language at school is not an attractive option. Although most primary schools now offer foreign language lessons to children as young as six, it is common for students to give up languages completely at 14 because many think it is more difficult to get good grades in languages than in other subjects.

Only 38 per cent of Britons speak at least one foreign language compared with 56 per cent in the rest of the European Union. As few as 18 per cent of Americans report speaking a language other than English. Foreign language teaching in the USA is not generally offered until about age 13–14 and motivation is not high, as Americans have to travel a long way to use a foreign language in a 'real' environment. In addition, both Britons and Americans expect the rest of the world to speak English.

While it is true that English is the most influential language in the world, it is estimated that 75 per cent of the world's population do not speak it, so the favourite argument of Americans and Britons that "everyone speaks English" is far from true. The most widely spoken language is Mandarin Chinese with an estimated billion native speakers. Spanish is the second language with more than 400 million speakers and English follows in third place with 380 million native speakers and some 1.8 billion speakers worldwide.

13 influential *einflussreich*
16 estimate *schätzen*

5

10

15

SPEAKING

L ▶ Interaktion (pp. 147–148)

2 Read the Info box, then work in small groups to discuss the following questions:

1 Why has English become the most influential language in the world?
Think about: advertising, business and trade, the British Empire, films and music, science and technology, political power.
2 After English, which language is the most important one to learn? Explain your choice.

The school where they speak 20 languages

1.06

16 months ago government inspectors gave Gladstone Primary School in Peterborough the lowest mark: 'inadequate' and ordered the school to improve. After a stressful 16 months, the school was graded 'good' in every aspect.

But that is not the reason why the 450-pupil school has made the national news.
5 Gladstone Primary is believed to be the only school in the country where none of its children speaks English as their first language, yet English is the main language of communication. Is the school a triumph of multiculturalism? And what is it like to be a pupil or a teacher there?

Across Britain, schools are becoming more multicultural. The challenges facing
10 Gladstone Primary, though, seem particularly acute. About 80 per cent of its pupils are from a Pakistani background: most speak Punjabi, but the school's 20 other languages include Dari, Pashto, Gujarati, Kurdish, Arabic, Lithuanian, Latvian, Russian, Polish, Slovakian, Czech, German and French. At break, six Year 5 girls all cheerily admit they couldn't speak English when they arrived at school.

15 Today Gladstone has 18 teaching assistants – one for each class – and ten of these are bilingual. The school is helped by additional local-authority funding for newly arrived pupils. 'Family support workers' liaise with parents (who may struggle with English) and visit families at home if pupils are absent from school. Other unique features include a buddy system, so new arrivals are paired up with
20 schoolmates who speak their language. Sixth-formers from other schools visit to teach science or take English classes. Then there is a regular arrangement whereby Year 5 pupils spend time at other schools with pupils who speak English as a first language.

Head teacher Christine Parker doesn't see Gladstone as a ghetto. "We've got more
25 diversity and we're very celebratory about that diversity," she says of the school's cultural mix. She argues that other predominantly white British schools (and there are plenty in the region) should forge links with multicultural schools. "They have as much of a responsibility to ensure that the children in their schools understand the diversity of Peterborough and have some real experience of that."

30 As Parker puts it, "Not only is most of the world bilingual, a lot of the world is multilingual. We're the odd ones out. When I was working in Pakistan, many of our friends spoke five, six, seven languages. We tend to have a fear about language, but different languages bring different ways of seeing the world."

(419 words)

Adapted from *The Guardian*

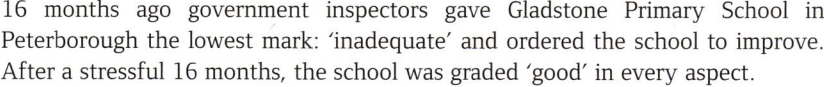

¹ **primary school** *Grundschule*
² inadequate *ungenügend*
² **improve** *sich bessern, besser werden*
³ grade *benoten*
¹⁴ cheerily *fröhlich*
¹⁶ **bilingual** *zweisprachig*
¹⁶ **local authority** *Kommunalbehörde*
¹⁷ family support worker *Familienhelfer/in*
¹⁷ liaise *als Verbindungsperson fungieren*
¹⁷ **struggle** *sich schwer tun*
¹⁹ **unique** *einzigartig*
¹⁹ **feature** *Eigenschaft*
¹⁹ buddy *Kamerad, Kumpel*
¹⁹ pair sb up with sb *jdn mit jdm zusammenbringen*
²⁰ sixth-former *Oberstufenschüler/in*
²¹ **arrangement** *Regelung*
²⁵ **diversity** *Vielfalt*
²⁵ be celebratory about sth *etw feiern*
²⁶ **predominantly** *überwiegend*
²⁷ forge links *Brücken schlagen*
³¹ **multilingual** *mehrsprachig*
³¹ be the odd-one-out *aus der Reihe fallen*

WORKING WITH THE TEXT

→ EXAM PREPARATION
Leseverstehen (p. 149)

L ▶ Interaktion (pp. 147–148)

3 Which measures were taken to improve Gladstone Primary? Make a list of six items in German. Write complete German sentences. You will find the answers in paragraph 4 *"Today Gladstone has 18 teaching assistants ..."*.

4 Discuss in class.

The text tells us that "Sixth-formers from other schools visit to teach science or take English classes". Would you like to teach in such a school? Why (not)?

5 Research on the internet.

In addition to English, there are 14 languages mentioned in the text. For each language, name at least one country or region where it is spoken by the majority of native speakers. If you can't, research the language on the internet and find out.

1.07

LISTENING

L ▶ Das Hörverständnis üben
(pp. 137–138)

6 **a** Listen to a radio interview with a teacher who works in a multi-cultural school and take notes.

b Listen again and do the following tasks using your own words.

1 Name at least three countries Isabel's pupils come from.
2 Explain why Isabel needs to know about her pupils' cultural backgrounds.
3 Describe a misunderstanding that can arise through lack of eye contact.
4 Explain why Asian or African students might be accused of cheating.
CHALLENGE!   5 Explain the difference between 'individualist' and 'collectivist' cultures.

COMPETENCE TRAINING: USING A DICTIONARY

L ▶ Umgang mit dem einsprachigen Wörterbuch (p. 136)

TIP
In a good dictionary you will find some or all of the following information about a word:
a part of speech (noun, verb, etc.)   **f** spelling
b grammar, e.g. countable or uncountable noun   **g** pronunciation
c preposition(s) used with the word   **h** other words in the same word
d the meaning(s) of the word   family
e how the word is used in context   **i** idioms which contain the word

7 Look at the dictionary entry and find the information a–i above.

Example: **a** *adj* (= adjective)

> **keen** [kiːn] *adj.*(**-er, -est**) **1** ~ (**to do sth/that ...**) eager, enthusiastic: *a keen swimmer • I'm not keen to go again. • She's keen that we should go.* **2** (of feelings, etc.) intense, strong, deep: *a keen desire, interest, sense of loss.* **3** (of the senses) highly developed: *Dogs have a keen sense of smell.* **4** (of a wind) bitterly cold **5** (idm) (**as**) **keen as mustard** extremely eager or enthusiastic
>
> **keen on sth/sb** (**a**) interested in sth/sb: *keen on playing tennis* (**b**) fond of sb/sth: *He's keen on my sister. I'm not very keen on jazz.* (**c**) enthusiastic about sth: *She's not very keen on the idea.* ▶ **keenly** *adv.* **keenness** *n*

DESCRIBING A CARTOON

8　Work in groups of three. Each person chooses one cartoon.

L ▶ Interpretation von Bildern und
Karikaturen (pp. 145–146)

C ▶ Working with cartoons and
pictures (p. 21)

a　Produce an uninterrupted two-minute discourse (in monologue) based on one of
the cartoons below.

→ **EXAM PREPARATION**
*Kommunikationsprüfung
(p. 150)*

b　Produce an uninterrupted three-minute discourse (in monologue) based on one
of the cartoons and the following quotation:

CHALLENGE!

> "Learning another language is not only learning different words for the same
> things, but learning another way to think about things."
>
> Flora Lewis, American journalist

SPEAKING

9　Read the reasons for learning a foreign language in the box below and then rank
them 1–8 in order of importance for you (1 = most important, 8 = least important).
Compare your ranking with a partner and give reasons for it.

Why should you learn a foreign language?

Learning a foreign language takes a lot of time and effort, but there are many reasons
why it is worth your while. Here are some of them:

1　**Increase your brain power.** Learning a language involves memorizing rules and
vocabulary, so your memory improves. Studies have shown that decision-making
skills improve, too.
2　**Enrich your travel experience.** Knowledge of the language will help you make
contact with local people and understand more of what is going on around you.
3　**Improve your employability.** In a globalized world, speaking foreign languages
will give you an advantage when it comes to finding a good job.
4　**Study or live in another country** – it will bring variety and adventure into your
life.
5　**Discover another culture.** Learning a language helps you understand how other
people think.
6　**Increase global understanding.** Better communication between nations can help
to promote world peace.
7　**Meet new people and find new friends.**
8　**Understand books, films and songs in the original language.**

ANALYZING AN ADVERTISEMENT

HANDS-ON TASK

10 Look at the online advertisement below and follow these steps:

1 Describe the advertisement.
2 Work with a partner and discuss the message of the advertisement. Would you take this advertisement seriously? Why (not)?
3 Design an online advertisement for a language course at a school in the USA or the UK. You can check out examples on the internet.

TEXT 5   Child labour

1 Have you ever had a job after school, at weekends or in the school holidays?
Work with a partner. If your answer to the question is 'Yes', tell your partner where,
when and why you work or worked. If your answer is 'No', give your partner reasons.

2 Describe the photographs.

L ▶ Interpretation von Bildern und
Karikaturen (pp. 145 – 146)

USA 1912

USA 2016

INFO

According to the International Labour Organization
the term 'child labour' refers to work that:
· is mentally, physically, socially or morally dangerous
  and harmful to children; and
5 · <u>interferes with</u> their schooling by:
· <u>depriving</u> them of the opportunity to attend school;
· <u>obliging</u> them to leave school <u>prematurely</u>; or
· requiring them to attempt to combine school attendance
  with excessively long and heavy work.

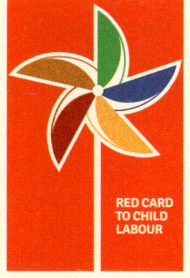

10 "In its most extreme forms, child labour involves children being <u>enslaved</u>, separated
from their families, <u>exposed to</u> serious <u>hazards</u> and illnesses and/or left to <u>fend for</u>
themselves on the streets of large cities – often at a very early age. Whether or not
particular forms of 'work' can be called 'child labour' depends on the child's age, the
type and hours of work performed, the conditions under which it is performed and the
15 <u>objectives</u> <u>pursued</u> by individual countries. The answer varies from country to country,
as well as among sectors within countries."

3 Read the Info box. Match the words and phrases below with the underlined words
and phrases in the text. If necessary, use a dictionary to help you.

aims | early | dangers | followed | has a negative influence on | look after | made into a
slave | makes it necessary for | takes away from | not protected from

27

1.08

Back to the bad old days?

In the early 20th century, a lot of effort was made to end the misery of children working in factories, so when the state of Maine, USA, made a new labor law loosening restrictions on employing minors, this made headline news. Under the old law, children under the age of 18 were allowed to work up to 20 hours a week and no later than 10 p.m. on school nights. These restrictions had been imposed in 1991 after complaints by teachers that students with part-time jobs were falling asleep in class. Under the new law students can work up to 24 hours a week and as late as 10.15 p.m.

Maine's child-labor laws are still stricter than in many other states, and the new changes are relatively modest. Recently, the state of Missouri considered allowing companies to employ children under 14 and lifting the limit on how many hours minors could work per day. It also proposed ending regular state inspections of companies that employ children.

Of course, federal restrictions still apply even if states abolish their child-labor laws. The Fair Labor Standards Act has limited the use of child labor since 1938. The aim of the Act and other legislation regulating the employment of children is to protect them from being exploited and ensure that the main focus is on their education.

Not surprisingly, the demand for loosening restrictions comes mostly from businesses that employ young people, especially fast-food companies. They want to be able to employ students on shift work, including night shifts. And they hope to get away with paying less than the minimum wage, arguing that minors who live at home with their parents can afford to work for less. In addition, children tend to be more manageable workers, more likely to accept poor working conditions and less likely to join a labor union.

These companies claim that fewer restrictions would have big advantages for young people – they would be more flexible in their choice of working hours and could gain valuable work experience – although it is not certain how valuable the experience of delivering pizzas late in the evening would actually be!

Research has shown that working most definitely has a negative effect on a young person's school performance. Studies show that students' grades suffer if they work outside school. Academic and behavioral problems have been linked to working too many hours, and students who work more than 20 hours a week are more likely to become high school dropouts.   (416 words)

5

10

15

20

25

30

WORKING WITH THE TEXT ....

L ▶ Lesen schwieriger Texte: Suche nach Einzelinformationen (pp. 134–135)

④ What does the text say about the following? Write your answers in full German sentences.

1 The changes made to the child labour laws in Maine.
2 The changes Missouri considered making to their child labour laws.
3 The main aims of the Fair Labor Standards Act.
4 Why companies that employ young people are hoping for fewer restrictions.
5 The reasons those companies give when they argue for a change in the rules.
6 The reasons why minors are often more manageable workers.
7 What research has shown about working students' academic performance.

WORKING WITH WORDS

5 Make compound nouns with the words below. Check your answers in the text.

Example: *child labor*

child | conditions | drop | experience | fast | food | head | high | *labor* (2x) | law | line | minimum | night | out | school (2x) | wage | work | working

6 **a** Find two words in the text with American English spelling. How are these words spelled in British English?

b Copy the table and complete it with the British English spellings of the American English words.

AE	BE	AE	BE	AE	BE
airplane		dialog		meter	
center		humor		neighbor	
catalog		license		program	
defense		liter		traveling	

7 Find the word that does not belong to these groups. Give reasons for your answers.

1 hardship, misery, suffering, well-being
2 employment, flexi-time, part-time, shift work
3 adult, minor, teacher, senior citizen
4 afford, earn, experience, wage
5 inflexible, rigid, strict, strong
6 ban, limitation, regulation, restriction

CHALLENGE!

LOOKING AT LANGUAGE

8 **a** Choose the best modal verbs (in italics) to complete the sentences.

G ▶ Modal auxiliary verbs (pp. 156–157)

1 You *don't have to / mustn't* work if you are underage. It's against the law.
2 I *might / must* get a summer job if my parents agree.
3 In the past little children *must / had to* work in factories.
4 A part-time job *mustn't / isn't allowed to* interfere with your education.
5 We have a cleaner at home, so I *mustn't / don't have to* help with the housework.
6 I'm sorry to *must / have to* tell you this, but you didn't get the job.
7 The law says that children *are allowed to / may not* have a part-time job unless their parents agree.
8 Children under the age of 13 *mustn't / might not* do paid work outside the home.

CHALLENGE!

b Complete these sentences with your own words, then compare your answers with a partner.

1 I hope I never have to … because …
2 I'd like to be able to … because …
3 I have never had to … because …
4 I think people should … because …
5 In my opinion nobody should be allowed to … because …

ROLE PLAY

L ▶ Interaktion (pp. 147 – 148)

9 Work with a partner. Decide on your roles and, after you have made some notes, role play the discussion between a parent and a son or daughter.

Student A: You are still at school. Your mum/dad doesn't want you to have a part-time job. But you have found a job you would like to do (what? where? when?). You have to persuade your mum/dad to let you work after school. Make a note of your arguments.

Student B: Your son/daughter is still at school, but he/she wants to take a part-time job. You are against it for several reasons. Make a note of your arguments.

WRITING

10 Check out the regulations for youth employment in Germany on the internet. Write an email to an American friend, giving him/her an overview of the regulations in English.

CROSSOVER TV

11 Child labour

Watch the video about the day in the life of a young Cambodian girl called Pharady and answer the questions.

1. What is Pharady's first task in the early morning?
2. What does she do instead of going to school?
3. What does the workers' pay depend on?
4. Why does Pharady have to go to work?
5. What is Pharady's dream job?

INTERNET RESEARCH

HANDS-ON
TASK

12 Read the Info box, then research on the internet and find the answers to the questions below.

INFO

At the age of 12, Canadian Craig Kielburger read a newspaper story about a Pakistani boy of his age who had been murdered for speaking out against child labour factories. The following day Craig and some school friends started a children's rights campaign called Free the Children, which has since become one of the most successful youth children's campaigns in the world.

Craig Kielburger at We Day in Vancouver, Canada (18.10.2012)

1. When was the Free the Children charity founded?
2. In how many countries is the organization active?
3. What are some of the programmes and campaigns the organization runs?
4. What is the organization's motto?
5. What is 'We Day'?
6. Who can attend 'We Day'?
7. Where does the organization's funding come from?

TEXT 6   The boomerang generation

....

1 Work with a partner.

a You have five minutes to make lists.

Student A: List the benefits of living at home after you have finished your education.
Example: *You can avoid the stress of flat hunting.*

Student B: List the downsides of living at home.
Example: *You will be treated like a child.*

b Compare your lists, then swap them. Add at least one more benefit or downside to your partner's list.

We make it easy for our children not to grow up

1.09

While attending college graduation recently, I watched many bright, young people cross the stage to accept their diploma, including my daughter. She, like many of her friends, does not have post-college plans and will probably move back home indefinitely.

5

A research center analysis of U.S. Census Bureau data found that 36 percent of the millennial generation, 18–31-year-olds, still live at home with their parents.
10 Sixty percent of all young adults receive financial support from their parents. These young people are hindered by a weak labor market, high cost of living and significant college debt.

While the job market and student debt are important contributing factors to the number of college students who move back home, I also believe the attitudes of
15 many parents and caregivers make it easy for our children not to grow up, to 'boomerang' back home.

In 1983, the year I graduated from college, I moved back home for six months and worked part-time while I searched for a professional job. Once I found a job, although I only made $1,000 per month, I found a small, inexpensive place of my
20 own that I shared with a friend. That was what was expected. While my mother still enjoyed spending time with me, she also really enjoyed my emerging independence.

About four million jobs in the US are currently unfilled. When it comes to this mismatch between unemployment numbers and vacant jobs, blame is cast in all
25 directions: job seekers are unwilling to move cities or work in unfamiliar positions; employers are holding out for the 'perfect candidate'; and schools just aren't providing the right skills.

This millennial generation is characterized by their willingness to trade off a higher paycheck for meaningful work, in the location they desire with the
30 flexibility to live the lifestyle they choose. Since those jobs are hard to find, one may argue that it's not that college grads cannot get a job, but that they are waiting for the 'perfect job' to land in their lap.

---

3 **stage** *Bühne*
7 **indefinitely** *auf unbestimmte Zeit*
10 **support** *Unterstützung*
11 **labor market** *Arbeitsmarkt*
12 **significant** *erheblich*
12 **debt** *Schulden*
13 **contributing factor** *Zusatzfaktor*
14 **attitude** *Ansicht, Einstellung*
15 caregiver *Bezugsperson*
21 emerging *neu entstehend*
24 mismatch *Diskrepanz*
24 **vacant** *offen*
28 millennial generation *Personen, die zwischen 1980 und 2000 geboren sind*
28 trade sth off for sth *etw gegen/für etw eintauschen*
32 lap *Schoß*

34 launch *in die Welt hinausschicken*
38 **self-reliant** *selbständig*
39 **resourceful** *findig, einfallsreich*
40 **sacrifice** *Opfer*
41 delay *hinauszögern*
43 **considerable** *beträchtlich*
44 purchase *kaufen*
45 **maintain** *(finanziell) unterhalten*
46 grad = graduate
Hochschulabsolvent/in
49 tempting *verlockend*
51 nudge *den Anstoß geben*
51 carve out sth out *sich etw aufbauen*

In my opinion, it is parents' responsibility to launch their children after college, letting them both succeed and fail on their own. If college graduates are funded by their parents indefinitely, they are robbed of important life and developmental experiences: gaining confidence in knowing they are in charge of their lives and can support themselves, learning how to be self-reliant and resourceful, understanding what is important to them, making compromises and sacrifices to get a start in a field that truly interests them. When we, as parents, make it too easy for our children, they delay stepping into full adulthood.

Besides the personal impact to young people, living at home after college also considerably affects our economy. Home sales are affected. The millennials are not buying homes at the rate of previous generations. They are also not purchasing furniture, or laying out their cash for all that it takes to maintain a home. There is a considerable impact to our economy when college grads end up sleeping in their childhood beds well into their late 20s.

I enjoy my daughter (and sons) as much as anyone, and there is nothing that makes me happier than having a house full of family. So it is tempting to encourage her to move back home to live. But, I believe my role as a parent is to gently nudge her along to her own uniquely carved-out life. She needs to feel good about the choices she is making. She needs to find her values and know how it feels to earn a lifestyle.

(595 words)

Adapted from *Huffington Post*

35

40

45

50

WORKING WITH THE TEXT

2 Read the text and list the reasons given . . .

1 why young people often go back home to live with their parents.
2 why it is not a good thing for young people to go back home to live with their parents.
3 for the mismatch between unemployment numbers and vacant jobs.

CHALLENGE!

3 Explain in your own words how the boomerang generation is having an impact on the economy.

4 a Match the sentence halves to make statements about the text. There is one sentence half in each list which cannot be matched.

1 The boomerang generation refers to young people who . . .
2 The writer thinks that after college her daughter will . . .
3 Research shows that more than two-thirds of all young people . . .
4 The writer's mother encouraged her to . . .
5 A high paycheck is not the most important factor for college grads who . . .
6 There is an impact on the economy when college grads don't . . .
7 The writer is tempted to . . .

a move out and become independent.
b buy and furnish their own homes.
c go back home to live with their parents.
d delay becoming adults.
e encourage her daughter to move back home.
f are looking for a job.
g are funded by their parents.

CHALLENGE!

b Complete the two unmatched sentence halves in your own words.

WRITING

5 "… 36 percent of the millennial generation, 18–31-year-olds, still live at home with their parents." (ll. 8–9)
Explain the quotation in relation to the text and then give examples why young adults may not want to move out of their parents' home.

→ EXAM PREPARATION
Textproduktion (p. 150)

DESCRIBING A CARTOON

6 a Work with a partner. Choose a cartoon each and produce an uninterrupted three-minute discourse (in monologue) based on the cartoons.

L ► Interpretation von Bildern und Karikaturen (pp. 145–146)

C ► Working with cartoons and pictures (p. 21)

→ EXAM PREPARATION
Kommunikationsprüfung (p. 150)

"I know the younger generation are living at home longer these days, but you're not exactly the younger generation anymore son!"

"This property comes complete with grown-up children left behind by the vendors."

b Discuss the problems of the boomerang generation in detail.

WRITING

7 The text says that young people are often looking for the 'perfect job'. Write a short description of your perfect job.

- full-time / part-time / flexi-time / fixed hours
- branch: science and technology, medicine, social services, finance, etc.
- teamwork / working independently
- working with people
- wage / salary / bonus
- travel opportunities
- challenging job / undemanding job / work-life balance
- chances of promotion
- teleworking from home
- small company / large company / self-employed
- annual leave / unpaid extra leave

COMPETENCE TRAINING: DESCRIBING CHARTS AND GRAPHS

TIP Charts show statistical information in a way that is easy to understand. It is often helpful to use charts and graphs to support your explanations in a presentation.

8 Match the chart types a–c with their names.

1 pie chart
2 bar chart
3 line graph

a    b 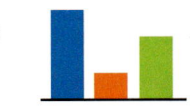   c

9 Here are some useful words for describing charts and graphs. Use them to describe what happened to sales in 1–6 below.

verb	+	adverb	adjective	+	noun	verb	+	adjective
increase		gradually	gradual		increase	be		steady
grow		rapidly	rapid		growth	remain		
rise		sharply	sharp		rise			
decline		slightly	slight		decrease			
decrease		slowly	slow		decline			
fall		steadily	steady		fall			

Sales last year

1	2	3	4	5	6
↑	↗	→	→	↘	↓

10 Describe the trends shown in the graph below. Use these expressions and the words from exercise 9 to help you. Compare your description with a partner.

Since 19..
In 19../20..
When ...
After ...

the number of young adults living with their parents in the UK
...

Young adults aged 20–34 living with parents in the UK, 1996–2014

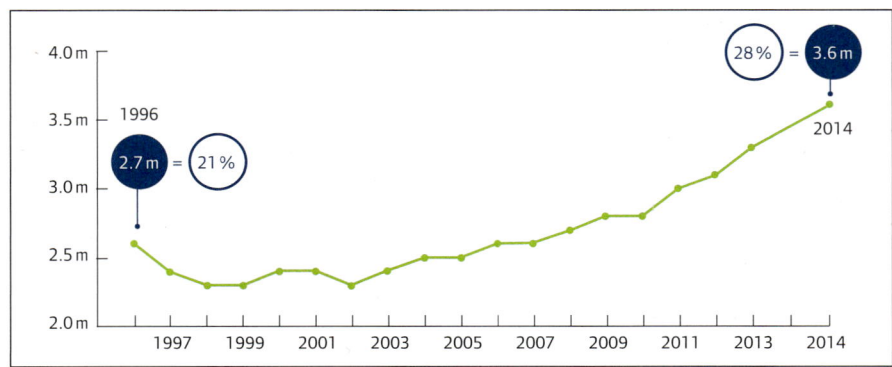

Source: UK Office for National Statistics

WORKING WITH WORDS

11 Match the family types 1–7 with the descriptions a–g. Which type of family would you most like to live in? Why?

1 multi-generational family
2 patchwork family
3 nuclear family
4 same-sex family
5 foster family
6 extended family
7 one-parent family

a a family with stepmother, stepfather and/or stepchildren
b adults bringing up children who are not legally their own
c children, parents and grandparents living together
d grandparents, aunts, uncles, cousins
e a family where children are raised by mother or father, not both
f mum, dad and their biological children
g gay or lesbian couples and their children

LISTENING

1.10

12 a You are going to listen to a radio interview with three members of a multi-generational family. Listen and take notes.

b Copy and complete the table in German with information from the interview.

→ **ZENTRALE KLASSENARBEIT**
Hörverstehen (p. 150)

	Vorteile	Nachteile
Daniel	…	…
Gary	…	…
William	…	…

SPEAKING

11 Work with a partner. Take turns to choose ONE picture from Topic 1. Don't let your partner see your choice. Describe the picture. Your partner has to find the picture you have described.

TEXT 1 Northumberland and the Borderlands

WARM UP

1 Look at the information below, then listen to the song.

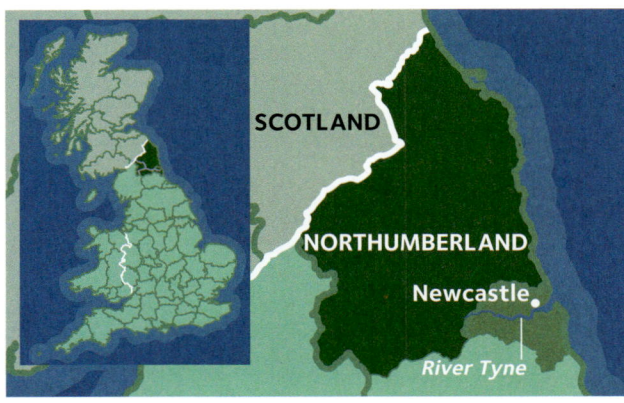

Mark Knopfler, who was born in Glasgow, Scotland, is a British songwriter, singer, film music composer, guitarist and record producer. In 1977 he co-founded the band Dire Straits. The group disbanded in 1995 and Knopfler went on to record and produce many hit songs. He is considered to be one of the greatest guitarists of all times and has won many awards for his music.

1.11

Fare thee well Northumberland

Mark Knopfler

Come drive me down to Central Station	
I hate to leave my River Tyne	
For some damn town that's godforsaken	
Fare thee well, Northumberland	
Although I'll go where the lady takes me	5
She'll never tell what's in her hand	
I do not know what fate awaits me	
Fare thee well, Northumberland	
My heart beats for my streets and alleys	
Longs to dwell in the borderlands	10
The north-east shore and the river valleys	
Fare thee well Northumberland	
I may not stay, I'm bound for leaving	
Bound to ramble and to roam	
I only say my heart is grieving	15
I would not gamble on my coming home	

0 fare thee well = farewell *Lebe wohl!*

3 damn *verdammt(e)*

3 godforsaken *gottverlassen*

7 fate *Schicksal*

9 alley *Gasse*

10 long *sich sehnen*

10 dwell *verweilen, bleiben*

11 shore *Küste*

13 be bound to do sth *dazu bestimmt sein, etw zu tun*

14 ramble *umherstreifen*

14 roam *herumstreunen*

15 grieve *trauern*

16 gamble on sth *auf etw wetten, auf etw setzen*

16 Geordie *Spitzname für jemanden aus Tyneside*

20

Roll on, Geordie boy, roll
Roll on, Geordie boy, roll
Roll on, Geordie boy, roll
Roll on, Geordie boy, roll

So drive me down to Central Station
I hate to leave my River Tyne
For some damn town that's godforsaken
Goodbye old friend of mine

25

Although I'll go where the lady takes me
She'll never tell what's in her hand
I do not know what fate awaits me
Fare thee well, Northumberland

So roll on, Geordie boy, roll

30

Roll on, Geordie boy, roll
Roll on, Geordie boy, roll
Roll on, Geordie boy, roll

Lyrics: © Universal Music Publishing Group

2 Which interpretation of the song do you agree with most? Give reasons.

a The singer is leaving his home to be with his girlfriend in another town.

b The singer has to leave his home because he has found a job in another town.

c The singer is forced to leave his home and he doesn't know what the future holds.

3 Scan the text *England's northernmost county* on page 38 and match the photographs to the most relevant sections.

L ▶ Lesen schwieriger Texte: Suche nach Einzelinformationen (pp. 134–135)

A

B

C

D

1.12

0 county *Grafschaft*
3 rampart *Schutzwall*
4 **incredible** *unglaublich*
8 skinny dip *nackt baden*
10 rage *wüten*
14 excavate *ausgraben*
16 uncover *entdecken*
17 **collapse** *Zusammenbruch, Zerfall*
18 **enrichment** *Bereicherung*
19 turmoil *Unruhe*
20 **decade** *Jahrzehnt*
20 **monastery** *Kloster*
21 **treasure** *Schatz*
22 **conquer** *erobern*
25 conquest *Eroberung*
26 raid *Überfall*
27 warrior *Krieger*
29 **inaccurately** *ungenau*
32 expanse *große Fläche*
33 bloodshed *Blutvergießen*
35 maraud *plündern*
36 tie *Bindung*
37 livestock *Vieh*
37 arson *Brandstiftung*
37 retribution *Vergeltung*
40 **aristocratic** *adlig*

*pronounced /ænɪk /

England's northernmost county

Northumberland with its history of invaders and bloody battles is a place to get away from the crowds.

Just 20 miles south of the Scottish border a 3,000-year-old earthen rampart offers an incredible view across the county of Northumberland. At certain times of the day, when the light is clear, you can see seven castles – Northumberland has more castles than any other English county. But very few people know this area and its attractions. Where else in the country can you walk along a sandy beach and meet only a handful of people, or skinny dip in a lake or waterfall knowing there's no-one around to see you? 5

Yet for centuries battles raged in this region, and here you can find the most important Roman monument in Britain, Hadrian's Wall, built by the Emperor Hadrian in 122 AD to keep out the 'barbarians' of northern Britain. For 73 miles, the 2,000-year-old barricade crosses the neck of England from west to east. 10

Northumberland's Roman sites have been excavated and studied many times since the ruins caught the attention of Victorian collectors, so it may come as a surprise to learn that archaeologists are still uncovering Roman artefacts today. 15

A few centuries after the collapse of the Roman Empire, Northumberland entered a long period of cultural enrichment and learning, much of it centred on the Church. But turmoil returned to the region when Vikings invaded in 793. They continued to invade Britain for seven decades, destroying the monasteries and stealing their treasures. 20

In 1066 the Normans conquered the south of England and moved north with their armies, murdering anyone who got in their way. They built many great castles and rebuilt the ruined monasteries.

From the Norman Conquest until the union of England and Scotland in the 17th century, Northumberland was the scene of raids by the Scots. One of the most famous Scottish warriors was William Wallace, who led the Scots in the First War of Scottish Independence against King Edward I of England at the turn of the 14th century. Wallace was inaccurately portrayed by Mel Gibson in the film *Braveheart*. 25

Many of the region's legendary battles took place in the mid-western part of the county where there is an expanse of countryside that has experienced more bloodshed than probably anywhere else in Northumberland. For a couple of hundred years until the mid-17th century, this was the Wild West of Britain, a lawless place where marauding clans in England and Scotland, who had stronger ties to family groups than to country, rode on horseback at night over the moors, stealing livestock, committing murder and arson, and seeking retribution. 30 35

Another claim to fame for Northumberland is Alnwick* Castle, one of the locations in the Harry Potter films. The castle, which was built in the 12th century, has belonged to Northumberland's most powerful aristocratic family, the Percys, for over 700 years. The family settled in Britain shortly after the Norman Conquest and bought the castle in 1309. They still live there today. 40

And as if there were not already enough reasons to visit Northumberland, the county has some of the best weather in the UK with an average rainfall of 865 millimetres compared with the national average of 1,125 millimetres. (541 words)

Source: Britain Magazine 45

WORKING WITH THE TEXT

4 Decide whether the statements about the text are true or false. Give reasons for your decisions in German.

 **EXAM PREPARATION**
Leseverstehen (p. 149)

1 Northumberland is a popular destination for lots of tourists.
2 It's surprising that there are still lots of Roman artefacts to be discovered in the region.
3 Christianity did not arrive in the region until the Vikings had left.
4 The 'Wild West of Britain' was the area along the coast.
5 The Percy family came to Britain in the 11th century.
6 In the film *Braveheart* Mel Gibson played a historical figure.
7 Alnwick Castle was built by the Percy family.

CHALLENGE!

5 a Make a list in German of attractions that Northumberland offers. You will find them in the first and second paragraphs of the text (up to "from west to east."). Five or even six items can be named.

 **EXAM PREPARATION**
Leseverstehen (p. 149)

b Compare your list with a partner.

6 a In your own words say what the numbers in the text refer to.

....
7 | 73 | 122 | 700 | 793 | 1,125 | 1309
....

b Make up questions to produce answers that contain these numbers.

CHALLENGE!

....
7 | 73 | 122 | 700 | 793 | 1,125 | 1309
....

WORKING WITH WORDS

7 Copy and complete the table with words from the text.

Verb	Noun	Adjective
attract	…	attractive
–	…	barbaric
…	conquest	–
…	destruction	–
enrich	…	–
–	…	independent
…	invasion	–
…	portrayal	–

LOOKING AT LANGUAGE

G ▶ The passive (pp. 160–161)

8 Use the words and phrases to write passive sentences.

1 Hadrian's Wall / build / to defend Roman Britain
2 Northumberland and its attractions / know / by only a handful of people
3 Britain / invade / by the Vikings / many times
4 Many monasteries / destroy / when the Vikings invaded
5 The south of England / conquer / by the Normans in 1066
6 The Scots / lead / into battle by William Wallace
7 The castle / still / inhabit / by the Percy family
CHALLENGE!
8 New Roman artefacts / still / uncover / today
9 Since Victorian times, Northumberland's Roman sites / study / many times
10 The castle / own / by the Percy family since 1309
11 A new Harry Potter film / shoot / at Alnwick Castle at present

COMPETENCE TRAINING: USING YOUR OWN WORDS

TIP
When you do comprehension tasks in speaking or writing, you often need to use your own words as much as possible. To help you do this, you can use other forms of the words in the text, as in the table in exercise 7. Or you can paraphrase – that means saying something in another way.

9 Rewrite the sentences using the words in brackets and words from exercise 7.

1 The Vikings continued to invade throughout the next seventy years. *(There were several …)*
2 Very few people know how attractive this area is. *(This area's … not well known.)*
3 The Norman Conquest of England took place in the 11th century. *(In the 11th century, the …)*
4 The Scots fought for their independence. *(The Scots wanted to …)*
5 The Vikings continued to destroy the monasteries for decades. *(The Vikings continued with …)*

10 Match the phrases/sentences to parts of the text with the same meaning. They are in the same order as in the text. Explain how the sentences have been paraphrased.

1 … and see very few people?
2 the narrowest part of England
3 Victorian collectors became interested in the ruins.
4 for seventy years
5 They built the ruined monasteries again.
6 The portrayal of Wallace was not accurate.
7 a place with no laws
8 One of the places where Harry Potter films were made.

WRITING

CHALLENGE!
➔ **EXAM PREPARATION**
Textproduktion (p. 150)

11 Local, regional and national governments all over the world have developed programmes to attract tourists to their area. Discuss the advantages and disadvantages of the development of tourism.

TEXT 2   Northern Ireland's peace walls

WARM UP

1 Explain the difference between:

England | Great Britain | The British Isles | The United Kingdom

2 Look at the cartoon and explain how it is linked to question 1.

INFO

The Troubles

'The Troubles' refers to a violent thirty-year conflict in Northern Ireland which began with a civil rights march in Londonderry on 5 October 1968 and ended (officially) on 10 April 1998 with the Good Friday Agreement. In those three decades violence on the streets of Northern Ireland was commonplace. Over 3,600 people were killed and over 50,000 injured.

10 At the heart of the Troubles was the conflict between the Protestant majority, the 'unionists' or 'loyalists', who wanted Northern Ireland to remain part of the United Kingdom, and the Catholic minority, the 'republicans', who wanted to become part of the Republic of Ireland. The conflict was, in fact, territorial rather than religious and had its roots in the centuries-old British occupation of Ireland.

15 The Irish Republic Army (IRA), the main republican paramilitary organization in Northern Ireland, demanded Irish unification and the withdrawal of the British, and they were determined to fight until this happened. On the other side, the major loyalist paramilitary organizations, the Ulster Volunteer Force (UVF) and the Ulster Defence Association (UDA), would do anything to prevent unification.

20 In 1969 riots broke out in Belfast and Londonderry, and British troops were sent to restore order. In 1972 the British government suspended the Northern Ireland parliament and imposed direct rule from London.

By 1994 both the republicans and the British Army had realized that the conflict could not be solved by military means. In that year the IRA announced a ceasefire. Several 25 attempts to find a political solution failed until the Good Friday Agreement, which restored self-government to Northern Ireland and brought an end to the Troubles.

8 commonplace *alltäglich*
16 unification *Vereinigung*
17 determined *fest entschlossen*
18 Ulster *Nordirland*
24 ceasefire *Waffenstillstand*

3 Look at the facts in the Info box and make a short summary about the Troubles. Use this outline and your own words.

The Troubles is the name given to … that lasted … It was not … conflict, but … between …, who …, and …, who … The main republican paramilitary organization, …, demanded that … should … and Ireland should … The … organisations, the UVF and the UDA, strongly opposed … After riots in …, … sent in. . . the Northern Ireland parliament … The Troubles ended …, when a political solution known as … meant that Northern Ireland …

1.13

³ **urban** *städtisch*
⁴ **erect** *errichten*
⁹ **graffitied** *mit Graffiti bemalt*
¹⁰ **sectarian** *konfessionell*
¹⁴ **reconciliation** *Versöhnung*
¹⁷ **community** *Gemeinde*
¹⁷ **restrict** *begrenzen*
²⁷ **sustainability** *Nachhaltigkeit*
³² **consent** *Zustimmung*
³⁸ **common** *häufig*

Belfast – a divided city

Like the Berlin Wall, the Cupar Way 'peace wall' in Belfast, has cut an urban landscape in half for decades. The wall, one of dozens erected by the British Army that divide the capital of Northern Ireland, has become one of the city's top tourist attractions.

Although the walls may look like monuments to the past to be graffitied and photographed, for the people living in their shadows, sectarian conflict between Protestant unionists (who historically have defined themselves as British) and Catholic nationalists (who favour joining the Irish Republic), is not a thing of the past. The decades of bloodshed, known as 'the Troubles', are over, but peace and reconciliation are not the same thing. A 2012 study showed almost 70 per cent of the people living near the walls fear for their safety without them.

Put simply, the walls prevent people from crossing between the Protestant areas on one side and the Catholic communities on the other. Some walls restrict access completely, while others use gates with limited opening hours to restrict movement.

In 1998 the historic Good Friday Agreement ended nearly 30 years of violence. The agreement involved a fundamental reshaping of Northern Ireland – a power-sharing arrangement allowing parties from both sides to be in government. Prisoners held for crimes relating to the Troubles were released, and the Protestant-dominated police force was reformed and re-named.

Politicians from both sides of the Atlantic have called for the walls to be removed as part of the peace and reconciliation process in Northern Ireland. But Rosie McGlone, who grew up in the shadow of the Cupar Way wall, says many people are sceptical about the sustainability of the peace deal. "People want to feel safe; that's not to say they hate their neighbours," she says. "People just don't feel secure enough to take the walls down. What if you had grown up in the Troubles? Seen the murders?"

Northern Ireland's government says it wants to bring down the walls by 2023, but will only act with the "engagement, consent and support" of the people living near them.

Dr Byrne from the University of Ulster, who co-wrote a report about people's attitudes to the walls, says: "Some of the walls have been up since 1969. That's two, three or four generations that have lived with them. When they've been there that long, and someone comes along and says 'we're going to take down your wall', the most common reply will be 'Why?'"

5

10

15

20

25

30

35

40 Apart from crowds of Protestants fighting night after night with the police in violent demonstrations over the city council's decision to stop flying the British flag every day, there has not been large-scale inter-community violence – of the type the walls were designed to prevent – for more than a decade.

45 So will the walls come down by 2023? "Never say never," says Dr Byrne, while Ms McGlone doubts it will happen. But everyone agrees that if the peace walls did come down, it would be a gradual process, not a dramatic event like the fall of the Berlin Wall.   (510 words)

Adapted from *Huffington Post*

[42] **large-scale** *in großem Umfang*
[42] **inter-community** *zwischen den Gemeinden*
[46] **process** *Vorgang*
[46] **event** *Ereignis*

WORKING WITH THE TEXT ....

4 **Decide whether the statements about the text are true or false. Give reasons for your decision in German.**

1 Tourists want to see the peace walls because they are part of Northern Ireland's history.
2 Most people who live near the walls want them to be removed.
3 It is not possible to cross to and from the Catholic and Protestant areas in Belfast.
4 The government will definitely remove the walls before 2023.
5 Dr Byrne thinks it possible that the walls will be removed by 2023.
6 There are those who don't believe the peace agreement will last.
7 There has been no violence in Belfast for more than a decade.

→ **EXAM PREPARATION**
Leseverstehen (p. 149)

CHALLENGE!

WORKING WITH WORDS ....

5 **Replace a word in these sentences from the text with a word from the box. There is one extra word.**

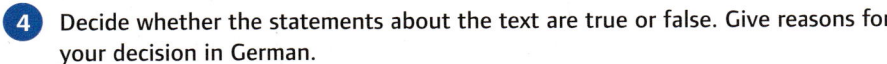

agreement | daily | durability | fierce | freed | harmony | limit | peaceful | put up

1 The wall is one of dozens erected by the British Army.
2 Some walls restrict access completely.
3 Peace and reconciliation are not the same thing.
4 A power-sharing arrangement allows the parties from both sides to be in government.
5 Prisoners held for crimes relating to the Troubles were released.
6 The city council decided to stop flying the British flag every day.
7 Many people are sceptical about the sustainability of the peace deal.
8 Crowds of Protestants fought night after night with police in violent demonstrations.

CHALLENGE!

6 **Fill in the missing prepositions, then scan the text to check your answers.**

1 There has been conflict … unionists and republicans … decades.
2 The walls were built to prevent people crossing … one area … another.
3 Many prisoners were being held …crimes … the British.
4 Many people who grew … near the walls are sceptical … the peace deal.
5 Politicians are calling … the walls to be taken ….
6 People who have lived with the walls … 1969 have a different attitude … them.
7 There has been little violence … … … some protesters fighting night … night.

LOOKING AT LANGUAGE

G ▸ Reported speech (pp. 158–160)

7 Work in pairs.

Student A: Tell your partner what Ms McGlone said using reported speech. Begin like this:
Ms McGlone said that many people were sceptical about …

Student B: Tell your partner what Dr Byrne said using reported speech. Begin like this:
Dr Byrne said that some of the walls had been up since …

1.14

LISTENING

L ▸ Das Hörverständnis üben
(pp. 137–138)

ZENTRALE KLASSENARBEIT
Hörverstehen (p. 150)

8 Four people from Northern Ireland
– Alison, Pat, Mary and Conor –
give their opinions on the topic of
the peace walls in a radio show.

Complete the sentences below in German.
Name two aspects for each statement.

Alison	möchte, dass die Peace Walls bleiben, weil …
Pat	ist der Meinung, dass die Peace Walls so bald wie möglich abgeschafft werden sollten, weil …
Mary	erinnert sich an ihre Kindheit, als …
Conor	sagt, dass es noch zu früh ist, die Peace Walls abzuschaffen, weil …

WRITING

EXAM PREPARATION
Textproduktion (p. 150)

9 a "Some walls restrict access completely, while others use gates with limited
opening hours to restrict movement." (ll. 17–18)

Explain the quotation in relation to the text and give further examples of how
walls and borders affect the lives of the people who live with them.

b Discuss the arguments in favour and the arguments against removing the peace
walls in Northern Ireland, as well as similar walls and borders in other places in
the world.

PROJECT

HANDS-ON
TASK

EXAM PREPARATION
*Präsentationsprüfung
(p. 151)*

10 a Research the following and present the results of your research to the class.

Bloody Sunday | decommissioning | Sinn Féin | The Anglo-Irish Agreement

b Use the information from your research and the information from the Info box on
page 41 to make a poster showing the main events during the Troubles in
chronological order.

SPEAKING

11 **a** Produce an uninterrupted three-minute discourse (in monologue) based on the cartoon and quotation below.

"There are two traditions in Northern Ireland. There are two main religious denominations. But there is only one true moral denomination. And it wants peace."

– David Trimble, British politician and leader of the Ulster Unionist Party from 1995 to 2005

EXAM PREPARATION
Kommunikationsprüfung (p. 150)

L ▶ Interpretation von Bildern und Karikaturen (pp. 145–146)

denomination *Konfession*

b Discuss the historical background of the Troubles in Northern Ireland with a partner.

CHALLENGE!

EXAM PREPARATION
Kommunikationsprüfung (p. 150)

COMPETENCE TRAINING: DEALING WITH UNKNOWN WORDS

L ▶ Umgang mit unbekannten Vokabeln (p. 135)

TIP

Guessing the meaning of words is a useful skill. Below are some general tips. The unknown words are underlined.

- Look closely at the root of the unknown word as well as any prefixes or suffixes. For example, if you know *comfort*, you can guess *comfortable*, if you know *belief*, you can guess *disbelief*, if you know *accuse*, you can guess *accusation*.
- Try to see from other parts of the sentence if the unknown word has a positive or a negative meaning. For example, if you read: *My parents were pleased with my achievement*, you can guess that *achievement* is something positive. If you read: *I felt dismayed when I saw the chaos that confronted me,* we can guess that *dismayed* must be a negative feeling.
- Synonyms can help you. For example: *I was really miserable; in fact, I was absolutely wretched*. We can guess that *wretched* is a synonym for miserable.
- Opposites can help you. For example: *Ben is a rather dull person, unlike his girlfriend, who is very lively*. Here with the help of the word *unlike*, we can guess that *dull* is the opposite of *lively*.
- Look out for other signal words. *For example* and *such as* tell us that examples of the word will follow: *The pipes transport fuels such as oil and natural gas. Because* tells us that an explanation of a word will follow: *It is called an biennial event because it takes place every two years.*

12 Guess the meaning of the underlined words. How did you guess?

1 Archeologists have unearthed many Roman artefacts.
2 Tom is such an obnoxious person that nobody wants to anything to do with him.
3 The exam regulations disallowed the use of dictionaries.
4 There has been a big increase in commodity prices such as coffee, sugar and wool.
5 The show was incredibly funny, in fact it was hilarious.

TEXT 3 **Living in a bankrupt city**

L ▶ Interpretation von Bildern und
Karikaturen (pp. 145 – 146)

WARM UP

1 Describe the photographs of Detroit, using your own words and the words from the box.

decaying | derelict | district | high-rise | skyline

INFO

The history of Detroit

In 2013 Detroit made history – once the heart of the US motor industry, it was the first large city in the USA to declare bankruptcy.

In June 1896 Henry Ford drove his first car on the streets of Detroit. In 1905 the Ford Motor Co. was founded there. In 1908 General Motors started up, and the Chrysler Corp was founded in the city in 1925.   5

During the Second World War, Detroit's defence industry boomed and job seekers – many of them black people from the south – arrived in large numbers. By 1950 Detroit's population stood at 1.85 million, making it America's fourth-largest city.

However, in the early 1970s after the oil crisis, more fuel-efficient, foreign-made cars were in demand, leading to a long period of crisis for Detroit's Big Three automakers,   10
and in 2009 Chrysler and GM declared bankruptcy.

Today, Detroit is one of the USA's poorest cities. About 30 per cent of its population live below the poverty line. 80 per cent of the population today are African-Americans, and the city has a long history of racial conflict. The first major confrontation between blacks and whites took place in June 1943, when 35 people were killed. In July 1967   15
inner-city residents fought police and National Guard troops in one of the biggest riots in US history, resulting in 43 dead and almost 1,200 injured.

By the 1970s, Detroit was considered to be a very dangerous city. The rate of violent crimes peaked in the 1990s, and although it has decreased since then, the city still has one of the highest crime rates in the USA.   20

As the city's fortunes declined, middle class and white residents began to leave. The population decreased to its lowest level in decades and the city was soon in serious financial trouble. Pensions and health benefits were cut, schools were closed and neighbourhoods abandoned.

Recently the city has experienced something of a revival. New projects are targeting   25
investment and some parts of the city could see major transformations in the future.

13 **poverty line** *Armutsgrenze*
14 **racial** *Rassen-*

2 Read the Info box and make a time line of Detroit's history.

L ▶ Lesen schwieriger Texte:
Suche nach Einzelinformationen
(pp. 134–135)

1.15

Will I be brutally murdered if I visit Detroit?

by Aaron Foley

If you're from Detroit and you tell people you're from Detroit, you get a pause, a brief stare and a "What's it like?" in a low voice. I get it. A lot.

5 Honestly, I get nervous talking about Detroit. For one, you're asked to provide a lot of information off the top of your head. So I usually take a deep sigh and start with an exasperated "Well …". Because living in a broken city that's also your hometown takes a lot of patience and compromise.

Here are some of the questions I get the most.

10 **What's it like to live in Detroit?**
It's not bad. Really. Things could always be better …
Do you live in downtown?
No. I live in the west side. We're dog owners, so we needed a backyard. We'd also like to own a house without having to sell our bodily organs for our mortgage.
15 A garage is a must. And besides, the world doesn't revolve around Midtown.
But how do you deal with the … (insert any city dysfunction here)?
Wouldn't it just be easier to move?
(sigh) I don't know a single Detroiter who hasn't talked about moving. I think about it every day. Stay or go? My emotions change when I (reluctantly) watch
20 TV news. I don't know, man. I'm good for now, but anything can happen. All I know is that my trash gets picked up on time, the city's tearing down houses little by little and it seems like there's always a new restaurant or something opening. I'd say life, for me, at least, is regular 90 per cent of the time.
What's the crime like?
25 Is crime bad in Detroit? Yes, and part of me has learned to live with it and part of me is mad as hell that it has to be this way. Usually I just keep my wits about me in unsure situations, make sure I engage my security system – something every house everywhere should have – at night and I'm extra careful about who I associate with.
30 **But the black population …**
Nope, stop. Can't speak for all black people just because I'm black. I can tell you what I think, but everyone here thinks differently about different things when it comes to race relations in Detroit. I can tell you this, though: a white family moved onto my street last year. They are the only white family on the street.
35 Their oldest kids go to the same high school I went to, and their younger kids play with all the black kids in the neighborhood. The wife of the household converses with the other women in the neighborhood like *Desperate Housewives*, and the husband drinks beer on his porch while keeping an eye on the kids. Sounds pretty normal, wouldn't you say?
40 **So what's the one thing Detroit needs?**
I don't know that, either. Look, all I know is this: I'm doing fine. Almost every time a house goes for sale in my neighborhood, someone buys it. All the time on Facebook, I see people that I knew from high school doing things like getting new jobs, buying a Chrysler 200 or celebrating a new and bigger apartment.

2 stare *Starren*
5 off the top of your head *aus dem Stegreif*
7 exasperated *entnervt*
8 **patience** *Geduld*
14 mortgage *Hypothek*
16 dysfunction *Fehlfunktion*
19 **reluctantly** *widerwillig*
21 **tear down** *abreißen*
26 **keep my wits about me** *meine fünf Sinne beisammen halten*
27 engage *einschalten*
33 race relations *Beziehungen zwischen ethnischen Gruppen*
36 converse *sich unterhalten*
38 porch *Veranda*

48 get sth together *mit etw die Kurve kriegen*
49 guess *Mutmaßung*

City services cut? I mean, they've been cut to the bone for some time now. But on   45
the upside, emergency management has promised (I know, I know, it's just a
promise) that city services would be fully restored.

I would love it if Detroit got its schools together. If that's the one thing Detroit
'needs', then that would be my best guess. But I don't know. Life is going on in
bankrupt Detroit. I don't know how else to explain it.   (615 words)   50

Adapted from *Jalopnik Detroit*

WORKING WITH THE TEXT

L ▶ Lesen schwieriger Texte: Detailverständnis (p. 135)

3 Read the text and do the following tasks using your own words as far as possible.

1 Describe people's reaction when the author says he is from Detroit.
2 Explain why the writer calls Detroit a 'broken city'.
3 Give three reasons why the writer has chosen to live in his part of the city.
4 Describe how the writer deals with crime in his city.
5 Quote parts of the text that show the writer is still hopeful for his city.

CHALLENGE!

6 Speculate on why the writer's emotions change when he watches TV.
7 Interpret the message the writer wishes to convey with his story about the white family.

WORKING WITH WORDS

4 Complete the sentences with one of the colloquial phrases from the text and one of the verbs in the box in the correct form.

an eye on | extra careful about | best guess | ~~off the top of your head~~ | to the bone | your wits about you

associate | be | cut | keep (2x) | ~~talk~~

Example: You don't have any facts. You are just *talking off the top of your head*.
1 If you are in a dangerous part of the city, you have to ...
2 Be ... the people you ... with.
3 I have to go out. Can you ... the kids?
4 City services have been ...
5 My ... that the one thing Detroit needs is schools.

READING

L ▶ Lesen schwieriger Texte: Grobverständnis (p. 134)

5 Skim the travel report on the opposite page. Does it give a similar impression of the city as the Aaron Foley's blog on page 47? What is the same, what is different? These phrases may help you:

I think both texts show that Detroit ...
Aaron Foley talks about ... and ... in the city, whereas the travel report ...
While Aaron Foley describes ..., the travel report focuses on ...
The travel report aims to ..., whereas Aaron Foley ...

Welcome to Detroit!

You have probably never considered
Motor City with its image as a symbol of
urban decay to be a vacation destination.
But the city that was once one of the
5 world's wealthiest still has lots to offer
behind its neglected, graffiti-covered
facades. Today, buildings that had been
abandoned for decades are finally being
demolished, making way for wide green
10 spaces. Several new hotels, restaurants
and art galleries have revitalized Detroit's
downtown area.

Historic buildings have been renovated – check out the Detroit Institute of Arts
and Michigan Central Station. For automobile fans there's the North American
15 International Auto Show, but that's in January – hardly the best time to visit the
Midwest. So perhaps it would be better to come in spring or summer and take a
Ford Rouge Factory Tour. In August there's the Woodward* Dream Cruise, a one-
day celebration of the automobile, with lots of parades, music and food. If you're
a jazz fan, you would enjoy the annual Detroit International Jazz Festival over
20 Labor Day** weekend. In any season, Detroit is a hub of sporting activity, so be
sure to catch a Tigers, Red Wings or Lions game during your stay. There you'll see
some of the finest baseball, ice hockey or American football respectively that you
can ever hope to see.   (213 words)

³ decay *Verfall*
⁶ **neglected** *vernachlässigt*
⁹ demolish *abreißen*
¹¹ revitalize *neu beleben*
¹⁷ cruise *hier: Fahrt*
²⁰ hub *Drehkreuz*
²² respectively *jeweils*

*Woodward Avenue is a north-
south state highway and one of
the principle avenues of Detroit.
In 2002 it was listed by the
government as a national
heritage (*Kulturerbe*) area
because it connects automobile-
related historic sites of the city.

Labour Day is a public holiday
in the USA on the first Monday
in September.

COMPETENCE TRAINING: MAKING NOTES FROM READING

TIP
Making notes is a useful skill for organizing the information in a text in a short form.
Leave out unnecessary words such as pronouns and articles. Use abbreviations,
symbols and short forms – for examples see **Competence training: Taking notes
while listening** on page 9.

L ► Notizen schreiben (p. 138)

6 a Copy the chart and complete the notes about Detroit as described in the
travel report.

signs of decay graffiti … …	events International Auto Show – Jan. … …
Improvements wide green spaces … …	sports … … …

b Give an illustrated presentation on Detroit including your notes from 6a and
further interesting aspects about the city.

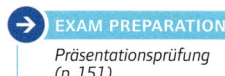

→ EXAM PREPARATION
*Präsentationsprüfung
(p. 151)*

1.16

L ▶ Das Hörverständnis üben
(pp. 137–138)

→ **ZENTRALE KLASSENARBEIT**
Hörverstehen (p. 150)

LISTENING

7 Laura Bradley, a teenager from Detroit, is talking about the history of Motown – the sound that changed America. Answer the following questions in German:

1 Warum ist Laura auf Motown stolz?
2 Wer hat die Firma gegründet und wo kam das Geld her?
3 Was ist der Ursprung des Namens „Motown"?
4 Das Museum ist in einem interessanten Gebäude. Was ist daran interessant?
5 Wann hat das Museum geoffnet?
6 Aus welchen Gründen hatte die Firma eine „charm school"?
7 Wie hat die Musik von Motown zur Rassenintegration beigetragen?

CHALLENGE!

M chael Jackson

PLANNING A VISIT

HANDS-ON
TASK

8 **a** Work with a partner. You have won a competition and the prize is a three-day visit to Detroit for two people. Follow the steps to plan your visit:

Step 1: Decide what you want to see or do and what you don't want to see or do. What are the reasons?
Step 2: Decide how much time you will need for each thing on your list and work out a timetable for your visit.

b Report your plans to the class. Use some of these words and phrases:

We'd like to … because… | We won't visit … because … | We'd rather … than … | So, on the first day, we're going to … | After that … | Later on, we'd like to … | The next day … | Afterwards … | Finally …

READING

L ▶ Lesen schwieriger Texte: Grobverständnis (p. 134)

9 *them* by the American writer Joyce Carol Oates is the story of a poor white family living in Detroit in the 1950s and 1960s. In the extract below, Jules, one of the main characters, is caught up in the 1967 Detroit riots. Read the text and decide which role (a–c) Jules plays in the riots.

a He is an active participant.
b He is a shocked and frightened eye witness.
c He is a passive observer.

¹ flow *strömen*
³ skid *rutschen, schlittern*
³ blare *heulen, plärren*

Riots in Detroit

Down the street flowed a great mob, and in front of it something was flying … many things … rocks, bottles? At the other end of the street, its target, was a police car parked sideways, as if it had skidded into this position. Its siren blared helplessly. Rocks and bottles rained upon it.

[…]

5

Through the smashed window of a grocery store women were stepping carefully, their arms already filled. A boy with too many jars and boxes dropped everything on the curb and cried out in disappointment.

[...]

10 A white woman, her nightgown showing beneath her raincoat, pushed past Jules to get hold of some cans … shrimp. The woman reminded him of his mother, though she was rather ugly, maybe crazy. She stood flat-footed, snatching cans of shrimp off the shelf and stuffing them into a shopping bag. Not even the rowdy little Negro boys could push her aside; she knocked them back with a blind sweep 15 of her arm.

Jules made his way back out to the street. The crowd had thinned out here. People were standing on rooftops, at windows, watching. Some Negro women were crying into their hands. Jules heard more sirens. A milk bottle flew past him and smashed on the sidewalk, but he thought it nothing personal, nothing.

20 Jules sat down on a porch step and watched. Some distance away a firetruck had stopped and the firemen, white men, were milling around. A knot of Negroes watched them. So this was really happening? The end on its way? It was like flaming gasoline poured out onto a flat surface, free to run in any direction, in all directions, urgent and beyond help. Jules smoked cigarettes and watched.

25 The fires were spreading. People were running up the street, their arms filled with clothes and bedding and kids. Some kids turned over a car and set it on fire. They cried out to one another in a language of shrieks, like large, dangerous birds. A couple paused to watch them, arms around each other. Jules could see their joy. He felt touched by it, drawn to it. Let everything burn! Why not? The city was 30 coming to life in fire. Hadn't he understood all along that this would happen?
(380 words)   From *them* by *Joyce Carol Oates*

6 smash *kaputt schlagen*	
7 jar *Konservenglas*	
8 curb *Bordstein*	
11 shrimp *Krabbe(n)*	
12 ugly *hässlich*	
12 snatch off *herunterreißen*	
13 rowdy *rauflustig*	
14 sweep *Schwung*	
21 mill around *umherlaufen*	
23 pour *gießen, schütten*	
24 urgent *dringend*	
26 bedding *Bettzeug*	
27 shriek *durchdringender Schrei*	
28 joy *Freude*	
29 touched *berührt*	
29 drawn to sth *zu etw hingezogen*	

WORKING WITH WORDS

10 a Find the American English words in the text above for the British English words below.

fire engine | pavement | petrol | shop | tin

b Work in small groups. What other differences between British English and American English do you know? Copy the chart and add five more examples to each section.

Vocabulary			
AE	**BE**	**AE**	**BE**
fall	autumn	vacation	holiday
…			
Spelling			
color	colour	center	centre
…			

1.17

c Listen to the way the British woman and the American man pronounce these words. What is the difference?

banana | car | schedule | status | tomato | vitamin | water | Z

LOOKING AT LANGUAGE

G ► The simple past, The past progressive, The past perfect (pp. 152–154)

11 Complete the summary of the text with the correct past tense form of the verbs in brackets.

As the mob ...¹ (move) off down the street, rocks and bottles ...² (fly) all around. Some of them ...³ (hit) a police car that ...⁴ (look) as if it ...⁵ (skid) into a sideways position at the end of the street. Jules ...⁶ (come) across a grocery store. Someone ...⁷ (smash) the window and people ...⁸ (carry) things out of the store. A little boy who ...⁹ (steal) a lot of jars and boxes, ...¹⁰ (drop) them as he ...¹¹ (leave) the store. Jules ...¹² (see) a white woman who ...¹³ (remind) him of his mother. She ...¹⁴ (take) cans of shrimp off the shelf. When Jules ...¹⁵ (go) back out on the street, the crowd ...¹⁶ (become) less dense. People ...¹⁷ (watch) and some women ...¹⁸ (cry). Jules ...¹⁹ (hear) sirens. Then he...²⁰ (sit) down on a porch step and ...²¹ (smoke) several cigarettes. Further down the street some white men ...²² (stand) around a firetruck that ...²³ (stop) some distance away. Jules ...²⁴ (notice) that the fire ...²⁵ (still spread) and people ...²⁶ (run) up the street with their kids and their belongings. One couple ...²⁷ (stop) to watch some kids who ...²⁸ (turn) over a car and set it on fire. Jules ...²⁹ (feel) touched by their joy. After all, he ...³⁰ (know) for a long time that this would happen.

CROSSOVER TV

2

12 Detroit rising from the ashes

Detroit, unable to pay its bills, declared bankruptcy. But there are signs that growth is returning to the once booming metropolis.

Deutsche Welle

a Before you watch, check that you know the meanings of the words below. Use a dictionary if necessary.

liability | shrink | venture | functionality | merge | component | administration | assemble

b Watch the video. What do these numbers refer to?

10 billion | 12 | 250,000 | 260 | 1,100

c Watch again and answer the questions.

1 Why is Detroit "a great place to start a company"? Give at least two reasons.
2 What is the function of the UpTo app?
3 According to Tifani Sadek, what should the city of Detroit do to encourage start-ups?
4 Why is it "natural" for manufacturers to build factories in Detroit?

TEXT 4 London's East End

1.18

L ▶ Lesen schwieriger Texte:
Suche nach Einzelinformationen
(pp. 134–135)

WARM UP ....

1 Read the poem from an online poetry forum. What does it tell us about life in the East End of London? Use your own words.

Life in London's East End

London's East End was a slum, old dears
A waste-hole for all the cast-offs and dregs
It weren't no place for those who had fears
Only fit for the street-jobbers
5   The kids who roamed and learned to be robbers

I remembers, in those days, old dears
When kids had to learn the rules, to cope
Jugs were used to bring home the beers
Screaming kids, an army
10 A dozen or more made the mothers go barmy

Two-up, two-down, me house; me dears
With a cold-water tap in the back-yard
Young women looked a hundred years
They never took any kid's crap
15 Nor the Old Man, with his leather strap

We urchins had a merry time, old dears
Dressed in rags, with plenty of dreams
We laughed through the hurts and tears
Living off our urchin wits
20 Till we wore those old blue borstal kits

It weren't as bad as this poem appears
If you was one of us, old dears!

Source: Plentyoffish > Poems about life in London's East End

² dregs *Abschaum*
⁴ street-jobber *Straßenhändler*
⁷ **cope** *zurechtkommen*
⁸ jug *Krug*
¹⁰ barmy *verrückt, plemplem*
¹¹ two-up, two-down *kleines Reihenhaus mit je zwei Zimmern oben und unten*
¹² **tap** *Wasserhahn*
¹⁴ crap (vulgar) *Unsinn*
¹⁵ strap *Riemen*
¹⁶ urchin *Straßenkind, Gassenjunge*
¹⁷ **rags** *Lumpen*
¹⁹ **wits** *Verstand*
²⁰ borstal *Jugendstrafanstalt*
²⁰ kit *Klamotten, Sachen*

INFO ....

The East End of London

The East End is the part of London north of the River Thames and east of the city's traditional business district, the City of London. In the 19th century, London became more industrialized and the population expanded. Manufacturing and trade grew especially around the docklands in the east. For a time, the Port of London was the
5   world's largest port. Poor people and immigrants came looking for work, but there was not enough housing for them, and many of them were forced to live in overcrowded, smelly slums. Soon the East End became synonymous with poverty, disease and crime. Its reputation was not improved when, in Victorian times, Britain's most notorious serial killer, Jack the Ripper, terrorized the East End.

⁴ **docklands** *Hafenviertel*
⁸ **notorious** *berüchtigt*

During the Second World War, the docklands were an obvious target for German bombs, and much of the East End was destroyed. In the 1950s many people moved out to new housing areas in the suburbs. The last of the East End docks was closed in 1980 and much of the area was redeveloped for housing, business and leisure. For example, Canary Wharf is home to Britain's banking and finance industry, now housed in some of the most impressive buildings in the city. Other huge building projects took place in the East End in preparation for the 2012 Summer Olympic Games. Yet some of the worst poverty in Britain can still be found in the East End of London.

East Enders often consider themselves the 'real' Londoners and call themselves 'Cockneys'. They speak a special dialect, and Cockney rhyming slang is almost impossible to for outsiders understand.

10

15

20

C ▶ Working with cartoons and pictures (p. 21)

2 Describe the pictures. Which sentence in the Info box links up with each of them?

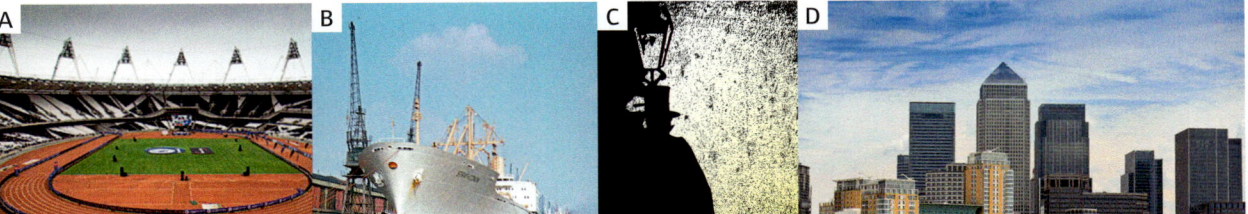

A   B   C   D

L ▶ Lesen schwieriger Texte: Grobverständnis (p. 134)

1.19

3 There are five synonyms for *heruntergekommen* in the text below. Skim the text and find them.

Shoreditch – London's hippest district

2 borough *Stadtbezirk*
8 undergo *durchmachen*
9 gentrification *Gentrifizierung*
10 dilapidated *heruntergekommen*
15 broker *Börsenmakler(in)*

Shoreditch, once a run-down urban area in the borough of Hackney in the East End of London, is today considered to be one of the hippest districts in the city. Like many other London districts, Shoreditch has undergone a process of 'gentrification', which means that property in dilapidated neighbourhoods is bought up and developed, making the area more attractive to the middle classes – to bankers, brokers, doctors and lawyers.

5

10

15

The positive side of gentrification is that derelict neighbourhoods are cleaned up, economic activity increases and crime rates decrease. But as the wealthier residents move in, the original lower-income residents and small businesses move out because they cannot afford the higher rents and taxes. Chains of coffee shops, sandwich bars and burger restaurants take over and small businesses are forced to close. In this way, high streets lose their diversity and begin to all look the same.

20

So what has been gained and what has been lost in Shoreditch through the process of gentrification? On the positive side, some ugly slum areas have been cleared, but unfortunately some attractive, historic buildings have also had to make
25 way for faceless new developments because it is quicker and cheaper to demolish decayed old buildings and build something new than it is to renovate them.

And of course, chain stores and franchises have moved in, but so far Shoreditch has managed to retain some of its own identity. The Columbia Road shops and flower market, which go back to Victorian times, went into serious decline in the
30 1970s, but were saved by local initiatives and growing affluence. Today a wide range of unusual shops makes it one of the most interesting shopping experiences you can have anywhere.

Since the neighbourhood has become more desirable, Shoreditch has become a magnet for the technology industry. In the heart of the district there is an old
35 roundabout that is now called 'Silicon Roundabout', because such a large number of tech companies have started up there. Although it will probably never compete with Silicon Valley in California, more businesses mean more jobs, and more jobs mean more affluence.

Life in Shoreditch has certainly improved for anyone looking for fun. A huge
40 number of entertainment venues have sprung up over the last few years. Shabby pubs have been replaced by smart wine bars and trendy night clubs. New restaurants and art galleries have appeared at a startling rate. And Shoreditch is a great place for street art. Love it or hate it, the streets are full of vibrant and colourful graffiti. Street artists from all over the world come here to paint some of
45 the most sophisticated graffiti you will ever see, and Shoreditch street art tours are one of the great new attractions of London.   (457 words)

22 **gain** *gewinnen*
24 **make way for sth** *einer Sache weichen*
25 **faceless** *gesichtslos, anonym*
27 **franchise** *Lizenzbetrieb*
28 **retain** *beibehalten*
29 **decline** *Verfall*
30 **affluence** *Wohlstand*
35 **roundabout** *Kreisverkehr*
40 **venue** *Lokal*
42 **at a startling rate** *in erstaunlichem Tempo*
43 **vibrant** *lebendig, pulsierend*
45 **sophisticated** *raffiniert, komplex*

WORKING WITH THE TEXT

4 Read the text and do the following tasks using your own words as far as possible.

1 Describe Shoreditch before gentrification.
2 Describe Shoreditch after gentrification.
3 Explain how Columbia Road was saved.
4 Outline what has been gained and what has been lost in Shoreditch through the process of gentrification.

L ▶ Lesen schwieriger Texte: Suche nach Einzelinformationen (pp. 134–135)

CHALLENGE!

WRITING

5 Discuss the advantages and disadvantages of the gentrification of a city district.

EXAM PREPARATION
Textproduktion (p. 150)

WORKING WITH WORDS

6 Find the opposites of these words from the text. They are in the same order.

1 rural   3 lovely   5 poverty   7 unfashionable
2 affluent   4 erect   6 narrow   8 lifeless

7 Which nouns DON'T go with the verbs from the text?

1 to undergo   a tragedy / medical treatment / a test / a transformation
2 to develop   an idea / politics / property / techniques
3 to gain   a competition / knowledge / status / weight
4 to demolish   an argument / a city / a house / a poster
5 to retain   charm / control / identity / experience
6 to take over   a business / a district / the initiative / somebody's property
7 to paint   a description / graffiti / a house / a portrait

LOOKING AT LANGUAGE

G ▶ The definite article (p. 157)

8 Put the definite article into the gaps if necessary.

1 Usually … graffiti is considered to be undesirable, but … graffiti in Shoreditch is special.
2 You can find … most sophisticated street art in the world here and … most of it is painted by excellent artists.
3 In the last decade, … life in Shoreditch has improved.
4 After … lunch, we'll go and look at … Silicon Roundabout.
5 … best time to visit London is in … May.
6 How did you travel to … Olympic Stadium, by … bus or by … car?
7 … English is a world language, but … English spoken by Cockneys is special only to them.

SPEAKING

L ▶ Interaktion (pp. 147 – 148)

9 Work in small groups to discuss the following:

a "High streets lose their diversity and look the same everywhere"
   Is this true for the town / city you live in? Is this a good or a bad thing?
   Explain your answers.

b "Love it or hate it – the streets are full of vibrant and colourful graffiti."
   Why might people love or hate graffiti? How do you feel about it?

10 Choose two of the graffiti slogans below and explain their message in your own words.

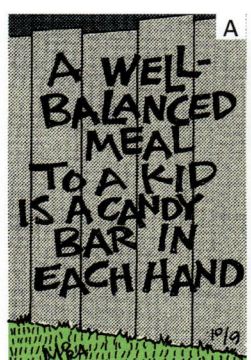

COMPETENCE TRAINING: MIND MAPPING

TIP

Mind mapping is a useful way of brainstorming and organizing your ideas before writing a text or giving a talk. Write the topic word or phrase in the middle then add branches for ideas connected with the topic word. Add as many ideas as you can.

L ▸ Mind Mapping (p. 139)

11 a Make a mind map of your city, town or district and its facilities.

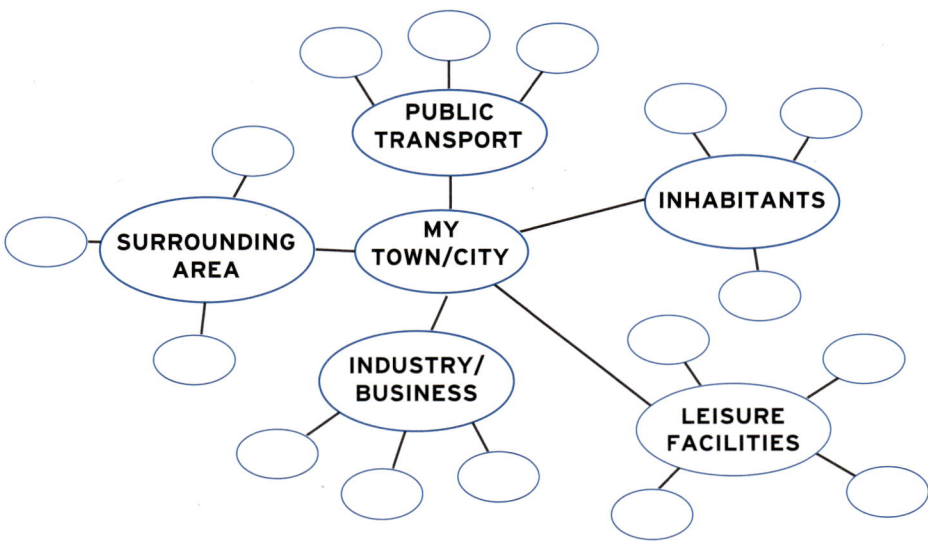

b Using the mind map give a three-minute talk on your city, town or district.

EXAM PREPARATION
Präsentationsprüfung (p. 151)

WRITING

12 Make a mind map of the perfect city and then write a description of it. Use the head words from the mind map in exercise 11.

SPEAKING

13 Work with a partner. Take turns to choose ONE picture from Topic 2. Don't let your partner see your choice. Describe the picture. Your partner has to find the picture you have described.

TEXT 1 Have I got talent?

1 a How would you define a 'celebrity'? Give some examples.

b Listen to the song *Celebrity* by The Subways and say which interpretation below you agree with most. Give reasons.

The song tells us that …
A the woman's ambition is to become a famous actress.
B the woman has no real friends.
C the woman doesn't have a clear idea of what she could be famous for.

2.01

¹ silver screen *Kinoleinwand*
³ arty *pseudokünstlerisch*
¹³ EastEnders *eine beliebte britische TV Serie*
¹⁵ bitch *lästern*
¹⁵ pretender *Blender/in, Angeber/in*
¹⁷ scramble *drängeln*
²⁴ etch *eingravieren*

Celebrity

She doesn't care about the silver screen
She doesn't care about the music business
She doesn't care about the arty scene
'cos all she knows is she wants to be famous!
She wants to ride in a chauffeured car
her photograph in the morning papers
'cos in this world it's who you are
and all she knows is she wants to be famous!

She wants to be a celebrity with her face in a magazine
She doesn't care how you get her there
She just doesn't want to be alone anymore

She doesn't care about the TV shows
unless of course it's about EastEnders
and Hollywood is where she wants to go
where she can bitch about the new pretenders
and everywhere there'll be screaming fans
scrambling just to get her picture
and then the world is in her hands
bigger than the Queen and so much richer
[chorus]
She wants to be a celebrity with her face in a magazine
She doesn't care how you get her there
She just doesn't want to be alone
She'd like to be the party queen who is etched in your memory
She doesn't care if you stop and stare
She just doesn't want to be alone anymore

The Subways at the Frequency Festival,
St. Pölten, 17.8.2012

5

10

15

20

25

30
She's got a dream and she'll never stop
until she's there sitting at the top
She doesn't care what she has to do
even if she has to step over you
and in the club with her famous friends
oh how the highs will never end
until the day when she hits the floor
when no one knows her anymore

35
[chorus]

Lyrics: EMI Music Publishing Ltd

c What are the singer's predictions for the woman's future?

d List the ways of becoming famous that are mentioned in the song and add references to the lyrics.

Example: *film star* (the silver screen, Hollywood)

e Add some more ways of becoming famous to your list in 1d. Name a person who has become famous in this way.

Examples: *Marry royalty – Kate Middleton*   *Excel at a sport – Kobe Bryant*

INFO

A new study has shown a dramatic shift in children's career aspirations. Twenty-five years ago, when children were asked what they wanted to be when they grew up, the top three career choices were teacher, banker and doctor. But today's five- to eleven-year-olds wish to be sports stars, pop stars or actors.

5 When today's parents were asked what they would like their children to do for a living, their top three favourites were lawyer (22 per cent), medical doctor (21 per cent) and entrepreneur (19 per cent). The children's desire for fame and celebrity suggests that media influence is more powerful today than parental advice, which is hardly surprising when the average 10-year-old spends four to five hours a day watching TV or using
10 digital media.

[1] shift *Wandel, Veränderung*
[1] aspiration *Ziel, Bestrebung*
[7] **entrepreneur** *Unternehmer/in*

Top ten career aspirations of today's pre-teens	Top ten ambitions of pre-teens 25 years ago
1 sportsperson 12%	**1** teacher 15%
2 pop star 11%	**2** banker 9%
3 actor 11%	**3** medical doctor 7%
4 astronaut 9%	**4** scientist 6%
5 lawyer 9%	**5** vet 6%
6 firefighter 7%	**6** lawyer 6%
7 medical doctor 6%	**7** sportsperson 5%
8 chef 5%	**8** astronaut 4%
9 teacher 4%	**9** beautician/hairdresser 4%
10 vet 3%	**10** archaeologist 3%

L ▶ Interaktion (pp. 147 – 148)

SPEAKING

2 Work with a partner. Read the Info box and discuss the following questions:

1 Why do you think so many young children want to become celebrities?
2 Which TV shows do you know that might encourage children to aspire to become rich and famous? How do they influence children?
3 Do you think these aspirations are harmful? Why (not)?

3 Make a survey of career aspirations now and in the past. Follow these steps.

1 Find out from your class what their dream jobs were when they were about ten years old. Make a ranking list like the one on the left in the Info box.
2 Find out from as many adults as possible (parents, teachers, …) what they wanted to be when they were children.
3 Pool your information in class and make another ranking list like the one on the right in the Info box.

**HANDS-ON
TASK**

🎧 2.02

¹ **apparently** *anscheinend*
⁶ **preferably** *möglichst, am liebsten*
¹¹ **charity** *Wohltätigkeitsorganisation*
¹⁶ **welfare** *Wohlergehen*
¹⁶ **revised** *überarbeitet, revidiert*
¹⁸ **contestant** *Teilnehmer/in an einem Wettbewerb*
²⁰ **guardian** *Erziehungsberechtigte/r*
²² **vulnerable** *verletzlich, wehrlos*
²³ **misleading** *irreführend*
²⁶ **barely** *kaum*
²⁷ **disenchanted** *desillusioniert*

Children in TV talent shows

Apparently the days are over when children wanted to grow up to be teachers or astronauts. Now many of them want to be actors, singers or YouTube personalities – anything as long as they can become famous – and preferably rich. Perhaps these widespread aspirations help to explain the growing number of children as young as four taking part in talent shows.   5

  10

However, Safermedia, a charity that campaigns for family-friendly media, has called for a ban on children under 16 taking part in TV talent shows. "Children are being put in stressful situations for the sake of entertainment. We constantly see children breaking down and weeping on TV because they can't deal with the pressure," said a spokesperson. "Talent shows take too many risks with children's   15 welfare." The organization is also calling for revised legislation not only for talent shows but also in the modelling and film industries.

The organizers of children's talent shows claim that the welfare of the contestants is their number-one priority, pointing out that there are strict rules on when children can perform and how long they can stay away from school. A parent or guardian   20 has to accompany the children at all times except when they are on stage.

But supporters of the ban believe that talent shows exploit vulnerable people and create false hopes, giving children the misleading idea that it is easy to succeed in the entertainment industry. In addition to the stress involved in performing to an audience of millions, children who win talent competitions are often catapulted   25 into stardom at an age at which they can barely cope with the media attention. Furthermore, their fame may not last, leaving them depressed and disenchanted and feeling that their career is already over at the age of nine or ten.

35 socialite *Salonlöwe,-löwin*
36 distorted *verzerrt*
39 **shallow** *oberflächlich*

30 Child psychologist Dr Monica Miller believes that talent shows and reality TV also corrupt children's values. "Children see footballers, pop stars and actors on TV and their lives look glamorous and exciting. They seldom realize that behind true talent there is a great deal of hard work." This is because, alongside celebrities with real talent, there are many who have little or no talent and are simply

35 'famous for being famous'. This applies, for example, to participants in reality TV shows, socialites or so-called 'It-girls'. As a result this culture of instant fame gives children a totally distorted picture. "Children should have their dreams and ambitions, but if they are not based in some kind of reality, they are going to be very disappointed." Dr Miller is also afraid that young people are becoming extremely shallow. "They are being encouraged to admire people not for what

40 they can do, but for the fact that they have appeared in the media and made a name for themselves." (461 words)

WORKING WITH THE TEXT ....

4 Decide if the statements about the text are true or false. Give reasons for your decisions in complete German sentences.

→ EXAM PREPARATION
Leseverstehen (p. 149)

1 Safermedia wants TV talent shows to be banned.
2 Only a parent or guardian can decide how long a child can stay away from school.
3 Early fame and fortune can leave children upset and disillusioned.
4 Dr Miller says that most celebrities achieve fame through a combination of real talent and hard work.
5 Dr Miller is concerned that children admire people for the wrong reasons.

5 a Match the sentence halves to make statements about the text. There is one sentence half in each list which cannot be matched.

L ► Lesen schwieriger Texte: Suche nach Einzelinformationen (pp. 134–135)

1 Children used to dream of …
2 Safermedia accuses TV talent shows of …
3 Organizers of TV talent shows claim that they …
4 There are celebrities with little or no talent who …
5 Vulnerable young people are often …
6 Contestants under the age of 16 …
7 The media attention surrounding winners of talent competitions …

a because they can't cope with the pressure.
b give top priority to child contestants' welfare.
c given the wrong impression of the entertainment industry.
d taking risks with the welfare of small children.
e becoming teachers or astronauts.
f is often too much for young children to deal with.
g must be accompanied by a parent or guardian at all times.

b Complete the unmatched sentence halves in your own words.

CHALLENGE!

WRITING ....

6 "Children should have their dreams and ambitions, but if they are not based in some kind of reality, they are going to be very disappointed." (ll. 36–37)
Explain the quotation in relation to the text and give further examples of the way the media can give children a distorted view of the world.

→ EXAM PREPARATION
Textproduktion (p. 150)

WORKING WITH WORDS

7 **a** Find the correct definitions a–h for the words 1–8.

1	socialites	a	travelling to famous film locations
2	It-girls	b	programmes that treat factual material in an entertaining way.
3	jet set		
4	A-list	c	people or acts known only for a single success
5	set jetting	d	the most famous and popular celebrities
6	infotainment	e	a TV series in which people's real-life activities are dramatized
7	one-hit wonders		
8	docusoap	f	people well known for going to fashionable parties
		g	fashionable, attractive, famous young women
		h	wealthy people who travel the world

b Think of examples of people, places or programmes for the words and phrases in 7a.

Example: **set jetting** *Visiting Alnwick Castle, which was the location for some Harry Potter films.*

LOOKING AT LANGUAGE

8 **a** Which of these linking words and phrases can you find in the text? Pay attention to how they are used there.

although | as a result | but | because | for example | furthermore | however | if | in fact| not only … but also | so that

b Complete the sentences with a word or phrase from 8a.

1 There are lots of popular talent shows in the UK, … *Britain's Got Talent.*
2 I don't know much about reality TV. …, I've never watched it.
3 People take part in TV talent shows … they can become rich and famous.
4 Children as young as four take part in these shows. …, there are strict rules on how long they can perform.
5 … the singer was only ten, he already had a powerful voice.
6 There was a lot of opposition to children in TV talent shows. … the government introduced new legislation.
7 Talent shows endanger children's welfare and … give them false hopes.

CHALLENGE!

G ▶ Relative pronouns and contact clauses (p. 165)

9 Make sentences with a beginning (1–8) and an ending (a–h). Join the phrases using a relative pronoun (*that, where, which, who, whom* or *whose*) only if it is necessary.

Example: *Isn't that the group that/which won the talent show?*

1	~~Isn't that the group~~	a	act won the show were from the UK.
2	The last talent show	b	the contestant sang was written by her father.
3	The theatre	c	I saw was X-Factor.
4	Malik is the boy	d	has an article about the winner?
5	The organizers with	e	~~won the talent show?~~
6	Where is the magazine	f	mother is very ambitious.
7	The children	g	I spoke said the children's welfare was a priority.
8	The song	h	the competition took place was in London.

LISTENING

2.03

10 **a** The radio show *Crossover Radio UK* interviews two mothers with opposing views on allowing children to compete in talent competitions. Copy and complete the table with their arguments in German.

→ **ZENTRALE KLASSENARBEIT**
Hörverstehen (p. 150)

Chloe	Molly

b Listen for the following phrases in English:

1 Das ist völliger Unsinn. *It's absolute nonsense.*
2 Verstehen Sie mich nicht falsch.
3 Das ist sicherlich schön für Sie.
4 Übrigens …
5 Wenn ich das sagen darf, …
6 Ich glaube nicht, dass Sie ihm einen Gefallen tun, wenn …
7 Abgesehen davon …
8 Nehmen Sie es nicht persönlich, aber …
9 Sie müssen einfach akzeptieren, dass Sie andere Ansichten haben.

CLASS DEBATE

11 Look at the question for debate below. The class divides into halves. One half makes a list of 'Yes' arguments, the other half 'No' arguments. Then present your arguments and debate the issue, using phrases from exercise 10b during your discussion.

Do TV talent shows exploit children?
• Yes, there should be stricter legislation to protect children.
• No, they are fun. Parents have to decide if their children can cope with taking part.

HANDS-ON
TASK

L ▶ Interaktion (pp. 147 – 148)

COMPETENCE TRAINING: VARYING YOUR VOCABULARY

TIP
Especially when writing, you will be able to express yourself in a more interesting way if you have a large vocabulary and don't always use the same words.

12 Which three words below can be used instead of each of the words 1–8?

1 say: *mention, argue, claim*
2 think
3 very
4 important

5 be about
6 nice
7 mostly
8 very interesting

argue | believe | claim | concern | deal with | enjoyable | essential | extremely | fascinating | feel | have to do with | highly | imagine | intriguing | lovely | major | mention | on the whole | pleasant | predominantly | really | significant | thought-provoking | to a large extent

TEXT 2   Life as a celebrity

WARM UP ....

→ **EXAM PREPARATION**
*Kommunikationsprüfung
(p. 150)*

L ▶ Interpretation von Bildern und
Karikaturen (pp. 145–146)

1 Describe the cartoon and explain its message.

A backup plan might be a good idea, in case 'being a celebrity' doesn't work out....

CAREERS ADVISOR

L ▶ Interaktion (pp. 147–148)

2 Complete the questionnaire, then discuss your answers with a partner.

1 What's the difference between being famous and being a celebrity?
2 Name five famous Germans. What are they famous for? What aspects of their private lives are reported in the press?
3 Which celebrity would you most like to spend a day with and why?
4 If you could be a celebrity for a day, who would you like to be and why?
5 Do you think celebrity and gossip magazines are harmless? Why (not)?
6 Do you read celebrity and gossip magazines? Why (not)?
7 Why do you think some celebrities commit suicide?

2.04

9 **embarrassing** *peinlich*
9 confession *Beichte*
10 splash sth across the media *über etw groß in den Medien berichten*
10 **rumour** *Gerücht*
13 mourn *trauern*
14 coffin *Sarg*

Prince Harry – the party prince?

How does it feel when you are three years old and you notice that people with cameras are following you and your mum everywhere you go? Then, as you grow up, you learn that your grandma is the Queen of England and one of the richest women in the world. You find out that your dad and your elder brother are future kings.

When you are twelve your parents go through a very public divorce with embarrassing confessions splashed across the media. There are even rumours that your dad is not your father at all. You are only thirteen when your beautiful mother dies in a tragic accident, and millions of people mourn with you and watch as you follow her coffin.

You'd like to be normal – but what does normal feel like? As His Royal Highness Prince Henry Charles Albert David of Wales you are never going to escape media attention, and that is hard to put up with.

5

10

15

20 At school you excel at sports, but the media prefer to focus on the fact that you are not good academically. After school you go to Australia to do a gap year working on a cattle farm. It's something that lots of young people do, but again for you every step is played out in public.

Then there are the scandals that hit the headlines simply because you are who you are – like the time you wore a swastika armband to a party. OK, it was a pretty stupid joke, but you never expected such a fuss. You were just young and 25 silly. If it had been anyone else, it would have never ended up in the media. And then those unfortunate mobile phone pictures of you naked at a party in Las Vegas. Shocking? The worst thing for you was that somebody in your private sphere took the photos and sold them to the press. Can you really trust anyone?

The media have often portrayed you as being interested only in blondes, guns, 30 aircraft and sport. Yet, you have served as a front-line soldier in Afghanistan, and invented and organized the Invictus games, a Paralympics' sports event for wounded or injured servicemen and -women. You have helped to set up a children's charity in the small African kingdom of Lesotho. With your elder brother you co-founded The Foundation of Prince William and Prince Harry, 35 which gives support to members of the armed forces and their families and to disadvantaged people. But will the media ever acknowledge that you are not the shallow party prince they claim you to be?

Unfortunately, you will never be allowed to draw attention away from your private life. The voracious global media will make sure of that. You are famous, 40 attractive and rich (you inherited £10 million from your mother on your 30th birthday), but don't you sometimes wish you could change places with an ordinary bloke – if only for a while?   (488 words)

20 cattle *Rinder*
23 swastika *Hakenkreuz*
24 **fuss** *großes Aufheben*
28 **trust** *vertrauen*
32 wounded *verwundet*
32 **serviceman/woman** *Soldat/in*
35 **armed forces** *Streitkräfte*
36 **disadvantaged** *benachteiligt*
36 acknowledge *anerkennen*
39 voracious *unersättlich, gierig*
40 **inherit** *erben*
42 bloke *Kerl*

WORKING WITH THE TEXT

3 Read the text and list in German in complete sentences:

1 four things Prince Harry has been criticized for.
2 six things Prince Harry can be praised for.

4 Discuss the following questions with a partner.

L ▸ Interaktion (pp. 147 – 148)

1 What are the advantages and disadvantages of being Prince Harry? Would you like to change places with him? Why (not)?
2 Why do we take such an interest in celebrities? What is their fascination?

WORKING WITH WORDS

5 a Find two- and three-word phrasal verbs in the text for these German words.

1 heranwachsen (para.1)
2 erfahren (para.1)
3 durchmachen (para. 2)
4 ertragen (para. 3)
5 sich abspielen (para. 4)
6 gründen (para.6)
7 landen
8 dafür sorgen

CHALLENGE!

65

b Use the English verbs from 5a in the correct form to complete the sentences.

1 She … a difficult time after her parents divorced.
2 I won't … your bad behaviour any longer.
3 What do you want to be when you …?
4 We wanted to go to Scotland, but … in Northumberland.
5 … the facts before you make a complaint.
6 Two years ago they … their own business.
7 How did you … where she lives?

6 Complete the sentences with the correct preposition(s).

....
after | at | for | forward to | out | up
....

1 I'm looking … meeting some famous people.
2 She often has to stay at home to look … her little sister.
3 Come and look … my holiday pictures.
4 You can borrow my tablet, but you must look … it.
5 Do you have time to look … this report?
6 My job is boring. I'm going to look … a new one.
7 I've lost my keys. Can you help me to look … them.
8 If you don't know the word, look it … in the dictionary.
9 Look …! You're going to break that lamp.

INFO

The British royal family and the German connection

In 1917 the British king, George V, decided to change his family's surname from Saxe-Coburg-Gotha to Windsor as a way of distancing the royal family from its German origins in the face of anti-German sentiment during and after the First World War.

The first German king to take the British throne was George I from the House of Hanover in 1714, and from then on until the present day the British royal family has had strong German blood ties. 35 of George V's many cousins were German and 44 half-German. Kaiser Wilhelm II, Britain's number-one enemy in the second decade of the 20th century, was one of George V's 79 (!) German or half-German cousins.   5

Prince Harry's great-great uncle Edward VIII, who gave up the throne in 1936 to marry an American divorcee, approved of Nazi ideology and was a supporter of Adolf Hitler. He once told a journalist that it would be tragic for the world if Hitler were overthrown.   10

There is no doubt about the current royal family's 'Britishness', and fortunately there is no longer any reason to hide their German past.

7 Read the Info box. Match the words and phrases below with the underlined words and phrases. If necessary, use a dictionary to help you.

....
brought down | divorced woman | feeling | present | relationship through birth |
the most important | when confronted with
....

LOOKING AT LANGUAGE

8 Complete the sentences with *will* or *going to* and the words in brackets.

G ▶ The future (pp. 155–156)

1 I think Prince Harry … (continue) to hit the headlines.
2 Look! Those paparazzi … (break) the car window!
3 Couldn't you get the latest *Hello* magazine? Don't worry. I … (lend) you mine.
4 I've taken some great photos of Harry and I … (post) them on Facebook.
5 I believe the new privacy laws … (come) into force next month.
6 We … (attend) the Academy Awards. We already have tickets.
7 Prince Harry … (probably, never, be) king.
8 Look out! The actor … (crush) by that crowd of fans. (*Passive!*)

CHALLENGE!

9 Work with a partner. Look at the sample horoscope below. Write a horoscope for your partner. Give your horoscope to your partner to read aloud and correct any mistakes he/she can find.

G ▶ The future (pp. 155–156)

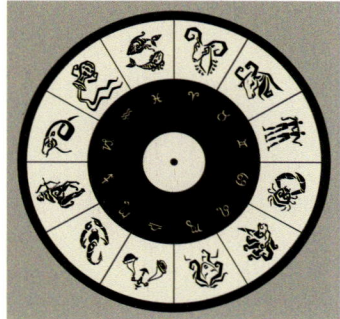

General: This week is going to be a good week for you. On Monday you are going to hear something that will please you and perhaps bring exciting new changes into your life.
Career: This week will probably be a good time to ask your boss about promotion, but he's not going to give you a pay rise, so don't even ask!
Romance: Soon a new and interesting person is going to enter your life, although you will probably not notice at first how important this person will become.
Health: There's a possibility that you will catch a cold, so dress up warmly.

SPEAKING

10 What do you think? Give reasons for your answer.

Celebrities may argue: Everyone has "the right to respect for his private and family life, his home and his correspondence" (Article 8 – European Convention on Human Rights). Therefore we have the right not to be filmed and photographed when we are not at work.

The press may argue: Everyone has "the right to freedom of expression … freedom to hold opinions and to receive and impart information and ideas" (Article 10 – European Convention on Human Rights). Therefore we have the right to inform the public about everything celebrities do.

Who, in your opinion, is right?

PROJECT

11 Work in groups. Make a list of the advantages and disadvantages of being rich and famous. Compare your lists with another group and then make a poster.

HANDS-ON TASK

L ▶ Arbeitsergebnisse präsentieren
(pp. 144–145)

L ▶ Mind mapping (p. 139)

COMPETENCE TRAINING: PRESENTATIONS

TIP
Seven steps to a successful presentation:
Step 1: Choose your topic.
Step 2: Research your topic.
Step 3: Prepare your talk – use a mind map to brainstorm your ideas.
Step 4: Organize your ideas into an introduction, main points and a conclusion.
Step 5: Practise your talk alone or with a friend or relative.
Step 6: Use visual aids – but not too many.
Step 7: Give your presentation. Before you start, take a deep breath, stand up straight,
look at your audience and speak slowly and clearly.

→ **EXAM PREPARATION**
Präsentationsprüfung
(p. 151)

12 Work with a partner. Choose one of the topics below for a presentation and research your topic at home. Then take turns to talk for three to five minutes. Your partner will copy and fill in the assessment sheet below. After your talk your partner will give you his/her feedback.

Topics
1 **A famous person I admire**
Talk about the life and work of a famous person of your choice.
2 **Films**
Talk about the last film you saw or a favourite film.
3 **A healthy lifestyle**
Talk about what constitutes a healthy lifestyle and your own habits.
4 **Teenage rebellion**
Talk about the ways in which teenagers rebel and their motives.
5 **Fashion**
Talk about brand names and fashion in clothes, electronic devices, etc. How important are brand names and fashion to young people in general and to you personally?

Assessment sheet

	☺	😐	☹		☺	😐	☹
Information (interesting? well researched?)				Pronunciation (easy to understand?)			
Structure (easy to follow?)				Grammar (only a few mistakes?)			
Body language (relaxed? eye contact?)				Vocabulary (wide range?)			
Fluency (gaps, breaks or hesitation?)				General impression			

☺ = very good   😐 = OK   ☹ = needs improvement

CELEBRITY QUIZ

 a   Do the quiz with a partner and find out how much you know about celebrities. Compare your answers with another pair.

1   In which TV show did the English band One Direction get to know each other?
 a Britain's Got Talent
 b The X-Factor
 c Pop Idol

4   Who plays the lead in iCarly?
 a Victoria Justice
 b Miranda Cosgrove
 c Vanessa Hudgens

2   In which series did Miley Cyrus get her breakthrough?
 a *Hannah Montana*
 b *Girl Meets World*
 c *Shake It Up*

5   In which Hollywood film did Heidi Klum play herself?
 a *The Twilight Saga*
 b *Mamma Mia*
 c *The Devil Wears Prada*

3   Justin Bieber is a(n) … singer and songwriter.
 a American
 b British
 c Canadian

6   Which American actor was born in Germany and had a German mother?
 a Bruce Willis
 b George Clooney
 c Tom Cruise

b   With a partner write a four-question celebrity quiz. Swap your quiz with another pair. Check each other's answers.

HANDS-ON TASK

WRITING

 Find a recent piece of news about a celebrity and write about it in English using your own words.

ROLE PLAY

 a   Explain the following quote in your own words.

"In future, everyone will be world famous for 15 minutes."   – Andy Warhol (artist)

b   Work in pairs and prepare a television interview for BBC World. One of you is the interviewer and one of you is one of the people below. Play your interview to the class. Make it as interesting as possible so that the class will enjoy listening to you.

L ▶ Interaktion (pp. 147 – 148)

- You were a passenger on a cruise ship that sank.
- You have just won an Olympic gold medal.
- You sailed round the world alone in a boat.
- You were attacked by a shark while you were surfing off Bondi Beach.
- You were on holiday on a South Pacific island when it was hit by a tsunami.

TEXT 3 **Celebrities and their charities**

WARM UP ....

1 With a partner think of five different ways that charities appeal for or raise money.

Example: *benefit concerts*

2 Work with a partner. You have five minutes to make a list of the charities and aid organizations that you know. Compare your list with another pair.

3 Skim the text to see if any of the charities on your list are mentioned.

2.05

0 **benefit** *profitieren*
1 **aid agency** *Hilfsorganisation*
5 link *in Verbindung bringen*
14 beneficiary *Nutznießer/in*
17 **NGO: non-governmental organization**
20 endorsement *Befürwortung, Unterstützung*
23 **cynical** *zynisch*
24 put sb off *jdn abschrecken*
28 outcome *Ergebnis, Resultat*
29 backing *Befürwortung, Unterstützung*

Who benefits most?

Emma Watson at the world premier of "This is the End", Regency Village Theater, Los Angeles, 2013

A While charities and aid agencies rely a great deal on celebrities to help them get publicity and promote their organizations, authors, actors, artists, musicians, sportspersons and supermodels like to have their names linked to good causes. When they lend their name to a charity, it rarely fails to attract some welcome publicity. But who benefits most, the charity or the celebrity? 5

B According to a study in the UK carried out by British academics, Professor Dan Brockington of the University of Manchester and Professor Spencer Henson of the University of Sussex, the answer is that the main beneficiaries are the stars themselves. 10 15

C The study involved 2,000 ordinary members of the public who were asked to link the names of seven well-known NGOs, including Amnesty International and the Red Cross, to a celebrity who promotes them. While the majority of those asked recognized the names of the organizations, more than two-thirds could not link them to a celebrity, suggesting that their endorsements have little effect. 20

D While the study shows that their involvement in good causes makes stars such as Angeline Jolie, George Clooney and Emma Watson even more popular, it would be cynical to say celebrities are only acting in their own interests. Although some people are put off by celebrity endorsement, doubting the motivation of the rich and famous, the researchers are careful to stress that, in general, the stars 25 are genuinely concerned about 'making the world a better place' and do not simply support charities for self-promotion – even though this may be the outcome.

E So if most people take little notice of celebrity backing, what then are the reasons why people choose to support a particular charity? The study shows that 30 people tend to support charities that are important to them because of personal or family connections, and not as a result of celebrity-endorsed promotion.

F   The charities themselves seem to be sceptical about the findings of the study. A spokesperson for the charity Comic Relief said: "Celebrities can reach millions of people, but people are often unwilling to admit that they are influenced by them. The fact that the majority of people know the brand names of NGOs and aid agencies shows that somehow our publicity has got through to them. After telethons such as the BBC shows on Red Nose Day, in which many celebrities take part, we receive millions in donations from the public. And without the help of celebrities like Bono and Bob Geldof, I don't believe so many children in poor countries would be going to school today."   (428 words)

[38] telethon *Spendensammelaktion im Fernsehen*
[39] **donation** *Spende*

WORKING WITH THE TEXT

4   Read the text and find out which paragraph (B–F) answers the questions.

1 What do some charities think about the findings of the study?
2 Who gets the most out of the celebrity-charity relationship?
3 How do people choose a charity to support?
4 What, according to the study, generally motivates celebrities to promote a charity?
5 What did the study involve?

L ▶ Lesen schwieriger Texte: Grobverständnis (p. 134)

5   Answer the following questions, using your own words as far as possible.

1 What do charities expect from celebrities?
2 Where did the study take place?
3 What are the six types of celebrity mentioned in the text?
4 What were the participants in the study asked to do?
5 What would be the cynical view of celebrities' involvement in charities?
6 Why is the spokesperson for Comic Relief sceptical about the findings of the study?

L ▶ Lesen schwieriger Texte: Suche nach Einzelinformationen (pp. 134–135)

CHALLENGE!

6   Decide if the statements about the text are true or false. Give reasons for your decisions in complete German sentences.

1 The study was carried out among British academics.
2 About one third of the people in the study could link the names of charities and celebrities.
3 Involvement in a charity has little or no effect on a celebrity's popularity.
4 The study proved that stars support charities out of self-interest.
5 Most people support a charity as a result of celebrity-endorsed promotion.
6 The Comic Relief spokesperson doesn't fully accept the findings of the study.
7 The spokesperson thinks that people are not greatly influenced by celebrities.

→ EXAM PREPARATION
Leseverstehen (p. 149)

CHALLENGE!

WORKING WITH WORDS

7   Find German equivalents of these English expressions from the text.

1 it rarely fails (l. 7)
2 act in their own interests (l. 23)
3 put off by (l. 24)
4 celebrity-endorsed (l. 32)

8   **a**   Find the nouns in the text for these verbs.

to benefit	to donate	to find	to motivate	to promote
to connect	to endorse	to involve	to organize	to publicize

71

b   Complete the sentences using the verbs in 8a in the appropriate form.

1   What usually … celebrities to lend their name to a charity?
2   Which charity do you think … most from next Saturday's telethon?
3   People support charities that are … to their own or their family's interests.
4   The study the university carried out … that most people know the names of NGOs.
5   Celebrities … millions of dollars to a variety of charities every year.
6   I'm … in a charity event to raise money for cancer research.
7   Last month a newspaper … the amounts donated to charity by Hollywood stars.
8   Sports stars can earn a lot of money by … sports equipment.

CHALLENGE!

c   Write your own sentences with the verbs from 8a that you did not use in 8b.

LOOKING AT LANGUAGE

9   **a**   Work in pairs. You have five minutes to find as many words in the text as possible that can be used as both nouns and verbs.

Example: *cause*

G ▶ Tenses (pp. 152–156)
The passive (pp. 160–161)

b   Use verbs you found in 9a in the correct tense in active or passive to complete the sentences.

1   Meryl Streep … in dozens of films. Last year she … in another box-office hit.
2   My dad … the same football team since he was a boy.
3   I'm starting university next month. I … maths.
4   All the journalist's questions … during the celebrity interview.
5   The actress said that she … (not) at all by linking her name to a charity.

CHALLENGE!

6   I … with her for ages, but I couldn't change her mind.
7   The star's name … to the name of a multi-millionaire.

COMPETENCE TRAINING: MEDIATION

TIP
Mediation is **not** translating. It means summarizing important information in another language. It can be either spoken or written. If written, your text should be somewhat shorter than the original text. Paraphrase the words if you don't know the English or German equivalent.

INFO

Charitybuzz is a for-profit internet company that raises funds for NGOs and charities in online auctions with celebrities and brands. The company was founded in 2005 by American Coppy Holzman, who realized he could link pop culture with technology to raise funds. He and his team persuaded 70 celebrities   5
and luxury brands to offer personal meetings, VIP tickets to shows, events or parties, invitations to film sets, vacations and other gifts to be auctioned online. The business grew quickly through word of mouth and, since its launch, it has raised more than $100 million dollars for charity. Auction experiences include entertainment, business, politics, sports, arts, fashion and other industries.   10

How it works:

A celebrity donates a lunch date, a company donates a gold watch, or a famous writer offers to name a character in his next novel after the winner of the auction. The auction goes online and people bid. The highest bidder wins the experience or the gift. At the
15   end of each auction Charitybuzz keeps 20 per cent to cover its operating costs. The rest goes to charity. The company's motto is 'Do good, live well'.

Top bids:

- The chance to spend the day with former President Bill Clinton to benefit the Clinton Foundation: Final bid of $250,000.
20 - The very first Chevrolet Volt car off the production line to benefit Detroit Public Schools. Final bid: $225,000.
- A tour of Facebook's headquarters with Company Director Blake Ross to benefit the Peace Corps. Final bid: $70,000.

10 Summarize the Info box in German for a friend who does not understand English.

L ▶ Mediation (p. 148)

ROLE PLAY ·

11 Work in groups of four. Imagine a situation where a famous celebrity wants to give a million dollars to a charity. He has four advisers who will help him decide who to give the money to. Play the roles of the advisers. You have to come to an agreement on how to divide up the money and who to give it to. You can give all the money to one charity, or you can divide it between a maximum of four different ones.

HANDS-ON TASK

L ▶ Interaktion (pp. 147 – 148)

Student A

These are the charities you would like to support:
1 A charity that looks after stray animals
2 A charity to help poor children in Africa
3 A charity that runs vocational training schemes for handicapped people

Student B

These are the charities you would like to support:
1 A charity doing research into cancer
2 A charity which aims to protect endangered species of animals worldwide
3 A charity that helps the homeless in Germany

Student C

These are the charities you would like to support:
1 A charity that supports poor, elderly people in Germany
2 A charity that helps street kids in Brazil
3 A charity that helps to establish schools in developing countries

Student D

These are the charities you would like to support:
1 A charity that helps unemployed young people in Germany to transform their lives
2 A charity which aims to build a village for homeless orphans in India
3 A charity for the victims of earthquakes and floods in developing countries.

2.06

LISTENING

→ ZENTRALE KLASSENARBEIT
Hörverstehen (p. 150)

12 Listen to a radio report about Laughing Man Worldwide, a charity sponsored by Hugh Jackman, an Australian actor. Take notes and then complete the following sentences in German.

Hugh Jackman at the launch of "Laughing Man Tea and Coffee", 5th Floor Bar, Harvey Nichols, London, 2012

1 Jackman kam die Idee für seine Firma, als …
2 Er war von Dukale zutiefst beeindruckt, weil …
3 Er versprach Dukale, dass er …
4 Jackman gründete Laughing Man Worldwide, …
5 Die im Laughing Man Café angebotenen Produkte sind …

READING

13 Find three sentences in the text below that do not belong there.

The search engine giant Google has started a new app that lets people give just $1 to a charity. When users open the *One Today* app, they are presented with several projects to which they can donate $1 with just one click. Some organizations have lost a lot of money this way. A spokesperson said, "Google has a long-standing commitment to supporting non-profit organizations, and to making the world a better place. A lot of   5
money has been invested in our new headquarters. We also hope that people will share their favourite projects on social media sites, so that even more people donate. 'Do good daily' is the motto." Charity shops are, of course, another option. As many people can afford an occasional $1 donation, the app has helped to raise a lot of funds for various charitable organizations because it has made donating simple and fun. There   10
is also a possibility of sharing with friends and an option to match friends' donations.

L ► Eine Stellungnahme schreiben (pp. 140 - 141)

COMPETENCE TRAINING: WRITING A COMMENT

TIP

When you write a comment, collect and present arguments for and against.
You can make a table or a mind map. Write your comment using the following outline.

Introduction: Statement of the issue in your own words
Development: Arguments for and against with reasons and/or examples
I agree with the statement / quotation because …
I disagree with the statement / quotation because …
On the one hand …, but on the other …
Conclusion: Restatement of opinion and summary of reasons
When I weigh up …
On balance I feel that …
My main reasons for this conclusion are …

WRITING

→ EXAM PREPARATION
Textproduktion (p. 150)

14 Look at the quotation. Explain the meaning in your own words. Comment on the message of the quotation.

"I'm sick to death of famous people standing up and using their celebrity to promote a cause. If I see a particular need, I do try to help. But there's a lot that can be achieved by putting a cheque in the right place and shutting up about it."

- Russell Crowe (actor and film producer)

TEXT 4   It's a digital world

L ▶ Interaktion (pp. 147–148)

WARM UP ....

1 Complete the questionnaire and then discuss your answers with a partner.

1 How long do you spend online on average each day?
2 What is the main reason you go online?
3 How many emails and texts do you send and receive on an average day?
4 What sort of social media do you use?
5 Which social networking sites do you use?
6 What is your favourite form of communication?

Is digital technology sending us out of our minds?

2.07

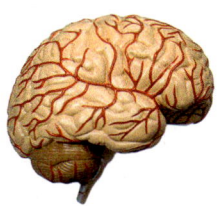

On the way to a recent meeting, my mobile phone ran out of juice. Suddenly, from being a 21st-century multi-tasker, I felt as if my legs had been chopped off. I couldn't look up the address where I was going, nor send an email or text saying I'd be late, nor call home.

The world felt lonely and alien: everyone in the street, apart from me, seemed glued to their smartphones. And I realized then that neurologist Susan Greenfield might have a point in her book *Mind Changes: How Digital Technologies Are Leaving Their Mark On Our Brains*. According to Greenfield, we have become such slaves to digital technology that it has begun to alter our brains.

Our constant need to check Twitter and Facebook updates; our inability to converse without constantly glancing at emails or text messages: this is addictive behaviour which, a generation ago, we would have found impossible to imagine. Today we accept it as one of the prices we pay for being modern.

But, argues Greenfield, it could be more worrying than that. Social networking may be worsening our communication skills; gaming could be making us more reckless; reliance on search engines may mean we're sacrificing deep knowledge and understanding; our ability to reinvent ourselves online may lead us to lose our sense of who we really are.

Her chapters on video games are especially scary. It turns out games are designed to be addictive, which is why it's not uncommon for gamers to play for ten hours at a stretch. And they stimulate the same functions in the brain associated with gambling, drug-taking and schizophrenia, flooding the front part of the brain with the addictive chemical dopamine.

The front part is the most impressionable part of the brain, not developing fully until your mid-20s. Gamers are often younger than that, which means, potentially, that they could be doing irreparable damage to their mental functions.

5

10

15

20

25

⁴ chop off *abhacken*
⁹ be glued to sth *an etw kleben*
¹¹ mark *Spur(en)*
¹² **slave** *Sklave, Sklavin*
¹² alter *verändern*
¹⁴ **glance at sth** *einen Blick auf etw werfen*
¹⁴ **addictive behaviour** *Suchtverhalten*
¹⁹ **reckless** *leichtsinnig*
¹⁹ **reliance on sth** *Abhängigkeit von etw, Angewiesensein auf etw*
²⁰ reinvent *neu erfinden*
²² scary *beängstigend*
²⁴ at a stretch *ohne Unterbrechung*
²⁵ gambling *Glücksspiel*
²⁷ impressionable *beeinflussbar*
²⁸ potentially *möglicherweise*

30 smug *selbstzufrieden*
32 **distracted** *abgelenkt*
43 sustained attention *anhaltende Aufmerksamkeit, Daueraufmerksamkeit*
46 **persuasive** *überzeugend*
47 **comprise** *umfassen*
47 conduct sth *etw durchführen*

Even if you're a non-gamer, you've no reason to be smug. Have you noticed how 30
much harder it is these days to concentrate on a long article? That's because social
media and the net are making our brains more easily distracted. Take, for example,
those hyperlinks you click on, mid-article, that take you somewhere different,
often making you forget what you were looking for in the first place. And if it's
bad for us, it's going to be worse for our children. 35

Sure, there are benefits: IQs are rising – believed to be the result of living in a
more stimulating environment. But our progress is slowing on tests that measure
verbal or problem-solving ability, or which require deeper understanding. We're
becoming like computers: super-efficient at processing information but hopeless
at interpreting it. 40

In other words, we're losing what it is to be human. For centuries, we have made
sense of our existence by telling stories. We still do this, of course, but we're
finding it harder to cope with complexity or anything requiring 'sustained
attention'.

Greenfield is not just a good communicator but a thoughtful, responsible scientist, 45
and the arguments she makes are well supported and persuasive. The past 20
years comprise the biggest experiment on the human brain ever conducted. For
good or ill, the human race is never going to be the same again.   (544 words)

Adapted from *Mail on Sunday* Ireland

WORKING WITH THE TEXT

L ▸ Lesen schwieriger Texte:
Suche nach Einzelinformationen
(pp. 134–135)

2 Read the text and do the following tasks, using your own words as far as possible.
Give your answers in complete sentences.

1 Describe how the writer felt when he was unable to use his mobile phone.
2 Interpret ll. 20–21 *"Our ability to reinvent ourselves ... our sense of who we
   really are"*.
3 Outline the dangers of video games, according to Greenfield.
4 Explain why we are becoming less human and more like computers.

CHALLENGE!

3 What are some of the problems that may be caused by overreliance on digital
technology? Make a list in complete German sentences. You will find all four items
in paragraph 4.

WORKING WITH WORDS

4 a Find adjectives in the text from these verbs.

1 impress   2 hope   3 persuade   4 think   5 worry

b Find verbs in the text from these nouns and adjectives.

1 conversation   2 imagination   3 loss   4 sacrifice   5 worse

c Find nouns in the text from these verbs and adjectives.

1 behave   2 complex   3 exist   4 rely   5 unable

5 Use the correct form of the words you found in exercise 4 to complete the sentences. Use each word only once.

1 His arguments were so … he managed to convince me.
2 His … to concentrate seems to have …
3 Our total … on automobiles is …
4 The child is at a(n) … age and he copies everything he sees.
5 I'm not … my day off to go shopping with you.
6 It is impossible to understand the … of human …

6 a Use the suffixes below to make adjectives.

-able | -al | -ful | –ive | -y

1 addict   2 doubt   3 culture   4 invent   5 sleep   6 enjoy

b Use the suffixes below to make nouns.

-ance | -ence | –ity | – ion | -ness | -ment

1 educate   2 curious   3 defend   4 dominant
5 available   6 forgive   7 disturb   8 achieve

7 a Find the opposites of these words in the text.

1 ability   2 possible   3 common   4 reparable

b Use one of the prefixes to make the opposite of these words.

-im- | il- | in- | ir- | un–

1 relevant   2 legal   3 patient   4 healthy
5 convenient   6 moral   7 literate   8 married

8 a What are the missing parts of the verbs?

infinitive	past simple	past participle
raise	…	…
rise	…	…

b Complete the sentences with the correct form of *raise* or *rise*.

1 IQs … in the last decade thanks to the stimulus of digital technology.
2 The sun … in the east.
3 Last week's benefit concert … a lot of money for charity.
4 If you want to ask a question, please … your hand.
5 The cost of living … only slightly last year.
6 The railway company … the price of tickets twice since January.

LOOKING AT LANGUAGE

G ▶ Gerund/Infinitive (pp. 162–163)

9 **a** **Complete the sentences below with a gerund or infinitive.**

1 Many of us have a constant need … emails. (check)
2 We pay a high price for … dominated by technology. (be)
3 It was impossible … the impact the internet would have 20 years ago. (imagine)
4 Computers are very good at … information but hopeless at … it.
   (process, interpret)
5 Lack of concentration is a result of … too much time with digital technology.
   (spend)
6 Even if you enjoy … video games, you shouldn't forget that they are designed …
   addictive. (play, be)

CHALLENGE!

7 Serious gamers are used to … games for hours at a stretch. (play)
8 One day you might regret … so much time in a virtual world. (spend)

G ▶ Participle constructions
   (pp. 165–166)

b **Rewrite these sentences, replacing the parts in italics with participle clauses.**

Example: I couldn't send an email or text *which said I would be late*.
         I couldn't send an email or text <u>saying I would be late</u>.

1 *While I was surfing the internet*, I found some useful information.
2 Many people find it difficult to deal with anything *that requires sustained attention*.
3 *As she is a responsible scientist*, her opinions should be taken seriously.
4 Hyperlinks take you somewhere else, *which makes you forget what you were reading first*.

CHALLENGE!

5 *Since he discovered that gaming is addictive*, he has given it up.
6 *After my mobile phone had run out of juice*, I was unable to send a message.
7 *When I had checked that my mobile phone was charging*, I went to bed.

READING

10 **These five sentences are missing from the text below. Decide where they belong.**

1 Just use your translation app.
2 GPS has taken over navigation.
3 Anyway, new technologies have always
   prompted strong reactions.
4 There's no need to learn.
5 Let's start with the car.

⁵ spatial *räumlich*
⁶ **superfluous** *überflüssig*

Is it true that the smarter our possessions are, the more incompetent we become?
Well, I have to confess that my smartphone is a lot smarter than I am, and now
that my house and car are getting smarter, I'll soon be the dumbest one around
here. It signals when I've forgotten to fasten my seatbelt or turn off the lights, so
my memory has less to do. I don't need my spatial skills because the car guides   5
me through parking. My ability to map read is now superfluous. OK, I still have
to steer and brake, but that will no longer be necessary when self-driving robotic
cars replace current models. The only decision I'll have to make is where to sit!

There's no longer any need to study grammar or spelling thanks to the spell check
on our computers. And you'll never have to learn to speak a foreign language.   10
Calculators and Excel spreadsheets make learning maths a waste of time – or at
least that's what my son tells me. But the jury's still out on that one.

Cooking? We'll just microwave ready-made meals we order on the internet and have delivered to the house. Handwriting? Forget it. You'll only need to be able to write your signature. The main thing is to master your keyboard and keypad.

But I'm not going to get on my high horse and talk about the dumbing down of the human race. I believe that, with the flood of knowledge and information around today, technology will help us stay smart. For example, it was once believed that travelling in a motor car faster than 10 kilometres per hour meant taking your life into your hands. And we all know what happened to that idea!

(318 words)

[15] **signature** *Unterschrift*
[16] **dumbing down** *Verdummung*

WORKING WITH THE TEXT

11 **Read between the lines.**

1 Is the writer for or against our reliance on technology? Give reasons for your answer.
2 Is the writer convinced by his/her son's arguments against learning maths? How do you know?

L ► Lesen schwieriger Texte: Suche nach Einzelinformationen (pp. 134–135)

WORKING WITH WORDS

12 **a** **Match the idioms 1–7 with their definitions a–g.**

1	get on your high horse	**a**	the final decision has not been made
2	take your life into your own hands	**b**	try to save money
		c	get fired from your job
3	the jury is still out	**d**	do something very risky
4	a piece of cake	**e**	really easy
5	fight a losing battle	**f**	try to do something where you will be sure to fail
6	tighten your belt	**g**	act as if you are more intelligent than other people
7	get the sack		

b **Choose the idiom from 12a which best fits the situation and use it to complete the sentence.**

1 She … and now she's unemployed.
2 I don't earn as much as I used to, so … .
3 A: Was the exam difficult? B: No, …
4 If you try to put a stop to progress, you …
5 … on whether technology is making us dumber or not.
6 There's no point … and judging others by your own standards.
7 Driving on the wrong side of the road, he …

CHALLENGE!

COMPETENCE TRAINING: DOING A PROJECT

TIP
A project consists of several steps:
Step 1: Read the task carefully and decide on your aims – what is the end product going to be, e.g. a graph, a chart, a poster, a class magazine, a web page?
Step 2: Decide on the tasks each member of the team will have.
Step 3: Research your topic. You can collect material by interviewing people, researching on the internet and/or asking an organization for brochures or posters.
Step 4: Present your project.

HANDS-ON
TASK

13 a   Work in small groups. Choose one of the following subjects to research amongst members of the group, their family and friends.

1   Which communication technologies are the most popular?
2   At what time(s) of day do people spend time on social media?
3   How many times a day do people check their email, Facebook messages, etc.?
4   What are people's favourite mobile phone apps?

b   Decide which type of visual aid – a poster, bar chart, pie chart or line graph – best illustrates your findings in 13a.

c   Present your project to the class. Compare your diagrams and posters with other groups. Are they similar or different?

WRITING

14 Write an email to an English friend. Describe the results of your class survey. Use some of the following words:

the majority   *a small minority*   *very few people*   *only x per cent*

INFO

⁰ divide *Kluft*

The global digital divide

Around 40% of the world's population has an internet connection today. In 1995, it was less than 1%. Unfortunately, there is still an enormous gap between the most and the least switched-on countries.

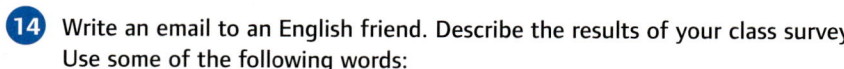

Percentage of population with access to the internet							
Norway	96.2	Germany	87	Indonesia	19.9	Malaysia	2.3
South Korea	91.1	USA	86.7	India	16.7	Sierra Leone	1.5
UK	89.9	Peru	40.9	Afghanistan	5.9	Myanmar	1.2

5

The inequality between populations with access to modern information and communications technology and those without is known as the 'global digital divide'. It is a gap that threatens to further deepen the social and economic inequality between developing and developed countries. Developing countries cannot hope to become part of the global economy without the modern tools to do so. Urgent action is needed at the local, national and international levels to bridge this divide, not only with the necessary infrastructure and equipment, but also with the essential know-how to use it.

10

INTERNET RESEARCH

HANDS-ON
TASK

15 'Close the Gap' is an international non-profit organization that aims to bridge the digital divide. Research on the internet and find out the answers to the following questions. Use your own words if possible.

1   How does the charity aim to bridge the gap?
2   How many projects does the charity have worldwide?
3   What are the first five steps in a project cycle?
4   What is the last step in a project cycle?
5   What is the first step in applying for a computer?

TEXT 5   Time for a digital detox

detox *Entgiftung*

WARM UP

1 Describe the cartoon and explain its message.

2 Choose the adjectives below that describe
how you feel when you can't use your
mobile phone. Explain why you feel that way.

anxious | awkward | bored | disconnected |
frustrated | liberated | lost | nervous | relaxed |
relieved | strange | uncomfortable

STAHLER
5/18

  EXAM PREPARATION

*Kommunikationsprüfung
(p. 150)*

L ▶ Interpretation von Bildern und
Karikaturen (pp. 145–146)

awkward *unbehaglich*

disconnected *abgeschnitten,
abgekoppelt*

liberated *befreit*

relieved *erleichtert*

2.08

⁴ implore *anflehen*

⁸ Internet Addiction
Disorder *Internetabhängigkeitssyndrom (IAS)*

¹⁰ withdrawal *Entzug*

¹² muster *aufbringen*

¹⁴ capitalize on sth *aus etw
Kapital schlagen*

¹⁶ insurance broker
Versicherungsmakler/in

¹⁸ prompt *veranlassen*

¹⁸ relinquish sth *auf etw verzichten*

¹⁸ **enrol in sth** *sich für etw
anmelden*

²⁴ trunk *Truhe*

²⁸ hike *Wanderung*

The unplugged weekend

Do you sleep with your smartphone or tablet
by your bedside? Do you check your email,
Facebook page or Instagram the moment you
wake up? Do your family members implore
5 you to look up from your phone? You might
need a digital detox.

Constant use of email, social media and constant news feeds can be damaging to
one's health, according to several recent studies. Internet Addiction Disorder (IAD)
is now a recognized problem. Indeed, when frequent internet users turn off their
10 devices, they undergo withdrawal symptoms similar to those experienced by drug
users, according to a study at Swansea and Milan universities.

But what if you simply can't muster the personal willpower to take even a day or
two away from your screens? You're not alone – and plenty of businesses are
looking to capitalize on your digital dependence. You could, for example, try a
15 weekend detox course in the countryside.

For Kim Beckett, 28, who works as an insurance broker in London, it was the
realization that she was addicted to WhatsApp and other social media that
prompted her to relinquish her phone and laptop and enrol in a tech-free workshop
weekend in the Brecon Beacons in Wales.

20 Called the 'Unplugged Weekend', the course, which takes place in a private house
in the Welsh hillside, is aimed at digitally-addicted executives. "When guests arrive
at Unplugged Weekend, we have a phone-handing-over ceremony to begin the
digital detox," said co-founder Lucy Pearson. "Everybody puts their phones in a
trunk, which we lock away for the weekend."

25 "It was a bit strange at first," said Beckett of letting go of her devices. "However,
you soon learned to switch off and not be constantly connected to the outside world."

Weekend guests are taught how to fill their time with things other than social media
and surfing the internet. Aside from classes in drawing and meditation, hikes and
yoga are also encouraged. "The absence of phones means guests are much more
30 social and can have uninterrupted conversations with each other," Pearson said.

Beckett turned her phone back on after her Brecon Beacons weekend with some reluctance. "I didn't want to be that person again, constantly going through my phone," she said. The biggest benefit: she learned to re-connect with people. "Most people, when they feel awkward or bored, get their phone out," Beckett said. Now she is much more mindful of getting lost in her devices. "Rather than going on my phone, I am going to make an effort to look around me. You realize you miss so many things that are going on right in front of you."   (435 words)

35

Adapted from the *BBC*

WORKING WITH THE TEXT

L ▶ Lesen schwieriger Texte: Suche nach Einzelinformationen (pp. 134 – 135)

3 Use suitable words from the text to complete the gaps.

Frequent internet users who are ...[1] to their digital devices often suffer ...[2] symptoms when they are no longer ...[3] to the outside world. People who recognize their digital ...[4] can go on a detox course, such as the Unplugged Weekend in Wales. There, in a private house, the course begins with a ...[5] where the guests hand over their phones, which are ...[6] away in a trunk for the weekend. Guests are ...[7] to spend their time doing sports or hobbies and to talk to other guests. The ...[8] of their phones means they have more time for uninterrupted ...[9] and can learn to ...[0] with people. It is worth making the ...[11] to overcome an Internet Addiction Disorder, which recent ...[12] have shown to be a danger to one's ...[13].

4 a What are the symptoms of Internet Addiction Disorder according to the text?

   b Complete the questionnaire to find out if you are suffering from IAD. Add up your points and look at the analysis below. Compare your results in class.

1 How often do you lose track of time when you are online?	1 2 3 4 5
2 How often do your family and friends complain that you spend too much time on digital devices?	1 2 3 4 5
3 How often do you neglect your homework and other tasks to spend time online?	1 2 3 4 5
4 How often do you lose sleep because of late-night internet sessions?	1 2 3 4 5
5 How often do you block out problems in your life by 'escaping' to the internet?	1 2 3 4 5
6 How often do you prefer to spend your time online than with friends and family?	1 2 3 4 5
7 How often do you think that life would be joyless without the internet?	1 2 3 4 5
8 How often do you get angry if someone disturbs you while using the internet?	1 2 3 4 5

1 = never   2 = rarely   3 = occasionally   4 = often   5 = always

Analysis
8 – 20 points: You are an average internet user and you have full control over your behaviour.
21 – 30 points: Your internet use is causing occasional problems in your life and you need to think about how to get it under better control.
31 – 40 points: Your internet use is causing some major problems in your life and you urgently need to get it under control.

5 With a partner draw up a list of Dos and Don'ts to help to overcome IAD. Compare
your list with two other pairs and in small groups make a poster.

WORKING WITH WORDS

6 Match the words 1–6 with the words a–f to form common compound nouns. Check
your answers with the text. Then find at least four more compound nouns in the text.

1	will	a	side
2	outside	b	broker
3	bed	c	feed
4	work	d	power
5	news	e	world
6	insurance	f	shop

7 Use compound nouns from the text to complete the sentences.

1 Kim couldn't go to sleep without her phone at her . . .
2 Kim couldn't muster enough . . . to leave her screens.
3 The house is located on a . . . in the Brecon Beacons.
4 Kim likes to keep in touch with the . . .
5 When Kim gave up her phone, she suffered from . . .
6 Kim works as a(n) . . .
7 She often watches American . . . such as CBNC, Europe.
8 Unplugged Weekend is a . . . for internet addicts.

8 **a** Only three of the verbs in each line are used in combination with the preposition
on the left. Decide which verb is the odd one out. Write a sentence each for TWO
of the other verbs.

1 **UP**   look | take | try | wake

Example: look | take | ~~try~~ | wake
            I <u>looked</u> the word <u>up</u> in the dictionary. He has <u>taken up</u> a new hobby.

2 **AWAY**   leave | lock | pass | throw

3 **DOWN**   calm | let | pass | read

4 **INTO**   grow | look | talk | want

5 **OFF**   call | put | think | turn

6 **OUT**   brake | break | cut | hand

b Write one sentence for the THIRD possible verb + preposition combination
in 8a 1–6.

CHALLENGE!

Example: What time do you usually <u>wake up</u> in the morning?

9 Work in small groups for a competition. Write an A–Z of different words to do with
communication. Write only one word for each letter. The group with the most words
after ten minutes wins the competition.

LOOKING AT LANGUAGE

G ► Countable and uncountable nouns (p. 166)

10 Choose the correct form of the verb. Sometimes both are possible.

1 The media is/are often criticized for lowering standards.
2 A lot of the information on the internet is/are not correct.
3 Politics plays/play an important role in every country.
4 Here is/are the latest news.
5 Economics is/are an interesting subject to study.
6 The government want/wants to introduce new legislation.
7 Your advice was/were very helpful.

CHALLENGE!

8 The police is/are looking for the driver of the stolen car.

2.09

LISTENING

L ► Das Hörverständnis üben (pp. 137–138)

11 a You will hear Jackie and Richard, who have an online podcasts-in-English service, talking about what happened when their internet connection was cut. Before you listen, check that you know these words and phrases.

Server not found

distracted | fiddling on the internet | flicking through a book | knitting patterns | recipe | subscribe | subscription | time-consuming

b Listen to the discussion. Which two internet activities do Jackie and Richard NOT mention?

checking emails | playing games | reading the news | researching information | Skyping | social networking | watching videos | uploading podcasts

ZENTRALE KLASSENARBEIT
Hörverstehen (p. 150)

c Listen again and complete these statements about the text in German.

1 Richard hat die Online Nachrichten am meisten vermisst, weil ...
2 Für Richard die positive Seite des fehlenden Internets war ...
3 Richard und Jackie sind sich einig, dass sie mehr Zeit verbringen, ihre Hobbies zu recherchieren, als ...
4 Jackie sucht Rezepte im Internet, obwohl sie ...

CHALLENGE!

5 Jackie und Richard haben fünf Tipps, wie man dem Internet entkommen kann, nämlich: ...

SPEAKING

L ► Interaktion (pp. 147–148)

12 Work with a partner. Decide if you agree or disagree with the statements below. Give reasons for your point of view. Use some of the phrases below.

1 The internet is the most important invention of the last 100 years.
2 People are becoming isolated because of technology.
3 Technology has made life much more complicated.

... has had a positive/negative effect on ...   *... has led to ...*
... has had negative consequences for ...   *... has been a positive step towards ...*
... has resulted in ...

WRITING

13 Choose one of the following topics and write an essay. Write about 200 words.

1 My life would be impossible without digital technology.
2 Technology has had a massive impact on private, professional and public life. Discuss the advantages and disadvantages of this impact.

L ▸ Einen Aufsatz schreiben (pp. 141–142)

CHALLENGE!

→ EXAM PREPARATION
Textproduktion (p. 150)

CROSSOVER TV

14 Media old and new

Nowhere is the newspaper market as competitive as New York. It is no longer enough to simply publish articles. To survive, newspapers must be innovative and adapt quickly to new trends.

3

competitive *konkurrenzfähig*
survive *überleben*
innovative *erfinderisch*

a Before you watch the video, check that you know the meanings of the words below. Use a dictionary if necessary.

public relations | awesome | thought leader | generate | address an issue | media outlet | point-and-click game

b Watch the video and do the tasks.

1 Describe what has changed for journalists like Jim Joseph.
2 Explain why newspapers like The New York Times would have no future without the internet.
3 Summarize Gabriel Dance's views on computer games linked to newspaper articles.
4 Write down three facts about the Half the Sky Movement game.

c With your partner, discuss the advantages and disadvantages of the following trends:

• Journalists writing blogs for online newspapers without getting paid
• Readers being able to publicly comment on online newspaper articles
• Online newspapers including interactive games which highlight issues from the articles

Especially consider how these trends affect the quality of journalism and how well-informed the public is.

The New York Times building in New York

TEXT 6   Television then and now

1 Compare the photographs. What is the same? What is different?

 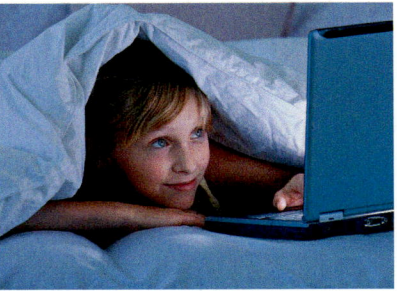

2 Interview two people and find out from them:

1 if they watch TV on a traditional set or on another device.
2 if they usually watch alone or with friends or family.
3 if they usually watch TV programmes as they are broadcast
   or do they record and/or download.

2.10

² landline *Festnetz*
⁶ main focus *Mittelpunkt*
¹³ perplexed *verdutzt*
¹⁷ era *Zeitalter, Ära*

The end of television?

Just as people began to realize a few years ago that a mobile phone was enough
and they didn't need a telephone landline, today people are increasingly giving
up their TV sets. Online streaming has given us total freedom to control our
viewing habits and watch anything from live news and sports to films and TV
programmes in our own time and on any device we choose.   5

In the second half of the twentieth century a television set was often the main
focus of the living room, and family, friends and even neighbours would gather in
front of it to share a viewing experience. They would eat 'TV dinners' and drink,
comment on on-screen events and afterwards discuss what they had seen. TV-
watching was a social activity. By contrast, watching TV-on-demand alone with   10
your laptop or tablet seems sadly anti-social.

Liz   Jenny   Ron   Dave

If you mention that shared viewing experience to many millenials, they will
probably give you a perplexed look because it's something they have never
known. Take Liz King, for example, a 20-year-old college student. Liz and most of
her friends don't have and don't want a television set. "When I see one in   15
somebody's living room, I just think it looks ugly, old-fashioned and unnecessary.
In the era of internet TV, laptops and tablets, why would anyone want to take up
space with a TV set?" she says.

"When I lived with my parents, the TV was always on," says Liz's flatmate Jenny Miller, "but since I came to study in London, I haven't owned a TV set. I don't need one. In a city like this there's always something to do. I'd rather be at a party, the cinema or theatre than watching TV on my iPad alone. The only time I ever watch TV is while I'm working out at the gym."

Ron Smith and his brother Dan usually watch their favourite programmes on their smartphones. "But," says Ron, "there are some programmes like the Olympic Games where you need a bigger screen." Since they are unwilling (and as students unable) to buy a TV set, the brothers have made a TV out of a spare computer and an Apple TV box. To help cover costs, they share streaming service passwords with their friends. Ron says: "One day I might buy a big, traditional TV set if I can afford it. But in the meantime I can live without one."

"I have to travel a lot for work, and I can watch the latest season of my favourite series on planes, in airports or hotels, or in a café waiting for a client," says 25-year-old Dave Jarvis, an electronics engineer from Bristol. "It's super-convenient and I don't waste any time."

Does this mean that the younger generation is watching less television? Certainly not. They still love television, but they are watching it in their own way – catching up with the latest news, sports or shows on their phones or tablets – anywhere, at any time.

(497 words)

19 flatmate *Mitbewohner/in*
27 spare *übrig geblieben*
31 season *Staffel*
33 super-convenient *megabequem*
34 **waste** *verschwenden*
36 catch up on sth *etw nachholen*

WORKING WITH THE TEXT ....

3 Read the text and answer the questions using your own words.

1 What made TV a 'social event' in the past?
2 What is Liz King's usual reaction when she sees a TV set?
3 How does Jenny Miller spend her free time?
4 How does Ron feel about traditional TV sets?
5 Where does Dave Jarvis watch TV?
6 How do modern viewing habits compare with those of the 20th century?

4 Find and change the one word in each sentence that makes it false.

1 A few years ago people began to give up their mobiles.
2 The TV was seldom on in Jenny's family home.
3 Jenny shares a flat with her parents.
4 Ron and his friend Dan watch TV on their smartphones.
5 Jenny hasn't owned a tablet since she came to London.
6 Today we are forced to watch TV at any time and any place.
7 Millenials are often interested when you talk about shared viewing.

5 Which of the people in the text said the following. Explain your choice.

1 "My family watched heaps of television when I was a kid."
2 "I'm on a business trip next week, but I'll still watch my favourite show."
3 "A TV set is such a useless piece of furniture."
4 "I'm simply too busy to watch TV."
5 "If we can get hold of the spare parts, we can make you one, too."
6 "I watched an interesting documentary while I was exercising this morning."
7 "I wouldn't rule out having a TV set one day."

L ▶ Lesen schwieriger Texte: Suche nach Einzelinformationen (pp. 134 – 135)

CHALLENGE!

CHALLENGE!

INTERPRETING A GRAPH ....

6 Look at the bar chart about TV viewing in the UK and do the tasks below.

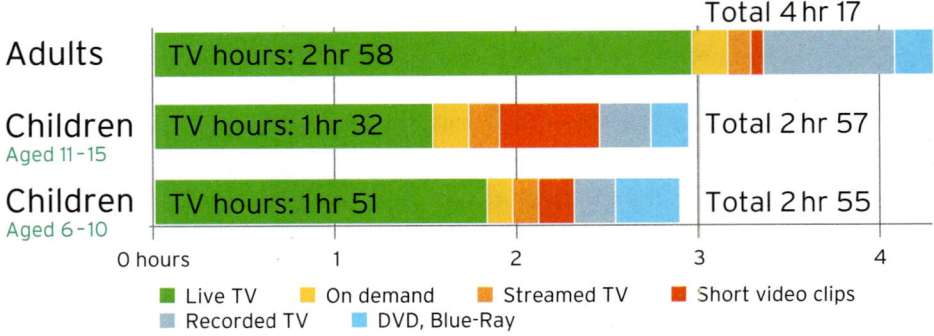

Watching TV
Minutes per day

	Live TV	On demand	Streamed TV	Short video clips	Recorded TV	DVD, Blue-Ray	
Adults	TV hours: 2 hr 58						Total 4 hr 17
Children Aged 11–15	TV hours: 1 hr 32						Total 2 hr 57
Children Aged 6–10	TV hours: 1 hr 51						Total 2 hr 55

Source: WEEKLY REACH

a Answer the questions.

Who watches the most and the least:
1 live TV?
2 TV on demand?
3 streamed TV?
4 short video clips?
5 recorded TV?
6 DVD, Blue Ray?

→ **EXAM PREPARATION**

Kommunikationsprüfung
(p. 150)

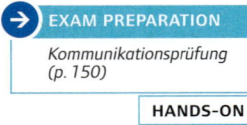

b Explain the diagram and comment on it, relating it to the future of video/
television viewing (two-minute monologue).

c In your notebook, draw additional bars for the above chart.

1 Draw one bar to show your own TV, video and DVD habits.
2 Work in small groups. Find out the average watching times of your group and add
a second bar.
3 Compare your group's bar with another group. Are they similar or different?

WORKING WITH WORDS ....

7 **a** Collect the adjectives in the text *Television then and now* and classify them into
the following groups:

(1) negative   (2) positive   (3) neutral
(4) used only for people   (5) used only for things   (6) used for both

b Choose two adjectives from each group and write a sentence putting them into
a context.

Example: *anti-social* (1) (6)
He was arrested for anti-social behaviour.

SPEAKING

8 Complete the questionnaire. With a partner, compare and explain your answers.   L ▶ Interaktion (pp. 147–148)

1 Television has destroyed family life.	1 2 3 4
2 Television makes people stupid.	1 2 3 4
3 Television is one of the best inventions of all times.	1 2 3 4
4 You can learn more from television than you can at school.	1 2 3 4
5 Television has brought the world closer together.	1 2 3 4
6 TV is chewing gum for the eyes.	1 2 3 4

1 = I couldn't agree more.   **2** = I agree.
3 = I don't really agree.   **4** = I completely disagree.

INFO

Studies show that American children watch on average about 25 hours of television a
week, and nearly two-thirds of American TV programmes contain some physical
violence. Violence is common not only in cartoons, thrillers and action films but also in
music videos and video games – almost 90 per cent of the most popular video games
5 contain violence. Before he or she reaches the age of 18, the average child will have
watched about a quarter of a million acts of violence, including more than 16,000
murders.

Before the age of four children are unable to distinguish between fact and fantasy and
may come to think that violence is normal. They can often be observed imitating
10 aggressive behaviour in their games. Children of all ages can gradually become
desensitized to violence. It becomes a fact of life and seems to them to be the only way
for the resolution of conflicts. Heroes are rewarded for their violent deeds and may
become role models for vulnerable young people, tempting them to use violent means
to solve their problems.

11 desensitized *unempfindlich,
abgestumpft*

CLASS DEBATE

9 Read the Info box and look at the statement for discussion below. The class divides
into halves. One half thinks up 'Yes' arguments, the other half 'No' arguments.
Then present your arguments and debate the issue.   L ▶ Interaktion (pp. 147–148)

Watching violence in the media and playing violent video games increases the
likelihood of aggressive behaviour, therefore the production of such material should
be banned.

SPEAKING

10 Work with a partner. Take turns to choose ONE picture from Topic 3. Don't let your
partners see your choice. Describe the picture. Your partner has to find the picture.

The state we're in – USA and UK

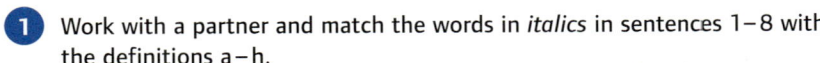

TEXT 1   The UK Parliament

WARM UP

1 Work with a partner and match the words in *italics* in sentences 1–8 with the definitions a–h.

1 Central government hoped that *devolution* would discourage break-away movements.
2 Scotland has its own parliament, while Northern Ireland and Wales each have an *assembly*.
3 Westminster Palace has been the *venue* for parliamentary debates since the 13th century.
4 The *civil wars* of 1642–1651 left England without a monarch.
5 A Scottish landowner was tried for *treason* and hanged.
6 King Charles I was *put on trial* and then executed.
7 The House of Lords was *abolished* by Oliver Cromwell in the 17th century.
8 Great Britain has been a *constitutional monarchy* for hundreds of years.

a a system where the powers of a monarch are defined and limited by a parliament
b a place where people agree to meet
c transfer of power to local or regional authorities
d taken to court
e wars between citizens of the same country
f ended, done away with, got rid of
g a group of people with limited powers who are elected as a government for a region
h the crime of betraying one's country

2.11

2 Pictures A–J are in the wrong order. Skim texts 1–10 and match them with the best picture.

History of the UK parliament

⁷ obliged *verpflichtet*

A

1 Talking shop
Before the 13th century Parliament was simply a talking shop for the king and rich men. By the 13th century, a parliament was when kings met up with English barons to raise cash for fighting wars – mostly against Scotland. Thanks to the Magna Carta of 1215, kings were obliged to ask before taking anyone's money.

5

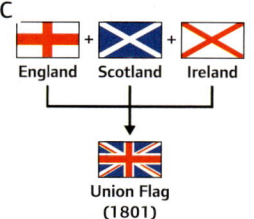

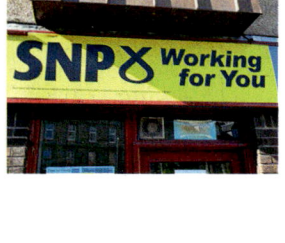

2 Palace of Westminster

The parliament of 1265 was the first to involve knights, not just the super-rich. And it was the first time elections were held. The venue was usually the Palace of Westminster. Today's 19th century building is home to the House of Lords and the House of Commons.

3 William Wallace and Scottish independence

Ireland had its own parliament from 1297 until 1800. Scotland also had its own parliament from the 13th century. When an English king declared himself King of Scotland, William Wallace, a Scottish landowner, started a rebellion. Wallace was eventually found guilty of treason and hanged.

4 First steps towards a UK parliament

It wasn't until 1542 that the seeds of a UK parliament were sown. To stop the Welsh coming under the influence of the Catholics, the corpulent and powerful King Henry VIII decided Wales would be ruled by England. By now Parliament was an established institution and Wales was allowed to send representatives. Henry called it an Act of Union, but it was more a forced marriage.

5 Parliament bites

The Commons got into its stride in the 1620s. They were turbulent years with fights in the chamber, and the king trying to arrest MPs, until Charles I dissolved Parliament for 11 years. He brought it back because he was short of money for a war with Scotland. But the struggle between Parliament and the king continued. In 1649 the king was put on trial and then executed.

6 Civil war and a brief UK Parliament

After the Civil War (1642–1651), England became a republic under Oliver Cromwell, who abolished the House of Lords and annexed Scotland and Ireland into a full union with a single parliament at Westminster. The 1654 Parliament was the first one in which the whole of Britain was represented. But Cromwell dissolved it pretty quickly when MPs refused to do his bidding.

---

11 knight *Ritter*
12 **election** *Wahl*
23 **treason** *Hochverrat*
24 hang sb *jdn hängen*
26 sow the seeds for sth *den Boden für etw bereiten*
27 corpulent *beleibt*
31 **representative** *Abgeordnete/r, Vertreter/in*
34 get into one's stride *in Schwung kommen*
37 **dissolve** *auflösen*
41 put sb on trial *jdn vor Gericht stellen*
41 **execute** *hinrichten*
44 annex *annektieren*
49 do sb's bidding *tun, was jmd will*

7 The Glorious Revolution

In 1660 the monarchy was restored and a two-house parliament re-established. But when King James II took steps to restore Catholicism, there was wide resistance. At the invitation of Parliament, William of Orange, a Protestant, invaded England and James fled. From then on Parliament laid down the rules – the beginning of Britain as a constitutional monarchy. The Act of Settlement ensured that there would be no more Catholic monarchs.

8 An expanding union

The 1707 Act of Union brought England and Scotland together with one king and no more Scottish Parliament. Scotland became a full member of the UK parliament. Ireland was brought into the UK with another Act of Union at the end of the 18th century after the campaign for Irish independence had been crushed. That was the end of the Irish Parliament until the division of Ireland in 1920.

9 Nationalist parties

The desire for independence has never gone away. The Scottish National Party was created in 1934 and won its first seat at Westminster in 1945. Welsh nationalists created Plaid Cymru in 1925 and had four Westminster seats by 1992. It is a peculiar situation for nationalist MPs – sitting in a parliament that they do not want to be a part of. For the Irish nationalist Sinn Fein, the answer is to win a seat but never turn up at Westminster.

10 Start of the break up?

When the Labour Party came into government in 1997, it hoped devolution would kill off Scottish nationalism. Along came a parliament for Scotland with powers to make laws on education, health and crime. For Northern Ireland and Wales, there were assemblies. A referendum on whether Scotland should separate from the rest of the United Kingdom was held in 2014, with 45 per cent voting for independence, resulting in promises of more powers to be devolved to Scotland.

(670 words)
Adapted from BBC.co.uk

50
55
60
65
70
75
80
85
90

WORKING WITH THE TEXT

3 What does the text say about the following? Use your own words as far as possible.

1 The UK Parliament in the 13th century
2 William Wallace
3 Events leading up to the execution of King Charles I
4 How William of Orange became king of England.
5 The Scottish National Party
6 The Scottish referendum on independence
7 The Acts of Union with a) Wales, b) Scotland, c) Ireland

L ▶ Lesen schwieriger Texte: Detailverständnis (p. 135)

CHALLENGE!

SPEAKING

4 Research on the internet. Find out more about ONE of the names below and give a three-minute presentation in class.

The Magna Carta | King Henry VIII | Oliver Cromwell | Act of Settlement

→ **EXAM PREPARATION**
Präsentationsprüfung (p. 151)

WORKING WITH WORDS

5 Copy and complete the table with the missing nouns and verbs.

verb	noun	verb	noun
abolish			influence
annex		invade	
	assembly	involve	
create			legislation
decide		oblige	
declare		marry	
desire		promise	
devolve		refuse	
dissolve			rebellion
	division	represent	
	election		resistance
establish			restoration
execute		separate	
	education		settlement
	government	suspend	
hang			trial

LOOKING AT LANGUAGE

CHALLENGE!

6 **a** Sometimes you may want to emphasize certain words or phrases when you are writing an essay or giving a presentation. You can do this using cleft (= divided) sentences. What is the difference between sentences A and B?

1 Using *It + to be …* (*that, who*) to give emphasis.
A *It was* in 1542 *that* the seeds of a UK parliament were sown.
B The seeds of a UK parliament were sown in 1542.

2 *What …* meaning *the thing that*.
A *What* I don't understand is why the monarchy was restored.
B I don't understand why the monarchy was restored.

b Write the following sentences with a different emphasis.

1 The Act of Settlement ensured there would be no more Catholic monarchs. *(It)*
2 I find it surprising that a foreign king was invited to rule Britain. *(What)*
3 William Wallace, a Scottish landowner, started the rebellion. *(It)*
4 The fact that Henry VIII had six wives fascinates a lot of people. *(What)*
5 Charles I's lack of respect for Parliament led to his downfall. *(It)*
6 I was really annoyed by his refusal to tell the truth. *(What)*

L ▶ Lernen neuer Vokabeln
(pp. 136 – 137)

COMPETENCE TRAINING: LEARNING NEW VOCABULARY

TIP

If you keep a vocabulary notebook, remember there are better ways of organizing vocabulary than alphabetical lists. Grouping words often helps us to remember them.
- word fields: POLITICS: assembly, central government, constitutional monarchy, devolution, election, legislation
- word families: elect, electoral, general/local/midterm election, electorate

Learn vocabulary by:
- using index cards,
- practising with a computer vocabulary trainer,
- putting sticky notes in prominent places,
- playing word games, e.g. Scrabble,
- doing crossword puzzles.

HANDS-ON
TASK

7 Find an online crossword-puzzle maker. Make a crossword puzzle using ten words from ONE of the texts you have read in Crossover. Use German words as the clues. Make sure you know the answers! Exchange crosswords with a partner. Tell him/her which text the vocabulary occurred in. Correct each other's answers.

CHALLENGE!

Instead of German words, use English clues for the words. Use a dictionary to help you.

READING

EXAM PREPARATION
Leseverstehen (p. 149)

8 Lesen Sie den Text *The United Kingdom Youth Parliament* auf Seite 95 und erstellen Sie Listen auf Deutsch:

1 MYP Aktivitaten (fünf Nennungen)
2 UKYP Themen (zehn Nennungen)

CHALLENGE!   3 Wie sich junge Leute in UKYP einbringen können (vier Nennungen)

The United Kingdom Youth Parliament

The UK Youth Parliament (UKYP) is a government-funded youth organization which gives a voice to 11- to 18-year-olds on issues that matter to them. The organization was founded in 2000. The idea originated from young people themselves, who felt that their needs were being ignored by their regular Members of Parliament (MPs).

Members of the UK Youth Parliament (MYPs) are elected to represent the views of young people in their area. Today UKYP has about 600 elected members – 369 seats for MYPs and 230 for Deputy MYPs – all aged between 11 to 18. Any young person of that age can stand for election or vote in elections, which are held by local authorities. Each local authority represents a UKYP constituency, and the number of MYPs in each constituency depends upon the number of young people in that area. In the past two years one million young people have voted in the UKYP elections.

MYPs hold meetings on a regular basis, organize events, make films, run campaigns and try to influence decision-makers on issues that concern their young constituents. In addition to voting, there are lots of ways for young people everywhere to get involved with UKYP. They can support campaigns, debate on online forums and lobby their local MP.

Amongst the major topics which have been dealt with in recent years was the question of voting at the age of 16. In the 2009 UKYP session in the House of Commons, MYP James Evans famously said: "At 16, we can marry our MP, we can sleep with our MP and we can have children with our MP. We can sign up in preparation for fighting and potentially dying for our MP. And suddenly we are not mature enough to vote for them. What an absolute disgrace!"

Other issues which have concerned the UKYP have been:
- a greener future for the planet,
- abolition of university fees,
- better job opportunities for young people,
- cheaper and better public transport for all,
- ending child poverty,
- minimum wage for every worker,
- more leisure facilities for young people,
- zero tolerance on bullying,
- youth crime and how to deal with it.

(363 words)

[1] government-funded *staatlich finanziert*
[3] originate *stammen*
[9] stand for election *kandidieren*
[10] **constituency** *Wahlkreis*
[14] run sth *etw durchführen*
[16] constituent *Wähler/in (eines Wahlkreises)*
[20] session *Sitzung*
[24] **mature** *reif, erwachsen*
[24] **disgrace** *Schande*
[27] **abolition** *Abschaffung*
[32] **leisure facility** *Freizeiteinrichtung*

WORKING WITH WORDS

9 Find 'political' words from the text *The United Kingdom Youth Parliament* to match the definitions. Then translate them into German.

1 the government of a city or area of the country
2 planned activities with a political aim
3 express your choice in an official way
4 choose a person for an official position
5 voters living in a particular area of the country
6 meeting of an official body
CHALLENGE!
7 the more powerful of the two parts of the British parliament
8 try to influence someone with political power

10 Which is the odd word out?

1 **to found**	an organization	an election	a political party
2 **to hold**	a speech	a meeting	an election
3 **to influence**	decision-makers	an opportunity	a decision
4 **to lobby**	a campaign	your local MP	decision-makers
5 **to represent**	an organization	a constituency	a topic
6 **to run**	a company	a campaign	a list
7 **to organize**	events	issues	campaigns
8 **to vote**	out of office	with your feet	an MYP

11 Use one of the prepositions to complete the sentences.

at | between | by | for (2x) | in | of | on (3x) | to (2x) | with

1 MYPs meet … a regular basis.
2 You can stand … election … the age of 11.
3 Young people's needs are often ignored … MPs.
4 UKYP deals … a lot of different topics.
5 Anyone … 11 and 18 can vote.
6 We have a policy … zero tolerance … bullying.
7 The UKYP gives a voice … young people … issues that matter … them.
8 I voted … the Labour MP … the last election.

SPEAKING

L ▶ Interaktion (pp. 147–148)

12 a Look at the list of issues in the text which have concerned the UK Youth Parliament. Rank the issues from one to ten according to their order of importance for you personally. One is the most important, ten the least.

b Explain your ranking to a partner.

c With your partner, add two more issues to the list that are important for you both. Explain to the class why they are important.

TEXT 2   Living and dying on Death Row

2.12

1 Read the poem and explain how it is linked to the Info box below.

Fleeting thought

I'm a fleeting thought in the minds of few,
housed in a 9 x 7, 63-square-foot cage
here on Florida's Death Row.
I deal daily with a never-ending
5 cycle of pain and loneliness that few
outside these walls even realize exists.
My pain and loneliness are not the normal
cycle of pain existing in the world
outside these concrete walls and razor-wire fences.
10 No, my pain and loneliness are way, way beyond
your comprehension. And it's a pain I'd
wish on no one, not even my worst enemy.
I bear a pain and loneliness that few
will ever know as I stand at my cell bars
15 staring far off into the distance at
a world I once knew, but will never know
again, yes … a world for which I have
become a fleeting memory to few,
and a non-existing soul to those I never knew.

© Ronald W. Clark

0 fleeting *flüchtig*
2 63 square feet *ca. 6 Quadratmeter*
2 cage *Käfig*
9 concrete *Beton*
9 razor wire *Stacheldraht*
14 bars *Gitter*
18 memory *Erinnerung*
19 soul *Seele*

INFO ....

'Death Row' is the name given to the section of a US prison that houses prisoners who are awaiting execution. Most Death Row prisoners are kept in solitary confinement in small cells for between 22 and 24 hours a day with little or no human contact. Visits from friends and loved ones are restricted and touching them is not allowed. Opponents
5 of capital punishment claim that prisoners' isolation and uncertainty of their fate is a form of torture, often leading to mental illness or suicide. A Death Row inmate in the USA waits an average of 15 years between sentencing and execution as a result of time-consuming appeals procedures. One inmate waited 40 years.

2 execution *Hinrichtung*
2 solitary confinement *Einzelhaft, Isolationshaft*
5 capital punishment *Todesstrafe*
6 torture *Folter*
6 inmate *Häftling*
8 appeal *Berufung*

What death penalty opponents don't get

2.13

In 1987, when he was 23 years old and in court on a drug charge, William Blake shot two sheriff's deputies in a failed escape attempt, killing one. At his trial, the judge presiding over his case expressed regret that New York did not have capital punishment, so he could not sentence Blake to death.

3 sheriff's deputy *Hilfssheriff*
5 **trial** *Gerichtsverfahren, Prozess*
6 preside *vorsitzen*
7 **regret** *Bedauern*
9 **sentence** *verurteilen*

Instead, for almost 30 years, Blake has lived in extreme isolation in a 7 x 9 cell. On some days he's allowed out for an hour to 'exercise' alone in a small pen. Because his sentence is 77 years to life, he is almost certain to die in prison. Because he is classified as both a cop killer and an escape risk, he may well spend the rest of his life in solitary confinement.

Recently Blake described his years in a New York state prison: "If I try to imagine what kind of death, even a slow one, would be worse than twenty-five years in the box, I can come up with nothing," he wrote. "Dying would only take a short time if you or the state killed me; in prison I have died a thousand internal deaths."

At the last count nearly 50,000 people in the USA were serving sentences of life without the possibility of parole – a number that has more than tripled since the early 1990s. In many states, the expansion – and the very existence – of life-without-parole sentences can be directly linked to the struggle to end capital punishment. Death penalty opponents often accept life without parole as a preferable option. But in reality, those prisoners are condemned to spend decades growing sick, old and finally dying in overcrowded, dangerous prisons.

Connecticut, in abolishing its death penalty in 2012, legislated a punishment even more harsh than life without parole. A new law decreed that those convicted of "murder with special circumstances" would be condemned to live out their sentences in solitary confinement. Though that requirement is codified into law only in Connecticut, it exists in practice throughout the nation. An unknown number of lifers have, like William Blake, been placed in permanent or indefinite solitary confinement.

Research has confirmed that even brief periods in solitary alter brain chemistry and produce psychiatric symptoms ranging from extreme depression to active psychosis. Some prisoners who have spent longer amounts of time in isolation describe it as a condition that slowly degrades both their humanity and sanity, turning them into blind animals. A study in New York found that prisoners in solitary confinement were five times more likely to kill themselves than those in the general population, despite the fact that it's never simple to commit suicide in a bare cell.

William Blake has said that while he cannot bring himself to take his own life, he would have welcomed the death penalty had he known what a lifetime in solitary confinement would be like. Perhaps the time will come when people like Blake – and the American public – are not forced to choose between such monstrous alternatives. In the meantime, it will be a shame if people who oppose state-sponsored death continue to advocate state-sanctioned torture.   (520 words)

Adapted from *Huffington Post*

WORKING WITH THE TEXT ··

L ▸ Lesen schwieriger Texte: Grobverständnis (p. 134)

2 Read the text and choose the statement that best summarizes what it says.

A The death penalty is a more humane punishment than life imprisonment.

B Life imprisonment is a more humane punishment than the death penalty.

C Neither the death penalty nor life imprisonment are acceptable ways to punish capital crimes.

3 Decide whether the following statements about the text are true or false. Give reasons for your answers in full German sentences.

→ EXAM PREPARATION
Leseverstehen (p. 149)

1 The judge at Blake's trial was pro capital punishment.
2 Blake hasn't left his cell for almost 30 years.
3 Blake thinks that death is preferable to life imprisonment.
4 According to a law in Connecticut, all convicted murderers are put into solitary confinement.
5 The Connecticut law has been adopted throughout the nation.
6 Nobody really knows what psychological effects solitary confinement has on prisoners.

INFO

Facts about the death penalty in the USA

- Over 8,000 people have been sentenced to death since 1976 and there have been 1,405 executions.
- Of all defendants executed, 782 were white, 486 black, 113 Hispanic and 24 other races.
5 • A study in California found that those who killed whites were over three times more likely to be sentenced to death than those who killed blacks.
- Studies have shown that a death penalty case costs about three times more than keeping someone in a high-security prison for 40 years. The costs are due to lengthy trials and repeated appeals.
10 • Lethal injection is the most common method of execution.
- Only two per cent of Death Row inmates are women. 43 per cent of Death Row inmates are white, 32 per cent black, 13 per cent Hispanic and the rest other races.

³ defendant *Angeklagte/r*
¹⁰ lethal injection *Todesspritze*

4 Using statistics from the Info box, make a poster with bar or pie charts for the following:

HANDS-ON
TASK

- the race of the defendants executed   • the race of victims in death penalty cases
- death row inmates by race

LISTENING ....
2.14

5 **a** Sie hören ein Podcast zum Thema Todesstrafe. EINE der folgenden Fragen wird in dem Gespräch NICHT beantwortet. Welche?

1 Woher stammt der Begriff ‚capital punishment'?
2 In wie vielen Ländern gibt es die Todesstrafe?
3 Warum sprechen sich die Vereinten Nationen gegen die Hinrichtung mittels Giftspritze aus?
4 Wodurch starb Gary Alvord?
5 Weshalb wurde Michael Selsor zum Tode verurteilt?
6 Wie viele Menschen sind irrtümlich zum Tode verurteilt worden?
7 Ist die Todesstrafe als Abschreckungsmittel effektiv?
8 Was verursacht dem Steuerzahler mehr Kosten – ein Todesurteil oder eine Verurteilung zu lebenslanger Haft?

b Hören Sie sich das Podcast noch einmal an. Machen Sie sich beim Hören Notizen und beantworten Sie die Fragen in 5a auf Deutsch in Stichworten.

WORKING WITH WORDS

6 The following word pairs are often confused. Complete the sentences by choosing the correct word from the pair.

1 *eventually – possibly*
   a He fell ill and . . . died.
   b Could you ... help me with this exercise?
2 *human – humane*
   a Sick animals are killed in the most . . . way possible.
   b The death penalty does not allow for . . . error.
3 *hung – hanged*
   a The criminal was caught and . . .
   b I . . . the picture on the wall.
4 *isolation – insulation*
   a You need to consider the facts in . . .
   b You can save heating costs if your house has good . . .

7 a Match the crimes 1–10 with their definitions a–j. Use a dictionary if necessary.

1	armed robbery	a	driving a vehicle under the influence of alcohol
2	arson	b	killing a person intentionally
3	blackmail	c	stealing from people's clothes or bags
4	burglary	d	deliberately setting fire to a building
5	drunk driving	e	taking goods that are for sale without paying for them
6	joyriding	f	taking someone's property by threatening them with a weapon
7	murder	g	forcing somebody to have sex against their will
8	picking pockets	h	stealing a car and driving around at high speed for fun
9	rape	i	breaking into a building to steal things
10	shoplifting	j	obtaining money by threatening to disclose unpleasant facts about a person

CHALLENGE!

b What do we call the offenders who commit the crimes 1–10 in 7a?

Example: **1** armed robbery ⇨ armed robber

SPEAKING

L ▶ Interaktion (pp. 147 – 148)

8 Work in small groups. Discuss which punishment would be suitable for the crimes.

inherit *erben*
probation *Bewährung*
fine *Bußgeld*
community service *Sozialdienst*
hold up *überfallen*

Crimes	Punishments
• a 16-year-old boy who stole pair of sports shoes from a department store • a woman who murdered her husband to inherit his money • a man who murdered his wife's lover • an 18-year-old arrested for drunken driving • a 16-year-old stopped for dangerous driving on his quad bike • an armed man who held up a bank • two teenagers caught joy riding • a man who raped a teenage girl	• probation (how long?) • a fine (how much?) • imprisonment (how long?) • community service (how long?) • the death penalty

COMPETENCE TRAINING: WRITING AN OUTLINE

TIP

Writing an outline is a good way to organize your ideas before writing an essay, or when preparing a presentation. You can see the typical structure for an outline below. Of course, you can add further main ideas with examples.

L ▶ Einen Aufsatz schreiben (pp. 141–142)

Title
Introduction: Outline of the topic

1st main idea	**2nd main idea**
1.1 Important fact	2.1 Important fact
1.1.1 Example or detail	2.1.1 Example or detail
1.1.2 Further example or detail	2.1.2 Further example or detail
1.2 Supporting fact	2.2 Supporting fact
1.2.1 Example or detail	2.2.1 Example or detail
1.2.2 Further example or detail	2.2.2 Further example or detail

Conclusion: Summary of points, summing up of arguments.

9   Copy and complete the outline below for an essay on the pros and cons of the death penalty (= dp) with six of the following points. One point is irrelevant.

- Killers are gone for ever.
- Main arguments against dp
- Main arguments for dp
- Many cases of wrong conviction
- Too many guilty people go free
- More humane
- Violent crime rates higher in death penalty states

conviction *Überführung*

The pros and cons of the death penalty

Introduction:	Long-standing discussion. Strong arguments both for and against dp
1st main idea	…
	1.1 Prevents re-offending
	1.1.1 …
	1.1.2 No chance of murderers escaping.
	1.2 …
	1.2.1 Life imprisonment is hell on earth.
	1.2.2 Modern execution methods are quick and efficient.
2nd main idea	…
	2.1 Tragic mistakes
	2.1.1 …
	2.1.2 Wrong decisions cannot be reversed.
	2.2 Not a deterrent
	2.2.1 …
	2.2.2 Murderers don't expect to get caught.
Conclusion	My own opinion

deterrent *Abschreckung*

WRITING

10   Discuss the pros and cons of the death penalty, using the outline you completed in exercise 9.

EXAM PREPARATION
Textproduktion (p. 150)

TEXT 3   Immigration

WARM UP ....

1 How much do you know about refugees and asylum seekers?

1 What is the difference between an asylum seeker and a refugee?
  a An asylum seeker only has political reasons for leaving their country; a refugee has economic reasons.
  b An asylum seeker has not yet had their asylum application accepted; a refugee has.
  c No difference. They are the same.

2 How many refugees were there in the world in mid-2015?
  a c. 6 million   **b** c. 16 million   **c** c. 60 million

3 How many of the world's refugees are under the age of 18?
  a about 50%   **b** about 25%   **c** about 10%

4 Which European country takes in the most asylum seekers per head of the population?
  a Germany   **b** The UK   **c** Sweden

5 How long on average does an asylum application take to process in Germany?
  a 7 weeks   **b** 7 months   **c** 2 years

6 How many asylum applications are rejected on average in the EU?
  a 75%   **b** 50%   **c** 20%

7 How many Germans were forced to leave their homes between 1944 and 1950?
  a about one million   **b** between five to six million   **c** at least 12 million

2 Check your answers at the bottom of the page. Did any of the answers surprise you? Why?

L ▶ Interaktion (pp. 147–148)

3 In small groups discuss the following questions.

  1 Why do people emigrate to other countries?
  2 Are there a lot of immigrants where you live?
  3 Do you think that immigrants are treated well in your country?
  4 What's the difference between political and economic migrants?
  5 Should all undocumented immigrants be sent back to their own countries?
  6 Has your town changed much in the last few years as a result of migration? How?
  7 Would you consider emigrating? Under what circumstances?

Key: 1b, 2c, 3a, 4c, 5b, 6a 7c

4 Find words in the word cloud to match the definitions.

1 a person who leaves their country to go and live in another
2 supporters of a certain American political party
3 a written plan for a new law
4 the opposite of 'legal'
5 the dividing line between two countries
6 a formal discussion
7 the rights of a citizen
8 the elected law-making body of certain countries
9 change, repair, update
10 an adjective from 'politics'

The novel *The Other Hand* was written in 2008 by the British author Chris Cleave. It tells the story of an undocumented Nigerian immigrant and a British magazine editor, who met during the oil conflict in the Niger Delta, and meet again in England several years later.

5 As a university student, Cleave had a temporary job in an asylum detention centre and wrote the book based on his experience of the hardships asylum seekers suffer in Britain. The novel deals not only with the treatment of refugees by individuals and the system, but also with issues such as British colonialism, globalization, political violence and human decency. The book has been on the bestseller lists in both the *Sunday Times*
10 and the *New York Times*.

I wish I was a British pound coin

Most days I wish I was a British pound coin instead of an African girl. Everyone would be pleased to see me coming. [...] A pound coin can go wherever
5 it thinks it will be safest. It can cross deserts and oceans and leave the sound of gunfire and the bitter smell of burning thatch behind. When it feels warm and secure, it will turn around and smile at you, the way my big sister Nkiruka used to smile at the men in our village [...]

10 Of course, a pound can be serious too. It can disguise itself as power or property, and there is nothing more serious when you are a girl who has neither. You must try to catch the pound and trap it in your pocket, so that it cannot reach a safe country unless it takes you with it. [...]

How I would love to be a British pound. A pound is free to travel to safety, and we
15 are free to watch it go. This is the human triumph. This is called *globalization*. A girl like me gets stopped at immigration, but a pound can leap the turnstiles and dodge the tackles of those big men with their uniform caps, and jump straight into a waiting airport taxi. *Where to, sir?* Western civilization, my good man, and make it snappy.

20 See how nicely a British pound coin talks? It speaks with the voice of Queen Elizabeth the Second of England. Her face is stamped upon it and sometimes when I look very closely I can see her lips moving. I hold her up to my ear. What is she saying? *Put me down this minute, young lady, or I shall call my guards.*

2.15

⁴ **desert** *Wüste*
⁶ **thatch** *Strohdach*
¹⁰ **disguise** *verkleiden, tarnen*
¹² **trap** *festhalten, einschließen*
¹⁶ **turnstile** *Drehkreuz*
¹⁷ **dodge sth** *einer Sache ausweichen*
¹⁷ **tackle** *Angriff, Tackling*
¹⁹ **Make it snappy.** *Aber flott!*
²³ **guard** *Wache*

Cullinan Diamond

25 **disobey** *nicht gehorchen*
25 sceptre *Zepter*
26 fuzzy *kraus*
28 **ID = identity card**
Personalausweis
29 **rule** *regieren, herrschen*
30 **desirable** *wünschenswert*
31 **Cullinan Diamond** *The biggest diamond ever found. Now part of the British Crown Jewels.*
32 **How dare you!** *Was erlauben Sie sich!*
37 **detention centre**
Internierungslager

L ▶ Lesen schwieriger Texte:
Suche nach Einzelinformationen
(pp. 134 – 135)

CHALLENGE!

If the Queen spoke to you in such a voice, do you suppose it would be possible to disobey? [...] Let me tell you, it is not the crown and the sceptre that have this effect. Me, I could pin a tiara on my short, fuzzy hair, and I could hold up a sceptre in one hand, like this, and police officers would still walk up to me in their big shoes and say, *Love the ensemble, madam, now let's have quick a look at your ID, shall we?* No, it is not the Queen's crown and sceptre that rule in your land. It is her grammar and her voice. That is why it is desirable to speak the way she does. That way you can say to police officers, in a voice as clear as the Cullinan Diamond, *My goodness, how dare you?* 25 30

I am only alive at all because I learned the Queen's English. Maybe you are thinking, that isn't so hard. After all, English is the official language of my country, Nigeria. [... but] learning came slowly to me. On the other hand, I had plenty of time. I learned your language in an immigration detention centre, in Essex, in the south-eastern part of the United Kingdom. Two years, they locked me in there. Time was all I had. (510 words) 35

Abridged from *The Other Hand by Chris Cleave*

WORKING WITH THE TEXT

5 **What does the text tell us about the following? Write your answers in full sentences using your own words.**

1 The advantages a British pound coin has that the writer does not have.
2 The writer's life so far.
3 The writer's attitude to the English language.

WORKING WITH WORDS

6 a **Complete these sentences from the text.**

1 A pound coin can go wherever it thinks it will be ...
2 When it feels warm and ..., it will turn around and smile at you.
3 It cannot reach a ... country unless it takes you with it.

b **What is the difference between *safe* and *secure*? What are the nouns from these two adjectives? Complete the sentences with the correct word.**

1 Seatbelts and headrests make travelling by car ...
2 When you go out, lock the door and make sure your house is ...
3 There was tight ... for the politician's visit.
4 Is it ... to go there at night?
5 Having reflectors on your bicycle is an important ... measure.
6 Locking up your bicycle is an important ... measure.

LOOKING AT LANGUAGE

G ▶ used to do (p. 163)

7 **Rewrite these sentences replacing the parts in italics with the correct form of *(not) used to* + verb.**

Example: *In the past* my big sister Nkiruka *smiled* at the men in our village.
My big sister Nkiruka used to smile at the men in our village.

1 *Many years ago I lived* in Nigeria.
2 *Previously I didn't drink* coffee, *but I do now*.
3 Dad, *did you often play* computer games when you were my age?
4 *In the past I didn't like* my neighbours, but now we get on well.
5 *Were you in the habit of eating* a lot of sweets when you were a kid?
6 *There was a time when I watched* TV a lot, but I don't have time now.
7 *I had to wear* a school uniform *when I went to school*.
8 *I could speak* Russian *a long time ago*, but now I've forgotten everything.

CHALLENGE!

INFO

The UK's immigration detention facilities are among the largest in Europe. About 30,000 persons, including children under the age of 18 and pregnant women, are kept in a number of so-called Immigration Removal Centres (IRCs). The centres are used to hold asylum seekers waiting for their case to be decided, and failed asylum seekers waiting to
5 be deported. Unlike other European countries, there is no restriction in the UK on how long detainees can be kept. As a result of lengthy bureaucracy, a period of detention can last indefinitely. Some detainees are forced to stay for a year or more because there is no real prospect of sending them back to their own country – because it is a conflict zone, for example, and airport or travel documents are unattainable.
10 Basic food and healthcare are provided. Rooms are usually shared by up to six people. Because of the sheer numbers involved, different dietary, religious, cultural and social needs can seldom be taken into consideration. Detainees are not allowed to work in the UK except within the centres themselves, serving food or cleaning.
Human rights campaigners have called for IRCs to be closed down, but the government
15 insists that detention is a vital tool to help deport those with no right to be in the UK.

[6] detainee *Gefangene/r, Häftling*
[9] be unattainable *nicht zu beschaffen sein*
[11] dietary *Ernährungs-*
[15] vital *unverzichtbar*

8 Describe the cartoon and relate it along with the Info box to aspects of British immigration. Produce an uninterrupted three-minute monologue.

→ EXAM PREPARATION
Kommunikationsprüfung (p. 150)

L ▶ Interpretation von Bildern und Karikaturen (pp. 145–146)

WORKING WITH A SONG

9 Listen to the song *City of Immigrants* by Steve Earle. First try to understand as much of the song as you can without looking at the lyrics. Which interpretation do you agree with most? Give reasons.

A The singer enjoys the multi-cultural diversity of his city.
B The singer says that immigrants have a good life in his city.
C The singer feels crowded out by all the immigrants who have come to his city.

2.16

City of immigrants

Livin' in a city of immigrants
I don't need to go travelin'
Open my door and the world walks in
Livin' in a city of immigrants
Livin' in a city that never sleeps
My heart keepin' time to a thousand beats
Singin' in languages I don't speak
Livin' in a city of immigrants

City of black
City of white
City of light
City of innocents
City of sweat
City of tears
City of prayers
City of immigrants

Livin' in a city where the dreams of men
Reach up to touch the sky and then
Tumble back down to earth again
Livin' in a city that never quits
Livin' in a city where the streets are paved
With good intentions and a people's faith
In the sacred promise a statue made
Livin' in a city of immigrants

City of stone
City of steel
City of wheels
Constantly spinnin'
City of bone
City of skin
City of pain
City of immigrants

All of us are immigrants
Every daughter, every son
Everyone is everyone
All of us are immigrants – everyone

Livin' in a city of immigrants
River flows out and the sea rolls in
Washin' away nearly all of my sins
Livin' in a city of immigrants

City of black
City of white
City of light
I'm livin' in a city of immigrants
City of sweat
City of tears
City of prayers
Livin' in a city of immigrants

5

10

15

20

25

30

35

40

45

50   City of stone
      City of steel
      City of wheels
      Livin' in a city of immigrants

      City of bone
      City of skin
55   City of pain
      City of immigrants

      All of us are immigrants, all of us are immigrants

© Exile on Jones Street Music, Neue Welt Musikverlag GmbH, Hamburg

10 Listen again, read the lyrics and do the tasks.

1 Look at these lines from the song. Which American city do you think it is about?
   Livin' in a city of immigrants (l.1)
   Livin' in a city that never sleeps (l.5),
   In the sacred promise a statue made (l.23)
   River flows out and the sea rolls in (l. 38)
2 Explain ll. 9–15 (City of black … City of prayers).
3 Explain ll. 25–31 (City of stone… City of pain).
4 What does the singer mean when he says: "All of us are immigrants" (l.33)?

MEDIATION ....

11 Read the text below Info box and say in German what you learn about Steve Earle.

L ▸ Mediation (p. 148)

Steve Earle was born in Virginia in 1955 and grew up in Texas. He began to play the guitar when he was eleven. At 16 he dropped out of school to follow a career in music. For thirty years he lived and played music in Nashville, Tennessee. But he spent all his money on drugs and alcohol, became unable to play and finally landed in prison. By
5 January 1995, Earle had overcome his addictions and made a successful comeback album *Train A Comin'*. In 2005 he won a Grammy[1] for Best Contemporary Folk Album for The *Revolution Starts Now*. Earle has also acted and written stories and plays. One of the reasons he decided to move to New York was to be near the theatre. Earle has been married seven times – twice to the same woman. He is well known for his liberal anti-
10 war and anti-death-penalty views.

[1]Grammy *Award given by the American National Academy of Recording Arts and Sciences for achievement in the record industry.*

12 Choose a song in English that you like and present it to the class.
Follow steps 1–4 below.

EXAM PREPARATION
Präsentationsprüfung (p. 151)

1 Find the lyrics to the song and prepare to explain any difficult words. Research the singer's biography.
2 In class, explain what the song is about and give a short biography of the singer.
3 Hand out the lyrics. Play the song and help your classmates to understand the lyrics.
4 Finally, tell the class why you chose the song.

2.17

LISTENING

13 **a** Listen to a British couple talking about immigration.

Copy and complete the table in German with information from the discussion.

> **ZENTRALE KLASSENARBEIT**
> *Hörverstehen (p. 150)*

Argumente für die Aufnahme von Migranten	Argumente gegen die Aufnahme von Migranten

b Give the arguments from 13a a ranking 1–3:

1 I absolutely agree.   **2** I partially agree.   **3** I totally disagree.

Compare your ranking with a partner. Give reasons for your ranking.

L ▶ Interaktion (pp. 147 – 148)

c With your partner, add two more arguments to each of the columns in the table in 13a. Compare your arguments with other pairs.

WRITING

14 "International migration is a global phenomenon that is growing in scope, complexity and impact."
(http://www.un.org/en/development/desa/population/theme/international-migration/)

Comment on the reasons why migrants leave their native countries.

INTERNET RESEARCH

15 Research on the internet, find the answers to these questions and report them to the class.

1 What is an EU Blue Card and who can apply for it?
2 When did Germany enact Blue Card legislation?
3 What requirements must be fulfilled in order to obtain an EU Blue Card?
4 How might the Blue Card system lead to a brain drain in developing countries?

brain drain *Abwanderung hochqualifizierter Arbeitskräfte*

TEXT 4   Young people and politics

WARM UP

1 Find somebody in your class who . . .

1 is interested in politics.
2 would like to be a politician one day.
3 knows who the German Vice-Chancellor is.
4 can name five ministers in the German Cabinet.
5 can name the prime minister of your federal state.
6 knows how many member states the European Union has.
7 believes that most politicians are too old to understand young people's interests.
8 thinks voting in elections is very important.

Why many young people don't vote

2.18

In the last mid-term elections in the USA less than a quarter of people aged 18 to 24 turned out to vote. In the last general election in Britain,
5 44 per cent of people of that age group voted, compared with 65 per cent of people of all ages, and there is not a single European country where the young turn out more
10 than older people. So why is it so difficult to get young people to vote?

Youth turnout has never been particularly high anywhere, but over the past few decades young people's participation in electoral politics has noticeably declined.
15 Older people like to say that the young are just lazy and apathetic, but surveys have shown that that is far from the truth. In fact, they indicate that today's young people are more liberal, cosmopolitan and politically engaged than previous generations. They take on more volunteer work than older people and are more likely to join NGOs. Many of them are genuinely concerned about political issues
20 such as war, the environment, the fight against poverty, tuition fees and the cost of home ownership.

One explanation for low turnout by young people may be that young people today feel that party politics is irrelevant to their lives. Young people are settling down much later than they used to – in 1970 the average American woman was just under 21 when she first married. Today women marry at 26 on average – if
25 they marry at all, and many young couples opt not to have children. Thus, there is little interest for them in how kindergartens and schools are run, and how local facilities such as playgrounds, parks and libraries are maintained.

A rather depressing explanation for young people's lack of interest is that many
30 believe politicians to be corrupt, cynical and out of touch, and there is no-one worth voting for. Charismatic politicians like Barack Obama, who was elected in 2008 and 2012 thanks to the unusually high youth turnout in the presidential elections, are few and far between.

[1] mid-term election *Zwischenwahl*
[3] turn out *zur Wahl gehen*
[13] **turnout** *Wahlbeteiligung*
[13] **particularly** *besonders*
[14] electoral politics *Wahlpolitik*
[15] **apathetic** *teilnahmslos, apathisch*
[16] indicate *erkennen lassen, zeigen*
[18] **volunteer** *ehrenamtlich*
[20] **tuition fees** *Studiengebühren*
[21] home ownership *eigenes Haus, eigene Wohnung*
[23] settle down *einen Haushalt gründen*
[26] opt *sich für etw/dafür entscheiden*
[30] out of touch *abgehoben*
[33] few and far between *dünn gesät*

35 tell sth apart *etw auseinanderhalten*
36 ballot *Stimmzettel*
38 perception *Wahrnehmung*

Other reasons young people give for not voting are not having enough information and not being able to tell the parties apart. Voter advice websites such as VoteMatch, Bite the Ballot and Vote For Policies are part of a trend aimed at counteracting two of the main reasons young people give for their reluctance to vote: lack of knowledge and the perception that all parties are the same. 35

There is one simple thing that politics could do to appeal more to young people: have politicians who are more representative of the country as a whole. In the last UK parliament, for example, only 22 per cent of MPs were female and four per cent were from an ethnic minority. Few young people can relate to 'rich, old, white men' – which is the way current governments appear to them. 40

(473 words)

WORKING WITH THE TEXT

L ▶ Lesen schwieriger Texte: Grobverständnis (p. 134)

2 Which statement best summarizes the text?

A Young people are not interested in politics and are too lazy to vote.
B Young people are too disillusioned with politics and politicians to vote.
C Young people are satisfied with their lives and don't think it is necessary to change things.

→ EXAM PREPARATION
Leseverstehen (p. 149)

3 Decide whether the following statements about the text are true or false. Give reasons for your answers in full German sentences.

1 A higher percentage of 18- to 24-year-olds voted in the last British general election than in the mid-term elections in the USA.
2 Youth turnout in elections used to be even lower than today.
3 Young people today are more apathetic than previous generations.
4 The writer has a negative opinion of young people.
5 There are very few politicians with personalities that appeal to young people.
6 Some important social groups were under-represented in the last UK parliament.

CHALLENGE!

4 Compare the text *Why many young people don't vote* with the text *The United Kingdom Youth Parliament* on page 95. Say whether it supports or contradicts the statements made in that text.

WORKING WITH WORDS

5 Complete the sentences using the following adjectives from the text. Two of the adjectives are not used.

average | charismatic | cynical | depressing | lazy | liberal | presidential | previous | simple

1 There is no … explanation why young people don't vote.
2 Young people today often have more … views than … generations had.
3 The next … election in the USA will take place later this year.
4 Barack Obama was one of the most … presidents the USA has ever had.
5 The … earnings in the country are about 1,000 euros a month.
6 Older people often say that the young are just too … to vote.

6 Match the words (1–8) from the text to the synonymous words and expressions (a–h).

1	decade	a	teaching, schooling
2	cosmopolitan	b	unwillingness
3	apathetic	c	present, ongoing
4	a single	d	at home anywhere in the world
5	reluctance	e	possessing something
6	current	f	ten years
7	ownership	g	one
8	tuition	h	uninterested

LOOKING AT LANGUAGE

7 **a** **Complete these sentences from the text.**

G ▸ Adjectives and adverbs
(pp. 163 – 164)

1 Youth turnout has never been … anywhere.
2 Many young people are … about political issues.
3 Barack Obama would not have been elected had it not been for … youth turnout.

b **Use a word from each column to complete the sentences. Use each word only once.**

Adverbs	Adjectives
absolutely	awful
awfully	better
badly	cheap
extremely	injured
happily	interesting
highly	kind
reasonably	married
slightly	qualified

1 It is … … … of you to help me.
2 I read a(n) … … … article yesterday.
3 The weather here is … … … .
4 The company is looking for … … staff.
5 The restaurant is … … … .
6 I feel … … … than I did yesterday.
7 The boy was … … … in the accident.
8 Tina and Tim are … … … .

SPEAKING

8 **a** **Complete the following sentences with your own ideas, then compare your sentences with a partner.**

1 In my opinion, most politicians …
2 If I were the German chancellor, I would …
3 The political system in my country is …

b **Work in small groups and exchange ideas. Elect one member of the group to report the results of the discussion to the class.**

L ▸ Interaktion (pp. 147 – 148)

1 Why are there fewer women than men in politics?
2 Should voting be made compulsory for anyone over 18?

GROUP PROJECT

9 Work in larger groups. Your group is going to form a new political party.

- Find a name for your party.
- Think up four policies your party will use in its election campaign:
  If we are elected, we will ...
- Tell the class the name of your party and describe its policies.
- Make ballot papers with the names of all parties listed.
- Hold an election.

WRITING

→ EXAM PREPARATION
Textproduktion (p. 150)

10 "... young people today feel that party politics is irrelevant to their lives."

Explain the quotation in relation to the text and give examples of ways in which politics could be made more attractive to young people.

READING

11 Read the online news article. Choose the sentence that best sums up Kimberly Guilfoyle's opinion.

A Uninformed people shouldn't vote.
B Beautiful young women are too stupid to vote.
C Young women should not be allowed to vote.

⁵ devote *widmen*
⁸ jury *Geschworene*
¹¹ variety *Vielzahl*
¹² retailer *Einzelhändler/in*
¹⁴ grant *gewähren*
¹⁴ wisdom *Weisheit*
¹⁵ raise children *Kinder erziehen*
¹⁶ health care *Gesundheitswesen*
¹⁷ like *hier: irgendwie*
¹⁷ care *Sorge*

Fox News host Kimberly Guilfoyle says beautiful young women should be excused from voting

Fox News Channel host Kimberly Guilfoyle believes that young, attractive women should be excused from voting so they can devote their time to online dating. ⁵

"It's the same reason why young women on juries is not a good idea. They don't get it!" she said on the news channel's daily talk show. ¹⁰

Guilfoyle, 45, who helped pay her way through law school modeling for a variety of retailers including Victoria's Secret, said young, beautiful women don't have the proper "life experiences to have a say in who holds elected office".

Instead, they should only be granted the privilege after they've gained wisdom from raising children, paying bills or dealing with real-world issues like a mortgage ¹⁵ and health care.

"They're like healthy and hot and running around without a care in the world," said Guilfoyle.

20   When co-host Bob Beckel noted that young women have "every right in the world" to sit on a jury, Guilfoyle said: "I just think, excuse them so they can go back on Tinder and Match.com."

On a later edition of the show, Guilfoyle said she had been joking. "I take the right to vote very seriously. I take the right to serve on a jury very seriously. I just think you should be informed when you do both things."

25   Her colleagues said that her comments had been taken out of context by the "liberal media".

(229 words)

Adapted from *New York Daily News*

[21] Tinder, Match.com *popular dating apps*

[22] **edition** *Ausgabe*

WORKING WITH THE TEXT

12   Use suitable words from the text in the correct form to complete the gaps.

Kimberly Guilfoyle, who is a …[1] on the Fox News Channel, made some …[2] on a …[3] that hit the headlines. She said that young women should …[4] their time to …[5] instead of voting or …[6] on a jury. Ms Guilfoyle, who studied …[7], said voting was a …[8] that should only be …[9] to women after they had …[10] children and had some experience of …[11] issues. Later Ms. Guilfoyle claimed that she …[12] and she had been quoted out of …[13].

MEDIATION

13   Read the Info box and make a timeline with the main facts in German.

HANDS-ON
TASK

L ▸ Mediation (p. 148)

INFO

Suffrage

'Suffrage' means the right to vote in political elections. 'Universal' suffrage means that the right to vote is not restricted by sex, race, religion, social status or wealth. In early democracies only a minority of the population, those with property and wealth, were allowed to vote. France was the first nation to introduce the right to vote for all male

5   adult citizens in 1792, and New Zealand was the first major country to grant universal male and female adult suffrage in 1893.

In the UK, it was not until 1918 that all male citizens over the age of 21 and female citizens over 30 were given the right to vote. By 1928 women had finally been given the same voting rights as men, and in 1969 suffrage was extended to everyone over 18.

10   In the USA, suffrage was determined to a large extent by the individual states, but various amendments to the Constitution meant voting rights for all adult males (1870), all adult males and females (1920) and all adult citizens over the age of 18 (1971).

In most US states, prisoners have no voting rights. In the UK, prisoners deprived of those rights took their case to European Court of Human Rights and won. Their

15   argument was that they shouldn't lose their status in civil society because they are in prison. Prisoners are still members of society, and voting has nothing to do with their punishment.

L ► Interaktion (pp. 147 – 148)

SPEAKING

14 Work with a partner. Exchange opinions on the following statement from the Info box:

"[Prisoners] shouldn't lose their status in civil society because they are in prison. Prisoners are still members of society, and voting has nothing to do with their punishment."

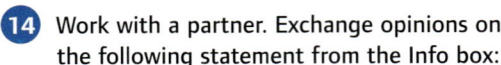

DESCRIBING A CARTOON

→ EXAM PREPARATION
Kommunikationsprüfung (p. 150)

15 Describe the cartoon and relate it to the Info box. Produce an uninterrupted three-minute monologue.

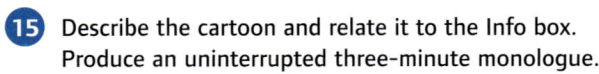

2.19

LISTENING

L ► Das Hörverständnis üben (pp. 137 – 138)

16 You are going to hear Jackie and Richard talking about International Women's Day.

  a Listen again. What happened in these years?

1893 | 1911 | 1923

  b Listen to the dialogue and explain these numbers.

2/3 | 1% | 8th | 10% | 20th | 75% | 100

→ ZENTRALE KLASSENARBEIT
Hörverstehen (p. 150)

17 Beantworten Sie die folgenden Fragen auf Deutsch in Stichworten.

  1 Wie wird Women's Day in China, Russland und Vietnam gewürdigt?
  2 Welches Thema stand am Anfang des Women's Day im Mittelpunkt?
  3 Was sagt Jackie über die Frauenrechtlerinnen der Vergangenheit?
  4 Warum ist es noch schwierig für eine Frau, Beruf und Kinder zu vereinbaren?
  5 Wie sieht Jackie die Zukunft und warum?

SPEAKING

L ► Interaktion (pp. 147 – 148)

18 Look at the statements below. Add TWO ideas of your own, then work in small groups and discuss the following statement:

Women today have all the rights they need. It is men who need to fight for equality.

> · Women on average live four or five years longer than men.
> · Young women are better educated than young men.
> · Men are the main victims of crime.
> · Women can have babies.
> · In some countries, men are obliged to do military service.
> · A woman can give up her job and stay at home and not be called a 'loser'.
> · It is acceptable for women to wear men's clothes but not for men to wear women's clothes.
> · …

TEXT 5   Elitist education in the UK

WARM UP

1   Read the Info box about private schools in the United Kingdom. With a partner, take turns to summarize the information in German for a friend who does not speak English.

L ▶ Mediation (p. 148)

INFO

Private schools in the United Kingdom

In the UK over half a million children are privately educated. Parents in the UK spend more on private schooling for their children than any other country in the EU because
5 private education is often thought to be superior to state education. Indeed, independent school pupils are three times more likely to get top grades at A-level than state school pupils, and 90 per cent of them
10 go on to higher education.

There are about 2,500 so-called 'independent schools', which are fee-paying, private schools. The name comes from the fact that the schools are independent of many of the regulations of state schools.

Fees average £14,000 a year for day places, and £26,000 for boarders, but there are
15 also scholarships for gifted children. Nearly half of independent schools are single-sex schools. Classes are much smaller than in state schools – a GCSE class may have between 10 and 15 pupils compared with 25 to 30 in state schools. Because private schools have more funds than state schools, they also tend to be better equipped.

Some of the older, more exclusive schools for 13- to 18-year-olds are known as 'public
20 schools', as they were the first schools open to the public. The top ten public schools in the UK have produced one in eight of the professional elite who run the country. Eton College, founded in 1440, is one of the best known and most expensive (£30,000 per year for boarders). Two of the school's most famous pupils were Princes William and Harry.

6 indeed *in der Tat*
8 A-level *Abitur*
5 independent school *Privatschule*
11 **regulation** *Vorschrift*
14 boarder *Internatsschüler/in*
15 scholarship *Stipendium*
16 GCSE = General Certificate of Secondary Education *entspricht etwa dem Realschulabschluss*

2   Look at the statements about private education. Which statements do you agree with and which do you disagree with? Give reasons for your answers.

- People shouldn't be allowed to buy a better education.
- Private education means that only the rich can get to the top.
- Special people need a special education.
- The existence of independent schools makes inequality in society even greater than it already is.
- There will always be more or less privileged people. That's life – accept it.

2.20

Elitist UK locks out diversity at the top

The UK is "deeply elitist" according to an analysis of the backgrounds of more than 4,000 business, political, media and public sector leaders. A small elite, educated at independent schools and Oxbridge, still dominate top roles, suggests the Social Mobility and Child Poverty Commission study. It says key institutions do not represent the public they serve.

The commission chairman said the UK's top jobs remain "disproportionately held by people from a narrow range of backgrounds. The institutions that matter appear to be a cosy club. [...] Locking out a diversity of talents and experiences makes Britain's leading institutions less informed, less representative and ultimately less credible than they should be," he warned.

The commission found that those who had attended fee-paying schools included:
- 71% of senior judges
- 62% of senior armed forces officers
- 55% of permanent secretaries (the most senior civil servants)
- 53% of senior diplomats.
- 44% of the *Sunday Times* Rich List
- 43% of newspaper columnists
- 36% of the Cabinet

This compares with seven per cent of the UK population as a whole who attend independent schools.

Figures for top people who went to Oxford and Cambridge universities paint a similar picture.

Some 75% of senior judges, 59% of the Cabinet, 57% of top civil servants, 50% of diplomats, 47% of newspaper columnists and 24% of MPs hold Oxbridge degrees.

In contrast, less than one per cent of the whole population are Oxbridge graduates, says the study. It asks whether top jobs are about what you know or who you know, and whether some talent is being locked out. It calls for more government effort to "break open" Britain's elite, by a number of measures – such as opening senior public sector jobs to a wider range of people.

The Headmasters and Headmistresses Conference (HMC) of top private heads called the study "unreasonable and unfair" and said that to suggest that a high number of people in positions of influence were there simply because they went to private schools was "lazy stereotyping and underestimates the diversity within the sector".

The HMC said the key to improving social mobility was to allow more young people access to independent schools through scholarships. It said their strength was in developing pupils' talents, creativity, character and individuality, as well as achieving high academic results.

(385 words)

Adapted from http://www.bbc.com/news/education-28953881

5

10

15

20

25

30

35

40

WORKING WITH THE TEXT

3 **a** **Match the sentence halves to make statements about the text. There is one sentence half in each list which cannot be matched.**

L ► Lesen schwieriger Texte: Detailverständnis (p. 135)

1 There would be more diversity in top jobs …
2 Key institutions do not represent the public because …
3 A large number of the professional elite who run the country …
4 While only one per cent of the UK population has attended Oxbridge, …
5 The HMC says that independent schools not only achieve high academic results …
6 Social mobility could be improved …
7 The HMC disapproves of the report because …

a it claims that it gives a false picture of the real situation.
b has made Britain's leading institutions less representative than they should be.
c they are dominated by an elite.
d come from a narrow range of backgrounds.
e 57 per cent of top civil servants hold an Oxbridge degree.
f if they were open to a wider range of people.
g by making more scholarships available.

b **Complete the unmatched sentence halves with your own words.**

CHALLENGE!

4 **Explain the title of the article in your own words.**

CHALLENGE!

WORKING WITH WORDS

5 **a** **Find jobs in the text to match the definitions 1–6.**

1 a public officer who decides cases in a court of law
2 a person who has been elected to represent people in Parliament
3 a journalist who writes for print media
4 a person employed to represent their country in another country
5 a woman in charge of a school
6 a person who works for the government

b **Complete the sentences with the jobs from 5a.**

1 The editor asked the … to submit his work by the end of the day.
2 My … advised me to apply for Oxbridge.
3 The … found him guilty and sentenced him to prison.
4 My father is a senior … in the Department of Energy.
5 For several years I worked as a … in the British Embassy in Berlin.
6 Jim got more votes than his opponent and became our local …

LOOKING AT LANGUAGE

6 **Put each of the linking words or phrases in a suitable place in the text below. Sometimes more than one answer is possible.**

L ► Einen Text sinnvoll gliedern (pp. 142–143)

as a consequence | but the fact is | despite | even more so | even though | however | in contrast to | moreover | one reason is | therefore

...¹ a long tradition of democracy, society in Britain, ...² other English-speaking countries such as the USA and Australia, is hierarchical. ...³ that as long as there is a monarchy and an aristocracy at the top of society, somebody has to be at the bottom. ...⁴ there is a strong awareness of social class in Britain and ...⁵ a strong sense of superiority and inferiority. In the past, ...⁶ than today, the family you were born into could determine your place in society. ...⁷, you would know all the 'right people', who would later help you to get on in life. Today, ...⁸, it is also possible to become part of the elite by having the right education. ...⁹ you have had to buy your way into the upper classes, you will still have a good chance of entering the 'corridors of power', thanks to the friends you made at school and university. Yes, there is a new elite, ...¹⁰ that there is still an exclusive group making decisions for the rest of us.

DESCRIBING A CARTOON

EXAM PREPARATION

Kommunikationsprüfung (p. 150)

7 Describe the cartoon and relate it along with the quotation to aspects of elitism in Britain. Produce an uninterrupted three-minute monologue.

"The best argument against democracy is a five-minute conversation with the average voter."
Winston Churchill, former British Prime Minister

SPEAKING

L ▶ Interaktion (pp. 147–148)

8 Does Germany provide equal opportunities in education? In pairs, discuss the different aspects of the question. Refer to the aspects mentioned in the mind map.

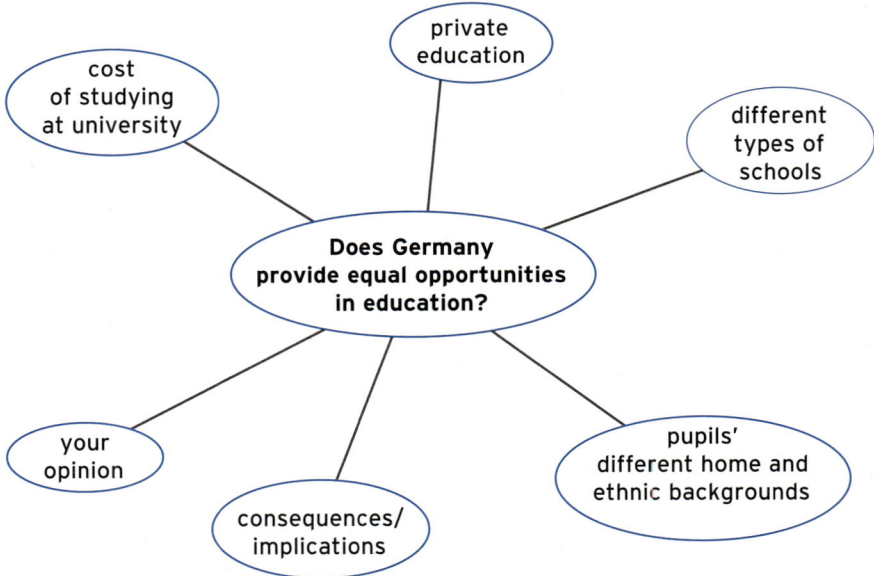

9 One paragraph of the following text is missing. Read Alternatives A to C below and decide which ONE best completes the text and in which of the places marked ...?... it belongs. Give reasons for your choice.

One in five adolescents not in school

While European and American parents agonize over the choice of school for their children, a total of 121 million children and adolescents worldwide have never started school or have dropped out, according to a United Nations report. Although in the last decade improvements have been made in schooling children of primary school age, 63 million adolescents have been denied their right to education.

...?...

Poverty is the greatest barrier to education. The highest out-of-school rates are in poor countries such as Eritrea and Liberia. In Nigeria, five per cent of children from rich families but sixty per cent of children from poor families don't go to school. Even if parents can afford to let their children go to school, poor countries mean poor classroom facilities and inadequate funds for teacher training. In several African countries, fewer than half of the teachers have had any training.

...?...

"To realize the promise of universal education for every child, we need to invest in three areas: getting more children into primary school; helping more children – especially girls – stay in school through the secondary level; and improving the quality of the learning they receive throughout their schooling," said UNICEF executive director Anthony Lake. "By working together and promoting greater investment, we can and must dismantle the barriers that stand in their way, one by one — and in doing so, deliver on our global promise of education for every child."

...?...

Alternative A: UNESCO says that although the pupil-teacher ratio has decreased in 121 countries at primary level, four million more teachers are needed to get all children into school. "Trained teachers remain in short supply in one-third of countries: in several sub-Saharan countries, less than 50% are trained," the report said.

Alternative B: That means that one in five adolescents are not in school, compared with one in 11 primary school-age children. Those most affected are young people living in conflict areas, child labourers, children with disabilities and girls living in countries where females are not allowed an education.

Alternative C: On the contrary, one in four young people in developing countries are unable to read a sentence, according to a UNESCO report, which warns that lack of or poor quality of education is more widespread than previously believed. In research published on Wednesday, the UN's educational, scientific and cultural body, suggests that 175 million young people lack even basic literacy skills.

² agonize over sth *sich über etw den Kopf zerbrechen*
⁵ drop out *die Schule abbrechen*
²⁵ dismantle *abbauen*
⁴² literacy *Lese- und Schreibfähigkeit*

WRITING

→ **EXAM PREPARATION**
Texproduktion (p. 150)

10 "By working together and promoting greater investment, we can and must dismantle the barriers that stand in their way."

Explain the quotation in relation to the text and give examples.

COMPETENCE TRAINING: PROOFREADING

TIP

Whenever you write a text, it is important to check it carefully to make sure there are no mistakes. If possible, wait for a while after writing your text before proofreading it, then follow this checklist:

1 Keep a list of mistakes you have often made in the past and look out for these in your text.
   A typical mistake is using the present perfect (*I have done*) instead of the past tense (*I did*).
2 Look out for grammar and spelling mistakes.
3 Look out for wrong collocations (*make a mistake* not **do a mistake*).
4 Look out for false friends (*bekommen ≠ become; aktuell ≠ actual*)
5 Read your text word-for-word aloud (or move your lips in a test). This helps you notice missing words.

11 The following text from a student's essay contains ten mistakes. Find them and write them down together with line number and correction. The first two have been highlighted.

Nick Duffell's excellent book *The Making of Them is examining* the British boarding school system. In the 21st century, British society is still characterized *from* a private education system originally created in Victorian times to produce gentleman to run the British Empire. Actually, some 25,000 British children aged 13 and under are in private boarding schools. Duffell not only analyzes the effect of boarding school life   5 on girls and boys while their school time but also in later life, looking at the kind of person the ex-boarder has become. Duffell, a psychotherapist, writes of his own experiment as a boarder and describes the pain of his clients and the damage that was made when they were separated from their families in an early age. He explores the effects of a 24/7 enviroment on children who cannot escape for months and years.   10 This book is a must for anyone who was unlucky enough to be sent to boarding school. Anyone interested in British culture, education and their attitude to children will enjoy to read it, too.

TEXT 6 The American Dream

1 Describe the pictures, then match the captions (1–6) to the photographs (A–F).

A

B

C

D

E

F

1 Home ownership
2 Mobility
3 Friendly neighbourhood

4 Prosperity
5 Freedom
6 Educational opportunities

What is the American Dream?

5
There are many definitions of the American Dream, but they all include the belief that in the United States of America each individual is free to strive for and achieve success and prosperity through hard work, and that everyone should have the same rights and the same opportunities.

10

15
The American Dream has its roots in the Declaration of Independence of 1776. This stated that "all men are created equal" and that everyone has the right to "Life, Liberty and the pursuit of Happiness". The term itself, however, was coined in 1931 by historian James Truslow Adams, who declared that "Life should be better and richer and fuller for everyone, with opportunity for each according to ability or achievement, regardless of social class or circumstances of birth". The idea that anyone can start out poor, work hard and become rich has persisted. To quote the African-American actress Whoopi Goldberg: "I am the epitome of what the American Dream basically said. It said you could come from anywhere and be anything you want in this country. That's exactly what I've done".

2.21
2 **include** *einschließen*
4 **strive for sth** *etwas anstreben*
4 **prosperity** *Wohlstand*
7 **root** *Wurzel*
7 Declaration of Independence *Unabhängigkeitserklärung*
9 **liberty** *Freiheit*
9 **pursuit** *Streben*
9 coin *prägen*
10 historian *Historiker/in*
11 **according to** *je nach*
12 **ability** *Fähigkeit*
12 **regardless of** *ungeachtet, unabhängig von*
13 **persist** *fortbestehen*
14 epitome *Inbegriff, Verkörperung*

21 **limitless** *grenzenlos*

21 **pursue** *verfolgen*

22 **purely** *bloß*

23 **focus on sth** *sich auf etw konzentrieren*

23 **narrowly** *eng*

28 **grip** *Griff*

28 **inaugural address** *Antrittsrede*

32 **honesty** *Ehrlichkeit*

32 **curiosity** *Neugier*

32 **loyalty** *Treue*

34 **force** *Kraft*

35 **faith** *Glaube*

35 **progress** *Fortschritt*

36 **preoccupation** *ständige (gedankliche) Beschäftigung mit etw*

Although the idea that just anyone can become a billionaire or the President of the United States is clearly absurd, the American Dream has been the inspiration for generations of Americans. Millions of immigrants of different nationalities, different ethnic backgrounds and different religions have come to America, the land of limitless opportunity, to pursue that dream.   20

But has the American Dream become a purely materialistic dream of consumerism? Has it come to focus too narrowly on making money, on following the 'dishwasher to millionaire', the 'rags to riches' idea that Hollywood films like to portray, pushing aside abstract values such as freedom, equality and democracy?   25

That is certainly food for thought, yet in years of economic recession the ideals of the American Dream have been remarkably strong. When Adams first coined the term, the USA was in the grip of the Great Depression. In his inaugural address in 2009, the year of the deepest economic recession since the Great Depression, President Barack Obama reminded the American people that: "Our challenges may   30 be new. But those values upon which our success depends – honesty and hard work, courage and fair play, tolerance and curiosity, loyalty and patriotism – these things are old. These things are true. They have been the quiet force of progress throughout our history."

The American Dream has always meant faith in progress, a belief that change for   35 the better is always possible. So while the preoccupation with consumerism may have to change according to economic developments, the ideals of freedom and opportunity will most certainly survive.   (436 words)

WORKING WITH THE TEXT

L ▶ Lesen schwieriger Texte: Suche nach Einzelinformationen (pp. 134–135)

2 Explain in English in your own words …

1 the origins of the term the 'American Dream'.
2 Whoopi Goldberg sees herself as the epitome of the American Dream.
3 why the American Dream has been an inspiration for generations of Americans and immigrants.
4 the materialistic aspect of the American Dream.
5 the importance of the American Dream in times of economic recession.
6 the future of the American Dream.

DESCRIBING A CARTOON

L ▶ Interpretation von Bildern und Karikaturen (pp. 145–146)

3 Describe the cartoon and explain its message.

INFO

The Great Depression

The Great Depression was a deep, long-lasting economic recession. It began in the United States soon after the stock market crash of October 1929, which sent Wall Street into a panic.

Banks failed and millions of investors lost their money.
5 Consumer spending and investment dropped. Because of lack of demand, factories closed and workers lost their jobs. By March 1930, 3.2 million people were unemployed compared to 1.5 million before the October crash. By 1933 some 13 to 15 million
10 Americans were unemployed, and by 1935 the unemployment rate in the US was over 20 per cent.

In February 1931 food riots broke out all over America. In the same month 6,024 Mexican Americans were accused of stealing jobs from 'real' Americans and were deported.

15 In 1932 Franklin Delano Roosevelt (FDR) was elected President. He introduced a set of programmes known as the 'New Deal' to promote economic recovery and social reform. In April 1938 FDR asked Congress to authorize $3.75 billion in federal spending. Yet unemployment remained high. The recession lasted until 1939, when World War II gave a boost to American industry.

4 Read the Info box and make a timeline of the Great Depression.

HANDS-ON
TASK

WORKING WITH WORDS

5 a Copy and complete the table with nouns from the text *What is the American dream?*

Adverbs	Noun	Adverbs	Noun	Adverbs	Noun
courageous	...	historic	(two words)	patriotic	
curious	...	independent	...	preoccupied	
equal	...	inspired	...	prosperous	

   b Match the nouns from 5a with the definitions.

1 ability to control fear
2 the state of not being controlled by anyone
3 having enough money and a fulfilling life
4 being treated in the same way and having the same chances
5 love for and loyalty to one's country
6 a strong wish to know something
7 obsession
8 an expert on past events
9 a person or thing that stimulates the mind to do something positive or creative

CHALLENGE!

6 **a** Match the idioms 1–7 with their definitions a–g.

1 give somebody food for thought
2 keep a lid on something
3 kill two birds with one stone
4 make somebody's day
5 stab somebody in the back
6 get to grips with something
7 go over the top (OTT)

a achieve two useful things with one action
b give somebody a reason to feel happy
c understand and deal with something
d give somebody serious ideas to think about
e exaggerate
f do something secretly to harm someone
g keep something secret

b Choose the idiom from 6a which best fits the situation and use it to complete the sentence.

1 While I work out at the gym, I listen to English vocabulary on my iPod. That way I …
2 I wouldn't trust Fiona. She's nice to your face, but she wouldn't hesitate …
3 My boss complimented me on my work yesterday and that really …
4 I'm finding it hard … these problems …
5 My parents' reaction was extreme. They … completely …
6 She doesn't want anyone to know she's getting married, so make sure …
7 Thanks for the information. You have …

LOOKING AT LANGUAGE

7 Each of the following sentences contains a mistake of the sort that German students of English often make. Find the mistakes and correct them. The clues in brackets will help you.

1 Yesterday, we must write an English test. (auxiliary)
2 *The Other Hand* is a novel from Chris Cleave. (preposition)
3 Jim had a shower when he heard the phone ring. (verb)
4 The food is good and it isn't expensive too. (adverb)
5 My mum is the best mum of the whole world. (preposition)
6 My parents have been happy married for twenty years. (adverb)
7 How do you call the prime minister of the UK? (question word)
8 When I don't see you tomorrow, I'll phone. (conjunction)
9 I learn English for a long time. (verb)
10 We took some notices during the lecture. (noun)

READING

8 Read the film synopsis and answer the questions below.

[0] synopsis *Zusammenfassung*
[8] shutters *Fensterläden*
[9] picket fence *Lattenzaun*
[11] despise *verachten*

American Beauty is an American film directed by Sam Mendes, starring Kevin Spacey as Lester Burnham and Annette Bening as his wife, Carolyn. The film shows what happens after a family has achieved its version of the American Dream. The Burnhams are the typical suburban family. Lester and Carolyn both have well-paid full-time jobs, and their daughter Jane is in high school.

Symbolically, they have a house with a red door, blue shutters and a white picket fence – the colours of the American flag. But behind the façade, Lester is bored with his job, Caroline is ambitious and materialistic and Jane despises her parents.

5

American Beauty, USA/1999 with K. Spacey and A. Bening, directed by Sam Mendes

10

Their neighbours, the Fitts, seem to be a typical conservative family, but their rebellious teenage son, Ricky, deals with marijuana. Carolyn begins an affair with a business rival, and Lester, longing for adventure, quits his job, buys a red sports car, begins to smoke pot (supplied by Ricky), and has sexual fantasies about Angela, his daughter's teenage cheerleader friend.

Each member of the Burnham and Fitt families has their secret dreams, which, one dark and stormy night, lead to a series of misunderstandings that would be comic if they didn't end in murder.

The film has won many awards including an Oscar for Kevin Spacey as Best Actor.

1 What does "a family has achieved **its** version of the American Dream" mean?
2 How would you describe a "typical suburban family"?
3 Would you like to see *American Beauty*? Why (not)?
4 Explain why the Burnham's red-white-and-blue house is "a façade".

CHALLENGE!

WRITING A FILM REVIEW

9 Work with a partner to complete the following task.

1 Talk to your partner and find a film you have both seen. Discuss the film and say what you liked or disliked about it. Was the film simply entertaining or did you learn something you didn't know before?

L ▸ Interaktion (pp. 147–148)

2 Working on your own, write a review of the film for the cinema section of your school magazine. Write:
   - a summary of the plot of the film
   - the actors' performance
   - what you liked/disliked about the film
   - conclusion/recommendation

HANDS-ON
TASK

Use the phrases below to help you.
… is a film by … starring … as …
The film is a feature film/documentary/…
The main theme/message of the film is …
The film tells us the story of …
… is great/weak in the main role because …
I found … both entertaining/ instructive/boring/too violent/really funny because …
What I especially enjoyed/disliked was …
In conclusion …
I would certainly (not) recommend …

3 You and your partner swap reviews. Read your partner's review, make notes and then suggest improvements and corrections.

4 Read your partner's comments. Write a revised version of your review to hand in for correction.

CROSSOVER TV

4

What is the American Dream?

10   a   Watch and listen to Americans answering the question: "What is the American Dream?" Which aspect of the American dream do the people interviewed NOT mention?

chance of a better life | freedom to choose your job | freedom to choose where you live | good family life | happiness | living in a safe neighbourhood | making money and getting rich | nice home | religious freedom | working hard and being successful

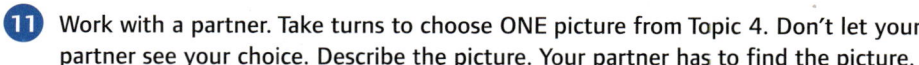

b   In answer to the question "How is America different from other countries" the speakers talk about freedom. What aspects of freedom do they mention?

c   What are the differences between the American Dream and dreams that German people have about their country and the way they want to live?

SPEAKING

11   Work with a partner. Take turns to choose ONE picture from Topic 4. Don't let your partner see your choice. Describe the picture. Your partner has to find the picture.

EXAM PRACTICE

Eating disorders in children and teenagers are soaring, but is the internet really to blame?

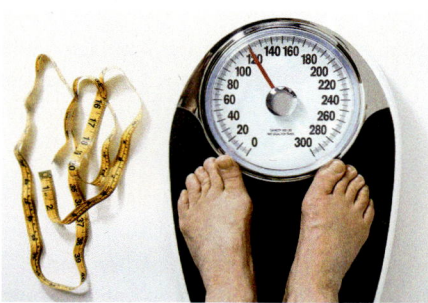

This weekend the *Independent on Sunday* exclusively revealed figures that show that the number of teenagers and young people with eating disorders had soared by 110 % in the last three years.

According to recent reports, the internet and social media websites like Facebook and Twitter are contributing to the growing trend in sufferers, particularly among young girls. It's an interesting suggestion, and most parents will be familiar with their children's constant engagement to social media sites via their laptops, tablets and mobile phones. Yet I for one have divided views on whether the internet is the major factor it is made out to be.

ChildLine, a counselling service for young people, says it has received more than 10,500 calls and online inquiries from young people struggling with food and weight-related anxiety in the last year. The  charity believes this dramatic increase could be attributed to several factors, including the increased pressure caused by social media, the growth of celebrity culture, and the rise of anorexia websites with their 'rules' and tips for getting thin.

Okay, it's understandable that they play a part in contributing to the pressures, but are social media sites entirely to blame? In reality, eating disorders are a result of a combination of factors built up over time. Peer pressure can play a major part, as can relationships, family troubles and academic concerns.

One advantage of the internet is that it is the most convenient and accessible means of communication for support. ChildLine said the proportion of children and young people who have used online channels to talk about eating problems was higher last year than for any other concern, giving an indication of how this issue is being played out on the internet. More than eight out of ten of ChildLine's counselling sessions about eating problems took place online, compared with only 19 per cent via the phone.

So if the internet is part of the problem troubling children and young people, then surely it is also part of the solution to tackling eating disorders.

Dr Nadia Micali, senior lecturer at University College London, and lead author of research into the diagnosis of eating disorders, said it was not yet clear whether the growth was down to increased awareness of the problem, leading to more diagnoses, or an actual rise in cases caused by factors such as social pressures. But she acknowledged: "One of the issues seems to be around a growing peer pressure to be thin."

0 soar *in die Höhe schnellen, stark ansteigen*
15 counselling service *Beratungsstelle*
19 attribute sth to sth *etw einer Sache zuschreiben*
28 proportion *Anteil*
38 be down to sth *auf etw zurückzuführen sein*
40 acknowledge *eingestehen*

⁴³ impact *Wirkung*

Speaking on the potential dangers of the internet, she said: "We as scientists haven't yet been able to fully examine the impact of social media and the internet. It's one of those things where, if it's not controlled, it could be harmful, but potentially it could be used by healthcare professionals in a good way."   45

The dangers of the internet may be largely understood, but due to the lack of evidence, it's questionable to claim that social media sites are the 'cause'. Instead of trying to point the finger, it's better to focus our attention on understanding why young sufferers are developing eating disorders in the first place.

After all, eating disorders are not simple, and to assume that any one factor is to   50
blame undermines the complexity of the illnesses.   (544 words)

From the *Huffington Post*

EXAM PREPARATION
Leseverstehen (p. 149)

TEIL 1: LESEVERSTEHEN

1 Entscheiden Sie, ob die Aussagen zum Text *Eating disorders in children and teenagers are soaring* richtig oder falsch sind. Begründen Sie Ihre Entscheidung auf Deutsch in vollständigen Sätzen.

Aussagen zum Text:
1 The author believes that social media are the major cause of eating disorders.
2 Most parents are aware that their children spend a lot of time online.
3 80 per cent of all the inquiries ChildLine receives are about eating problems.
4 Dr Micali believes that the increase in eating disorders is definitely a result of greater awareness of the illness.
5 The internet can be a useful tool in helping young people with eating disorders.

2 Im Text werden einige mögliche Gründe für Essstörungen erwähnt. Erstellen Sie eine Liste auf Deutsch (sieben Nennungen). Schreiben Sie vollständige Sätze.

EXAM PREPARATION
Textproduktion (p. 150)

TEIL II: TEXTPRODUKTION

Bearbeiten Sie Aufgabe 1 und Aufgabe 2.

1 According to the text "if the internet is part of the problem ..., it is also part of the solution" (ll. 34–35). Compare the positive and negative sides of the internet and social media sites.

2 Wählen Sie <u>eine</u> der beiden Alternativen aus:

Alternative 1: Analyze and discuss the reasons why the number of young people with eating disorders is increasing.

Alternative 2: Who or what, in your opinion, determines the 'beauty ideal' of a generation and how does it become generally accepted?

Should anti-tattoo discrimination be illegal?

Tattoos are more popular than ever, but workers can be dismissed from or denied jobs because of their body modifications. Some want protection under employment law. Should they get it?

You're perfect for the job. You have all the skills and experience the company is looking for, but there's a problem. If you have a tattoo, you might lose your job or not even get one in the first place.

One in five Britons now has a tattoo, according to research cited by the British Association of Dermatologists. Among US thirty-somethings the estimate rises to two-fifths and tattooed individuals are now firmly part of the mainstream.

But employers have not all kept pace with changes in attitudes. A report last year for the British Sociological Association found managers frequently expressed negative views about the image projected by noticeably tattooed staff.

While ink was an asset in some industries, such as those targeting young people, most of the interviewees felt there was a 'stigma' attached to visible markings, according to Andrew Timming of St Andrews University, who carried out the study.

Words like 'untidy', 'repugnant' and 'unsavoury' were all used to describe the impression clients were likely to gain of the organization if someone decorated in this way was hired.

Some enthusiasts for skin markings insist this is deeply unfair. A number of e-petitions have been organized against tattoo-related discrimination.

34-year-old Mathew Whelan from Birmingham, who describes himself as the UK's most tattooed man, has led a campaign to protect the employment status of people with body modifications. He has personally lobbied government ministers for a level playing field for those with tattoos. "If someone can do a job, they should be equal with the next person who has the same CV," he says. Tattoos are more than simply a lifestyle choice, he argues – they are an expression of someone's identity, just as much as their religion or other beliefs.

Policies which restrict tattoos are commonplace in the UK. The Metropolitan Police bans them on the face, hands and above the collar line, as well as any which are "discriminatory, violent or intimidating". Airlines frequently place restrictions on tattoos among cabin crew.

Firms have every right to decide who represents them, argues human resources consultant Sandra Beale. "An organization that wishes to project a smart, professional image, or whose clients would likely be put off, is entitled to ban or limit body modifications," she says – workers can choose whether they prefer having a tattoo or a job. "For an employer, if they employ them in a customer-facing role, it could have an impact on reputation and doesn't portray a good corporate image," she says.

Nonetheless, the sheer number of younger people with tattoos suggests that attitudes are likely to change over time.

---

[9] cite *zitieren*

[13] keep pace with sth *mit etw Schritt halten*

[16] asset *Pluspunkt*

[20] repugnant *abstoßend*

[20] unsavoury *unappetitlich*

[28] level playing field *Chancengleichheit*

[29] CV = curriculum vitae *Lebenslauf*

[34] intimidating *einschüchternd*

[37] consultant *Berater/in*

[38] be entitled to sth *zu etw berechtigt sein*

43 tackle sth *etw anpacken*

Employers – especially those seeking specialist skills – may find they can't afford to exclude talent. In an effort to tackle a recruitment shortfall, the British Army is reported to be considering relaxing its rules to allow tattoos on the face, neck and hands.

45

However, says Timming, "There will be certain genres of tattoos that would never be normalized. Any kind of racist symbols would be a death sentence in terms of your job prospects." (534 words)

From *BBC News Magazine*

EXAM PREPARATION

Leseverstehen (p. 149)

TEIL 1: LESEVERSTEHEN

1 Entscheiden Sie, ob die Aussagen zum Text *Should anti-tattoo discrimination be illegal?* richtig oder falsch sind. Begründen Sie Ihre Entscheidung auf Deutsch in vollständigen Sätzen.

1 In the United States, the majority of people in their thirties have a tattoo.
2 Being tattooed is not always a disadvantage for job seekers.
3 Mathew Whelan has lobbied employers to give equal rights to tattooed people.
4 Sandra Beale believes that it is unfair for employees to discriminate against tattooed people.
5 In future, employers may be forced to employ people with any kind of tattoos.

2 In dem Text werden einige Gründe genannt, weshalb Arbeitgeber tätowierte Personen nicht einstellen. Erstellen Sie eine Liste auf Deutsch (vier Nennungen). Schreiben Sie vollständige Sätze.

EXAM PREPARATION

Textproduktion (p. 150)

TEIL II: TEXTPRODUKTION

Bearbeiten Sie Aufgabe 1 und Aufgabe 2.

1 Answer the question in the headline *Should anti-tattoo discrimination be illegal?* Give reasons for your answer.

2 Wählen Sie eine der beiden Alternativen aus:

Alternative 1: Discuss the reasons why people may choose 'body modification' such as tattoos, piercing or cosmetic surgery.

Alternative 2: Conflict over tattoos highlights the fact that people of different ages often have different ideas about what is acceptable and what is not acceptable. Comment on this and give other examples of the 'generation gap'.

KOMMUNIKATIONSPRÜFUNG

→ EXAM PREPARATION
*Kommunikationsprüfung
(p. 150)*

1 **a** Monologisches Sprechen
Produce an uninterrupted five-minute
discourse based on the cartoons and
quotations below.

*"Advertising is the art of convincing
people to spend money they don't
have for something they don't need."*
Will Rogers

*"The media's the most powerful entity
on earth. They have the power to
make the innocent guilty and to make
the guilty innocent, and that's power.
Because they control the minds of
the masses."* Malcolm X

b Dialogisches Sprechen
Discuss in depth the topics or issues
raised in 1a.

*". . . No, he can't really fly . . . No, the bad guys don't
really have a ray gun . . . No, this cereal really isn't the
best food in the whole world . . . No, it won't make you as
strong as a giant . . ."*

2 Discuss the information given in the pie chart and bar graph and say how it is
related to the cartoon.

How teenagers spend their money

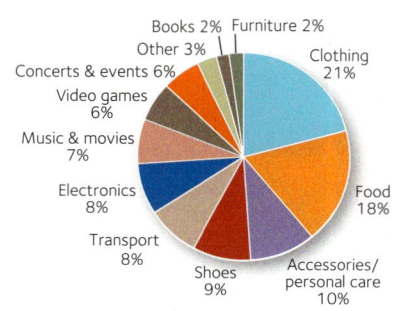

" I need enough for popcorn and a movie. "

Teen spending vs. adult spending (% share of total spending)

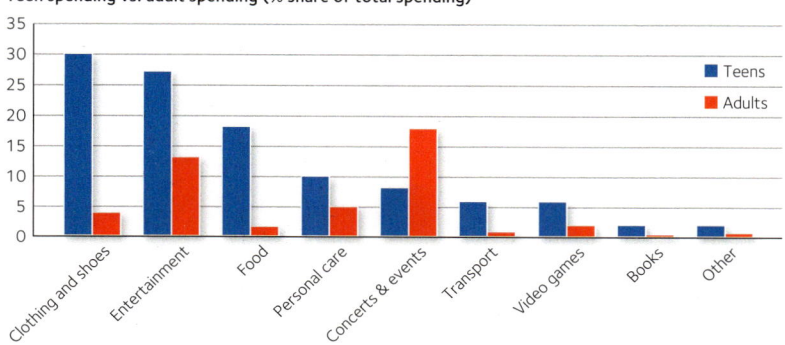

3 a Monologisches Sprechen
STUDENT A: Produce an uninterrupted five-minute discourse based on the two cartoons below.

"What happened in school today? Read my blog."

"In return for an increase in my allowance, I can offer you free unlimited in-home computer tech support."

STUDENT B: Produce an uninterrupted five-minute discourse based on the two cartoons below.

COULD YOU TEXT JAMIE TO COME DOWN FOR DINNER, AND TEXT BECKY TO COME IN FROM THE GARDEN, AND TEXT ME WHEN YOU'RE ALL SEATED

SOCIAL NETWORKING

b Dialogisches Sprechen
Discuss the advantages and disadvantages of modern technology for you personally.

c Sprechen in der Triade
Discuss in depth the topics or issues raised in 3a and 3b.

ROLE CARD

(Topic 1, Text 1, Exercise 11)

Student B

- Your parents want to influence your choice of hairstyle, clothes/friends.

- You don't care what other people think.

- You haven't got enough pocket money for all the things you want to buy, or to go out with your friends.

- Your grades at school are not great, but you are happy to be average.

Useful language:

What's wrong with …?

I'm not a child any more.

It's my life.

I want to make my own decisions/ choices/mistakes.

I don't care what people think.

How did you feel when you were my age?

LERNSTRATEGIEN

REZEPTION

Lesen schwieriger Texte

Texte werden zu unterschiedlichen Zwecken gelesen. Manchmal braucht man nur zu wissen, worum es geht, dann reicht in der Regel ein aufmerksames Überfliegen des Textes. Oft müssen gezielt Informationen herausgesucht werden, dann kommt es darauf an, die richtigen Schlüsselwörter zu finden. Will man sich gründlich mit einem Text auseinandersetzen, um z. B. Fragen zu beantworten oder einen Aufsatz dazu zu schreiben, ist gründliches, möglicherweise zweimaliges Lesen erforderlich.

Grobverständnis: Sich einen schnellen Überblick über einen Text verschaffen (*Skimming*)
Manchmal werden Sie im Buch aufgefordert, einen Text schnell zu lesen, um das Thema grob zu erfassen.

1. Schritt: Suchen Sie nach Anhaltspunkten, die Ihnen Aufschluss über den Textinhalt geben: Überschriften, fett gedruckte Wörter, Bilder und Bildunterschriften.

2. Schritt: Sind Sie noch unsicher, lesen Sie die ersten und letzten Sätze jedes Absatzes. Bleiben Sie nicht an Einzelwörtern, schwierigen Zitaten usw. hängen.

Suche nach Einzelinformationen im Text (*Scanning*)
Bei vielen Textverständnisfragen oder Aufgaben vom Typ *True or false* geht es darum, schnell die gesuchte Information im Text zu finden.

1. Schritt: Suchen Sie den Text nach Schlüsselbegriffen für die gesuchten Informationen ab. Geht es etwa um die Meinung des Autors zu einem bestimmten Thema, halten Sie nach Wörtern wie *think, believe, opinion* usw. Ausschau. Geht es um Informationen zu einem Thema, rufen Sie sich ein paar Schlüsselbegriffe in Erinnerung, nach denen Sie Ausschau halten. Manchmal hilft es, sich den gesuchten Begriff als gedrucktes Wort vor dem geistigen Auge vorzustellen.

2. Schritt: Gehen Sie falls nötig mit dem Finger die Zeilen entlang, während Sie suchen. Wenn Sie sich wie oben beschrieben vorbereitet haben, springen Ihnen die gesuchten Begriffe sofort ins Auge.

Detailverständnis: Gründliches Lesen *(Close reading)*

Lesen Sie nicht einfach drauflos. Ein paar einfache Schritte helfen Ihnen, den Text besser zu verstehen, ohne sich in Details zu verlieren.

1. Schritt: Der erste Schritt sollte darin bestehen, sich ein grobes Verständnis vom Textinhalt zu verschaffen (siehe oben). So werden Sie unklare Stellen besser in den Gesamtzusammenhang einordnen können. Es ist hilfreich, sich die wichtigsten Stichwörter kurz zu notieren. Zu dem Text *Elitist UK locks out diversity at the top* auf S. 116 könnten Sie nach kurzem Überfliegen aufschreiben: *The text is about the disproportionately large number of people from independent schools and Oxbridge in top jobs in the UK.*

2. Schritt: Machen Sie sich die Struktur des Textes bewusst. Wo ist die Einleitung? Welcher Teil enthält die Hauptinformationen, und wie sind sie aufgebaut (Zwischenüberschriften, Absätze usw.)? Achten Sie auf Strukturwörter wie *only, but while, that's why, while, however* usw., mit denen der Verfasser seine Argumentation gliedert.

3. Schritt: Lesen Sie den Text nun aufmerksam. Notieren Sie sich Schlüsselstellen (z. B. im Text auf S. 116: *Locking out a diversity of talents and experiences makes Britain's leading institutions less informed, less representative and ultimately less credible than they should be.* Schlagen Sie Wörter beim ersten Lesen nur nach, wenn die Bedeutung des ganzen Satzes an ihnen hängt. Oft lässt sich die wesentliche Bedeutung durch den Kontext erschließen.

4. Schritt: Notieren Sie sich den Textinhalt in strukturierter Form, etwa einer Mind Map oder einer Liste (Themen, pro/kontra). Fügen Sie auch Formulierungen hinzu, die Ihnen später helfen, sich in eigenen Worten über den Textinhalt zu äußern. Schlagen Sie jetzt das notwendige Vokabular nach.

▶ Notizen schreiben, S. 138
▶ Mind Mapping, S. 139

Umgang mit unbekannten Vokabeln

Fragen Sie sich bei neuen Vokabeln immer, ob sie für das Verständnis des Zusammenhangs unbedingt notwendig sind. Nachschlagen kostet Zeit und hilft oft nicht beim Verständnis des wirklich Wichtigen.

Erschließen der Bedeutung aus dem Kontext

- Ein Wort, das unbekannt scheint, kann z. B. mit einem anderen, Ihnen bekannten Wort verwandt sein (Ableitungen wie *aggressor* von *aggressive*). Oder das Wort hat einen bekannten Wortstamm und einen angehängten Wortteil, mit dessen Hilfe Sie die Bedeutung erkennen können (*formal – **in**formal, clockwise – **anti**clockwise, change – change**able**, stupid – stupid**ity***). Manche Wörter haben Ähnlichkeiten mit einem deutschen Wort (vgl. etwa *initial* und „Initialen", *potential* und „potenziell").
- Sind Sie sich immer noch nicht sicher, kann der Satzzusammenhang Aufschluss geben. Machen Sie sich zunächst die Wortart bewusst: Suchen Sie nach einem Substantiv? Wofür steht das gesuchte Substantiv wahrscheinlich – für ein Gebäude? Eine Person? Handelt es sich um ein Adjektiv, das die Situation näher beschreibt oder jemanden charakterisiert?
- Schauen Sie sich die folgenden Sätze an und versuchen Sie die Bedeutung der fett gedruckten Wörter aus dem Zusammenhang zu erschließen:
- *Business is bad at the moment and we don't expect it to **rally** for at least a year. All the signals are very **inauspicious**, I'm afraid.*

Umgang mit dem einsprachigen Wörterbuch

Machen Sie sich mit Ihrem Wörterbuch vertraut, so dass Sie die Symbole, Abkürzungen und die Lautschrift verstehen und die Hilfen, die vorne und hinten im Wörterbuch oder auf Zusatzseiten angeboten werden, nutzen können. Auf der folgenden Seite sehen Sie ein Beispiel eines typischen Wörterbucheintrags.

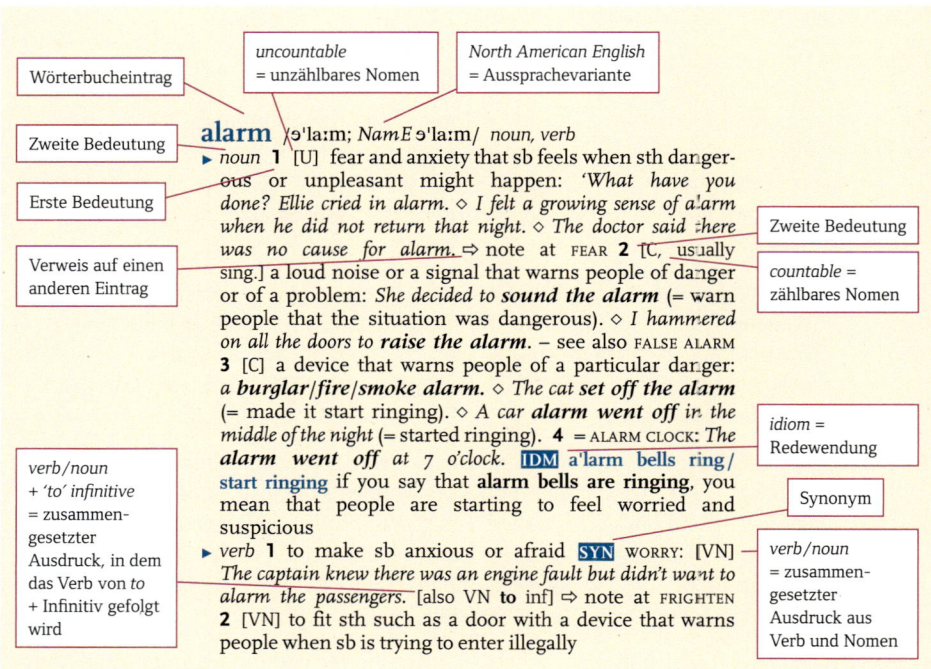

- Notieren Sie sich alle Wörter, deren Bedeutung Sie suchen, und schlagen Sie dann alle hintereinander nach.
- Lesen Sie nicht den gesamten Eintrag, sondern beschränken Sie sich auf die Verwendung Ihres Stichworts in der gesuchten Wortart (z. B. Sie suchen *alarm* als Verb, also ignorieren Sie den ersten Teil des oben stehenden Eintrags). Den entsprechenden Abschnitt mit allen zusammengesetzten Ausdrücken und den Beispielsätzen, die Ihnen helfen zu unterscheiden, in welchen Zusammenhängen welche Bedeutung zutrifft, müssen Sie dann allerdings gründlich lesen.
- Schauen Sie sich auch die Einträge in der unmittelbaren Umgebung Ihres Stichworts an, um eine Vorstellung von dem Wortfeld zu bekommen.
- Notieren Sie sich die passende Bedeutung, damit Sie sie nicht wieder vergessen.

pay (noun)	– Bezahlung, Gehalt, Lohn
payslip	– Gehaltsabrechnung
pay day	– Zahltag
pay-off	– Abfindung
pay (verb)	– zahlen
pay for sth.	– etw. bezahlen
pay off	– auszahlen
pay as you go (phone)	– prepaid(-Handy)

Lernen neuer Vokabeln

Es gibt verschiedene Möglichkeiten, Vokabeln zu lernen – suchen Sie sich die, die Ihnen am besten liegt. Eines gilt jedoch für alle Methoden: Wörter prägen sich am besten ein, wenn man nicht nur das Stichwort aufschreibt, sondern auch noch dazugehörige Ausdrücke, Synonyme, Gegenteile, verwandte Wörter und Verwendungsbeispiele, evtl. auch Aussprachehinweise. Besonders wichtig sind zusammengesetzte Ausdrücke. Dazu gehören auch *phrasal verbs* (*set about, put off* usw.). Der Eintrag für das Stichwort *pay* könnte z. B. so aussehen:

Natürlich brauchen Sie nicht gleich komplette Wörterbucheinträge aufzuschreiben. Überlegen Sie sich jedoch, welche Ableitungen Ihnen zu dem neuen Wort schon bekannt sein könnten oder in welchem zusammengesetzten Ausdruck es Ihnen begegnet ist. Lassen Sie Platz für spätere Hinzufügungen, so dass die Einträge nach und nach „wachsen".

Karteikarten: Sie benötigen Karteikarten und einen Karteikasten mit mehreren Abteilungen. Schreiben Sie das englische Wort mit den dazugehörigen Ergänzungen auf eine Seite einer Karteikarte und die deutschen Bedeutungen auf die Rückseite. Sobald Sie ein Wort wissen, wandert es von der ersten in die zweite Abteilung des Karteikastens. Die Wörter in der zweiten Abteilung schauen Sie sich in größeren Abständen nochmal an, um diejenigen, die Sie wissen, dann in die dritte Abteilung fürs Langzeitgedächtnis abzulegen. Was Sie nicht wissen, kommt zurück in die erste Abteilung, die Sie sich möglichst oft an-schauen sollten.

Vokabelheft: Wenn Sie im Unterricht neue Vokabeln mitschreiben wollen, bietet sich ein Vokabelheft an. Benutzen Sie ein zweispaltiges Heft, damit Sie eine Spalte leicht bedecken können. Gestalten Sie das Lernen weniger schematisch, indem Sie die Seiten, die Sie lernen wollen, zufällig auswählen und ab und zu mal Deutsch–Englisch statt Englisch–Deutsch lernen.

Wortfamilien: Fertigen Sie Listen mit Wortfamilien an, um sich zusammen mit einem neuen Wort auch noch seine Ableitungen einzuprägen (*approve – approval – disapprove – disapproval – approving*).

Wortfelder: Die beste Methode, Wortfelder, also zusammenhängende Wortgruppen zu einem Thema zu lernen, sind Mind Maps, also grafisch angelegte Wortnetze. Diese Methode ist gut geeignet, um den Themenwortschatz für eine Klassenarbeit zu lernen. Um den Schlüsselbegriff herum werden einzelne Oberbegriffe für die wichtigsten Aspekte des Themas herum angeordnet. Um jeden Oberbegriff werden nun die dazugehörigen Vokabeln herumgeschrieben. Zum genauen Vorgehen siehe unten S. 139.

▶ Mind Mapping, S. 139

Vokabeltrainer: Wer gerne am Computer lernt, findet problemlos einen geeigneten Vokabeltrainer im Handel. Solche Software enthält meistens vielerlei Übungen, die das Vokabellernen unterhaltsam und spielerisch gestalten. Achten Sie darauf, dass es sich um eine Software handelt, die auf Ihre Schulart abgestimmt ist. Es gibt auch zahlreiche kosten-lose Online-Vokabeltrainer im Internet.

Wortspiele und Kreuzworträtsel: Wortspiele z. B. *Scrabble* und Kreuzworträtsel bieten auch eine gute Möglichkeit, Ihren Wortschatz auf spielerische Art zu erweitern: siehe die BBC-Internetseite http://www.bbc.co.uk/worldservice/learningenglish/quizzes/ crossword/.

Das Hörverständnis üben

Um gesprochenes Englisch zu verstehen, z. B. in Unterhaltungen, Telefongesprächen, Vor-stellungsgesprächen, im Fernsehen u. a., sollten Sie sich gut auf die jeweilige Situation vor-bereiten. Oft beeinträchtigen der Akzent, Hintergrundgeräusche und andere Störungen das Verständnis so, dass man sich auf das Wichtigste konzentrieren muss. Eignen Sie sich die unten beschriebene Methode an, wenn Sie die Hörverständnisaufgaben in *Crossover* bearbeiten. Damit lassen sich Barrieren bei schwierigen Hörtexten leicht abbauen.

Vor dem Hören
- Lesen Sie die gesamte Aufgabenstellung sorgfältig durch. Nutzen Sie alle Hilfen, die Ihnen zur Verfügung stehen – Abbildungen, Überschriften usw.
- Schreiben Sie wenn möglich **Schlüsselbegriffe** auf und rufen Sie sich, wenn genug Zeit ist, kurz wichtige Wortfelder zum Thema in Erinnerung.

Während des Hörens

- Hören Sie sich den gesamten Hörtext zunächst in Ruhe an, um zu verstehen, worum es geht. Machen Sie in dieser Phase keine Notizen.
- Achten Sie bei einem zweiten Hören nur auf die für die Aufgabe wichtigen Informationen. Konzentrieren Sie sich nicht auf einzelne Wörter und Ausdrücke, die Sie nicht verstehen.
- Achten Sie auf Ausdrücke, die den logischen Gedankengang verdeutlichen, z. B. *however, in my view, in conclusion* usw. Sie helfen Ihnen, den roten Faden nicht zu verlieren.
- Notieren Sie Informationen nur **stichpunktartig**, nie in ganzen Sätzen. Dabei kann ein Raster sehr hilfreich sein. In diesem Beispiel handelt es sich um den Wandel der Geschlechterrollen in unserer Gesellschaft:

	changed role	reasons	consequences
men			
woman			

- Verwenden Sie Zeichen, Abkürzungen und Wortverkürzungen, um beim Notieren Zeit zu sparen:

Zeichen		Abkürzungen		Wortverkürzungen	
=	*the same as*	e.g.	*for example*	govt	*government*
≠	*not the same as*	km	*kilometres*	impt!	*important*
+	*and*	w., w/o	*with, without*	kids	*children*

Nach dem Hören

- Formulieren Sie Ihre Stichpunkte so schnell wie möglich aus – vielleicht können Sie später Ihre Aufzeichnungen nicht mehr lesen oder ihre Wortverkürzungen nicht mehr verstehen.
- Versuchen Sie, alle Fragen zu beantworten. Wenn Sie einige Informationen nicht verstanden haben, stellen Sie eine begründete Vermutung an.

PRODUKTION

Notizen schreiben

Es ist sinnvoll, sich beim Lesen und Hören eines Textes Notizen zu machen. So können Sie später leichter auf die Informationen zurückgreifen.

Beim Lesen

Auf den ersten Blick scheint es ziemlich leicht, sich beim Lesen eines Textes Notizen zu machen. Trotzdem fällt es vielen schwer, wirklich kurze, sinnvolle Stichpunkte zu notieren. Oft führt die Sorge, etwas Wichtiges auszulassen, dazu, dass ganze Sätze des Originaltextes abgeschrieben werden. Damit verliert man nicht nur Zeit, sondern es wird später auch schwierig, seinen Text in eigenen Worten zu formulieren.

Hier einige Tipps, damit Sie diese Falle umgehen:

- Geben Sie Ihren Notizen eine Überschrift, die Ihr Thema klar umreißt.
- Gehen Sie den Text durch und filtern Sie die wesentlichen Unterthemen heraus, die Sie als Überschriften verwenden können.

▶ Detailverständnis, S. 135

- Halten Sie Ausschau nach Signalen wie Hervorhebungen, Wiederholung und bedeutungtragenden Adjektiven wie *huge, incredible, devastating* usw. Diese zeigen, was der Verfasser für wichtig hält.
- Notieren Sie nur Stichwörter, nicht ganze Sätze.
- Verdeutlichen Sie den logischen Aufbau der Informationen, z. B. indem Sie bestimmte Punkte in einer Liste untereinanderschreiben, Themen durch Leerzeilen voneinander abheben oder die wichtigsten Begriffe unterstreichen.

Beim Hören

In diesem Fall ist es schwieriger Notizen zu machen, da man oft sehr schnell schreiben muss. Man muss sich auf das Wesentliche konzentrieren und sollte Abkürzungen verwenden, damit man den Faden nicht verliert. Tipps dazu siehe in dem Abschnitt „Das Hörverständnis üben".

▶ Das Hörverständnis üben,
S. 137 – 138

Mind Mapping

Eine Mind Map ist eine sinnvolle Methode, Begriffe übersichtlich anzuordnen. Sie eignet sich z. B. zum Vokabellernen, zum Brainstorming, zum Ideensammeln und zur Vorbereitung eines Aufsatzes oder einer Präsentation.

▶ Umgang mit unbekannten
Vokabeln, S. 135

1. Schritt: Schreiben Sie den Oberbegriff (wenn es um Wortfelder geht) bzw. das Thema (wenn es um eine Ideensammlung geht) groß in die Mitte.

2. Schritt: Schreiben Sie die wichtigsten Begriffe zum Thema um den Oberbegriff herum; sie sollten durch „Äste" mit dem Oberbegriff verbunden sein.

3. Schritt: Fügen Sie nach demselben Prinzip weitere Wörter und Ideen zu den einzelnen Unterthemen hinzu. Je spezieller, desto kleiner die Verzweigungen, d.h. der Weg vom Thema nach außen führt vom Allgemeinen zum Speziellen. Sie können jederzeit und überall neue Ideen hinzufügen.

4. Schritt: Heben Sie wichtige Begriffe durch farbige Markierungen und Symbole hervor.

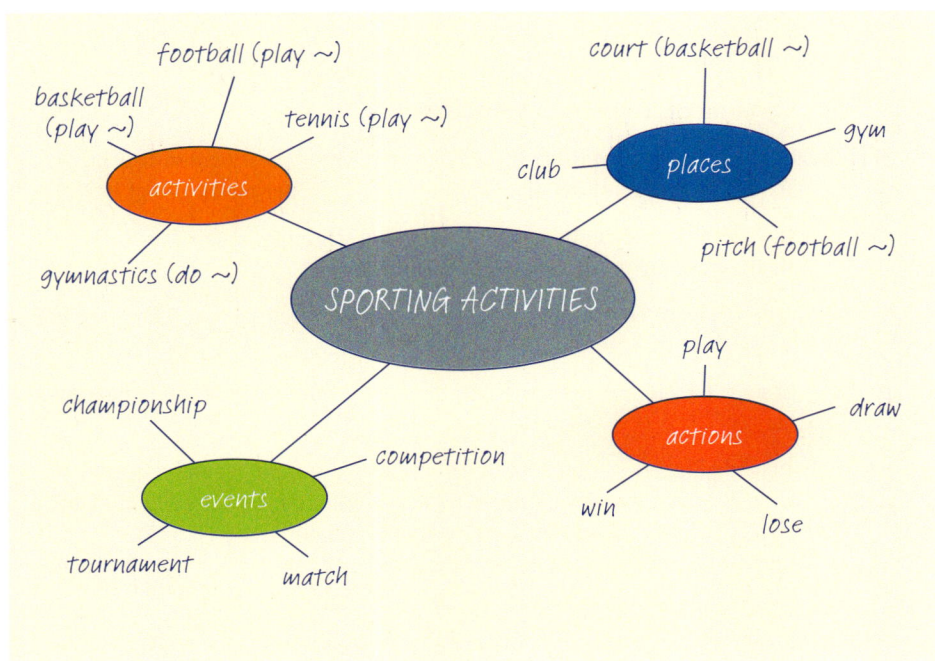

▶ Lesen schwieriger Texte,
S. 134 – 135

Fragen zum Text beantworten

Bevor Sie mit dem Schreiben beginnen, vergewissern Sie sich, dass Sie den gesamten Text verstanden haben. (Nicht jedes Wort ist wichtig – überlegen Sie sich, ob Sie die Bedeutung des Satzes auch verstehen, ohne jedes Wort zu kennen.) Lesen Sie die Aufgabenstellung immer genau, um zu verstehen, worauf es bei der Beantwortung genau ankommt – ein häufiger Fehler ist das „Vorbeischreiben" an der Frage. Achten Sie auch darauf, keine Informationen zu „verpulvern", die Sie möglicherweise für die Beantwortung einer anderen Frage benötigen.

- Wenn Sie im Buch nichts anstreichen dürfen, machen Sie sich Notizen in Form von Stichpunkten und Listen, anstatt ganze Sätze aus dem Text herauszuschreiben. In der Klassenarbeit bzw. Prüfung sollten Sie die wichtigsten Passagen im Text markieren. Am besten markieren Sie alles, was für eine Textverständnisfrage wichtig ist, mit einer bestimmten Farbe, und nehmen dann eine andere Frage für die nächste Textverständnisfrage.
- Verwenden Sie in der Antwort die Zeitform der Fragestellung.
- Verwenden Sie so viele Synonyme und Umschreibungen der Begriffe und Formulierungen aus dem Text wie möglich, z. B. *recently – in recent years; violent crime – crime involving violence; think – believe; to a great extent – largely; when she was a child – in her childhood* usw.
- Suchen Sie Signale im Text wie Hervorhebungen, Wiederholungen und bedeutungtragende Adjektive und Adverbien wie *absolutely, unbelievably, amazing.* Dies sind Signale dafür, was der Verfasser für wichtig hält.
- Versuchen Sie nicht, Ihre eigene Meinung einzubringen, wenn dies nicht in der Fragestellung gefordert ist.

Formulierungen für das Schreiben über den Text
- *According to the author, …*
- *The article goes on to say that …*
- *The text says that …*
- *The author makes the point that …*

Eine Stellungnahme (*comment*) schreiben

Bei einer Stellungnahme geht es darum, Ihre Meinung zu einem bestimmten Thema darzulegen. Wichtig ist, dass Ihre Meinung begründet und mit Beispielen belegt ist.

1. Schritt: Machen Sie sich genau bewusst, worüber Sie schreiben sollen. Lesen Sie die Aufgabenstellung mehrmals durch.

▶ Notizen schreiben, S. 138
▶ Mind Mapping, S. 148

2. Schritt: Machen Sie sich Notizen. Ordnen Sie Ihre Stichwörter übersichtlich an, z. B. in einer Mind Map, einer Liste oder einer Übersicht.

3. Schritt: Schreiben Sie einen Einleitungssatz, der sich auf die Aufgabenstellung beziehen sollte.

▶ Einen Text sinnvoll gliedern,
S. 142 – 143

4. Schritt: Behandeln Sie jedes Argument in einem Absatz. Handelt es sich um ein Pro-/Kontra-Thema, können Sie erst die Pro- und dann die Kontra- Argumente anführen. Verdeutlichen Sie Ihre Argumentation durch die Verwendung von Strukturwörtern; hierzu siehe die Liste auf der hinteren Umschlagklappe dieses Buches (*Language for Writing*).

5. Schritt: Bringen Sie Ihre Argumentation in einem prägnanten Schlusssatz auf den Punkt.

Einen Text zusammenfassen

Die Fähigkeit, einen gelesenen Text zusammenzufassen, ist nicht nur wichtig, um den Text richtig zu verstehen, sondern sie hilft auch bei anderen Situationen, in denen Sie Informationen aus einem Text auf das Wesentliche reduzieren müssen. Zu solchen Situationen gehören z. B. die Beantwortung von Textverständnisfragen oder eine Mediation.

▶ Fragen zum Text beantworten, S. 140

1. Schritt: Lesen Sie den Text so oft wie möglich, bis Sie sicher sind, alles verstanden zu haben.

▶ Mediation, S. 148

▶ Detailverständnis, S. 135
▶ Umgang mit unbekannten Vokabeln, S. 135

2. Schritt: Fassen Sie in ein oder zwei einleitenden Sätzen zusammen, worum es in dem Text geht, z. B.: *This article is about genetic modification. It deals with the advantages it could bring to farming, especially in underdeveloped countries.*

3. Schritt: Machen Sie sich bewusst, welche Informationen für den Leser wichtig sind, indem Sie *Wh*-Fragen beantworten: *Who? What? When? Where? Why?*
z. B.:
– *Who: geneticist Yang Huanming*
– *What: decoded the rice genome*

4. Schritt: Machen Sie sich Notizen in Form von Stichwörtern.

▶ Notizen schreiben, S. 138

5. Schritt: Schreiben Sie Ihren Text. Beachten Sie dabei folgende Punkte:
- Lassen Sie Unwesentliches weg. Dazu gehören etwa Beispiele, Aufzählungen, Namen, Zitate usw.
- Verwenden Sie so weit wie möglich Ihre eigenen Worte.
- Vermeiden Sie es, zu dem Text Stellung zu nehmen. Dies gehört in der Regel nicht zur Aufgabenstellung.
- Denken Sie daran, Zitate in indirekte Rede umzuwandeln.

▶ Reported speech, S. 158–160

6. Schritt: Kontrollieren Sie Ihren Text auf Fehler und vergewissern Sie sich, dass Sie alle wichtigen Aspekte des Textes berücksichtigt haben.

Einen Aufsatz schreiben

Im Laufe der Oberstufe, in der Abiturprüfung und auch später, z. B. im Studium, werden Sie immer wieder Aufsätze zu unterschiedlichsten Themen schreiben müssen. Es ist sinnvoll, sich von Anfang an einige Regeln zu eigen zu machen, um das Vorgehen möglichst zu automatisieren und sich gleich auf den Inhalt konzentrieren zu können. Dies ist besonders wichtig, wenn es – wie in der Abiturprüfung – auf die Zeit ankommt.

1. Schritt: Verschaffen Sie sich Klarheit über Ihr Thema. Welche Aspekte gehören dazu, welche nicht?

▶ Notizen schreiben, S. 138
▶ Mind Mapping, S. 139

2. Schritt: Machen Sie ein Brainstorming, indem Sie alle Ideen aufschreiben, die Ihnen zum Thema in den Kopf kommen. Wichtig: Die Ideen sollten Sie gleich in eine Struktur bringen, um nicht in einem Wust von ungeordnetem Gekritzel zu enden. Zur Strukturierung eignen sich z. B. Listen oder Mind Maps.

3. Schritt: Überlegen Sie sich einen Aufbau für Ihren Text. Dies kann z. B. in Form einer Mind Map geschehen, die Sie nummerieren, um die Reihenfolge der Ideen zu verdeutlichen. Eine andere Möglichkeit ist eine Übersicht (*outline*) wie die folgende:

> *Should old towns be closed to private vehicles?*
> **Einleitung:** Umreißen des Themas
> **Hauptteil:** Ausführung zum Thema, z. B.:
> *1. Disadvantages for business*
>   *1.1 Job losses*
>   *1.1.1 retail trade*
>   *1.1.2 fewer tourists*
>   *1.1.2.1 less money for tourist attractions*
>   *1.1.2.2 job losses in cafés etc.*
>   *1.2 What about town centre residents, delivery vehicles etc.?*
> *2. Advantages, positive effects on town and people*
> *…*
> **Schluss:** Zusammenfassung, Fazit

▶ Einen Text sinnvoll gliedern, S. 142–143

4. Schritt: Schreiben Sie Ihren Text. Lassen Sie Platz für Korrekturen, Änderungen oder Ergänzungen. Wichtig: Verdeutlichen Sie Ihre Argumentation durch die Verwendung von Strukturwörtern; hierzu siehe die Liste auf der hinteren Umschlagklappe dieses Buches (*Language for Writing*) und den Abschnitt „Einen Text sinnvoll gliedern".

5. Schritt: Überprüfen Sie Ihren Entwurf auf:
- **Rechtschreibfehler** (z. B. gleichlautende Wörter wie *there/their*, *meet/meat* usw.)
- **Grammatikfehler** (z. B. Gebrauch der Zeitformen; *-ly*-Endung für Adverbien)
- **Wortwahl** (z. B. Wiederholungen; *False friends* wie ‚aktuell' ≠ *actual*, ‚eventuell' ≠ *eventual*, ‚spenden' ≠ *spend*, ‚zum Schluss' ≠ *at last*)
- **Satzbau** (z. B. unvollständige Antworten, die mit *Because* beginnen)
- **Gedankenführung** (z. B. Klarheit des Ausdrucks; Verwendung von Strukturwörtern wie *However, On the other hand, In addition, As a result* usw.)

Einen Text sinnvoll gliedern

Wann immer es darum geht, einen zusammenhängenden Text zu schreiben, sei es eine Antwort auf eine Frage zum Text, einen Aufsatz, eine Zusammenfassung o. Ä., ist es ganz wichtig, seine Gedanken in einen logischen Zusammenhang zu bringen, damit der Leser den Faden nicht verliert. Dies alles gilt ebenso für mündliche Präsentationen, nur werden Sie dabei Ihre Materialien nicht Wort für Wort ablesen, sondern frei sprechen. Daher ist es wichtig, Formulierungen für die Gliederung auch mündlich parat zu haben.
Die wichtigsten Strukturwörter finden Sie auf der hinteren Umschlagklappe dieses Buches (*Language for Writing*). Im Folgenden sehen Sie einige Beispiele, wie man diese Formulierungen in einen Text einbauen kann.

Argumente gliedern

- In his text 'The world's changing energy supplies' Knapp discusses many aspects of energy and the environment. _Firstly_, he states that … _Secondly_/_Then_ he goes on to say that … _Another point_ he makes is that … _Finally_, …

Eine Begründung anführen

- _Due to_ / _Because of_ / _As a result of_ all the discussions about renewable sources of energy …
- Renewable energy has been talked about a lot. _Therefore_, the public …
- Renewable energy has been talked about a lot, _so_ the public …

Aspekte ergänzen

- Brian Knapp states that many renewable sources of energy include high development costs.
- _In addition_, / _Moreover_, he points out that these energy forms still only meet a small percentage of the world's rising energy requirements.
- _In addition to_ / _Besides_ / _As well as_ mentioning the high development costs of many renewable forms of energy, Knapp points out that these energy forms still only meet a small percentage of the world's rising energy requirements.

Einen Gegensatz ausdrücken

- _Although_ the demand for cheap energy continues to rise, our current main sources of energy – fossil fuels – are running out.
- _In spite of_ the rising demand for cheap energy, our current main sources of energy are running out.
- _While_/_Whereas_ the demand for cheap energy continues to rise, our current main sources of energy are running out.
- Our current main sources of energy are running out. _However_, / _Nevertheless_, the demand for cheap energy continues to rise.
- _On the one hand_, our current main sources of energy are running out; _on the other hand_, the demand for cheap energy continues to rise.

Beispiele anführen

- The writer is of the opinion that nuclear fusion is a safe energy source compared with other energy sources, _for example_ / _for instance_ / _such as_ / _e.g._ …

Ein Fazit ziehen

- _As a consequence,_ / _All in all_, / _Consequently_, Brian Knapp thinks that …
- _To sum up_ / _To conclude_, I would like to say that …

Diese Strukturwörter (_connectors_) sollten Sie sich so zu eigen machen, dass Sie sie möglichst in jedem Text verwenden. Dadurch gewöhnen Sie sich eine genaue und logische Ausdrucksweise an. Achten Sie auch beim Lesen von Texten auf Strukturwörter; so können Sie der Gedankenführung leichter folgen.

Die Arbeitsergebnisse präsentieren

Die Fähigkeit, wirkungsvoll vor einem Publikum zu referieren, ist wichtig im Berufsleben und zunehmend auch in der Schule. Dabei kommt es nicht nur auf den Inhalt an, sondern auch darauf, wie anschaulich Sie den Inhalt „verpacken", d. h. dass Sie Ihren Vortrag leicht nachvollziehbar gliedern, abwechslungsreich gestalten und lebendig illustrieren.

Vor der Präsentation

1. Schritt: Bereiten Sie Ihr Thema gründlich vor und machen Sie sich dabei Notizen auf Englisch.

2. Schritt: Prüfen Sie Ihre Stichpunkte sprachlich und vergewissern Sie sich, dass Sie alles richtig aussprechen (anhand der Lautschrift in einem Wörterbuch oder der Aussprachebeispiele in gängigen Online-Wörterbüchern oder auf Wörterbuch-CD-ROMs).

3. Schritt: Überlegen Sie sich, wie Sie Ihren Vortrag interessanter und lebendiger machen können (Anschauungsmaterial, Audiobeispiele, Anekdoten usw.).

4. Schritt: Organisieren Sie alle Hilfsmittel, die Sie benötigen (Beamer, Flipchart usw.).

5. Schritt: Üben Sie die Präsentation, am besten vor Zuhörern.

Während der Präsentation

1. Schritt: Steigen Sie nicht gleich mitten ins Thema ein, sondern geben Sie einen Überblick über Ihre Präsentation.

2. Schritt: Machen Sie es den Zuhörern leicht, indem Sie sich klar ausdrücken, kurze Sätze benutzen und langsam sprechen.

3. Schritt: Die Zuhörer bleiben am ehesten interessiert, wenn Sie Ihre Präsentation so abwechslungsreich wie möglich gestalten: Ziehen Sie zwischendurch Anschauungsmaterial (Photos, Videos, Grafiken usw.) heran und teilen Sie Handouts aus. Wenn Sie Folien benutzen, halten Sie sie klar und übersichtlich, anstatt sie mit Grafiken zu überladen.

4. Schritt: Achten Sie auf Ihre Körpersprache: Wenden Sie sich dem Publikum zu, halten Sie Blickkontakt mit den Zuhörern, sprechen Sie langsam und deutlich und benutzen Sie Gesten, um den Inhalt zu verdeutlichen.

5. Schritt: Fassen Sie zum Schluss das Wichtigste zusammen. Bedanken Sie sich bei den Zuhörern für ihre Aufmerksamkeit und ermuntern Sie sie, Fragen zu stellen.

Useful phrases

Introduction	My name is … and I would like to talk about …
	I've chosen this topic because …
Structure	I would like to divide my talk into … parts.
	In the first part, I will …
	First …, then …, after that … . Finally …
	Next I would like to take a look at …
	My next point is about …
Giving examples	As an example … / For example, …
	Let me give you one/a couple of example(s).
Explaining	That means …
	Let me explain in more detail / that again.
	Generally speaking …

Using visuals	Here you can see …
	The next picture shows …
Finishing	I'd like to finish by summarizing …
	That brings me to the end of my presentation.
	Thank you for listening.
Question time	Are there any questions?
	I would be happy to answer any questions.
	I'm not quite sure I understood your question.
	I'm afraid I don't know exactly, but I can find out.

Interpretation von Bildern und Karikaturen

Am besten eignen Sie sich einen Grundstock an Formulierungen zur Beschreibung und Interpretation von Bildern und Karikaturen an. Achten Sie darauf, sich auf die wesentlichen Bildaussagen zu konzentrieren, anstatt sich in Details zu verlieren. Halten Sie die folgenden Schritte ein, um Ihre Antwort sinnvoll zu gliedern:

1. Schritt: Beschreibung des Bildes. Betrachten Sie alle Einzelheiten der Bildvorlage, aber beschränken Sie sich bei der Beschreibung auf die Elemente, die für die Aussage wichtig sind.

Verwenden Sie bei der Beschreibung der Bildinhalte das *Present progressive* (außer bei Verben, die gewöhnlich nicht in dieser Zeitform vorkommen).

▶ The present progressive, S. 152

Zu dem Cartoon auf S. 10 könnten Sie z. B. so anfangen: *The cartoon shows two teenagers, a boy and a girl. The boy is overweight and he is sitting in front of the computer, glued to the screen. The girl is very slim. She is weighing and measuring herself. Some open bottles of pills are lying next to the two teenagers. They could be slimming pills or drugs. …*

Vorsicht: Das *Present progressive* gilt nur für die Handlungen und Situationen, die im Bild dargestellt sind, nicht für die Verben, mit denen Sie den Cartoon beschreiben und interpretieren (*The cartoon **shows**/**describes** … / It **seems** as if the person on the left …*).

2. Schritt: Interpretation des Bildes. Wenn Ihnen das Bild nicht viel sagt, können Sie dies in Ihre Interpretation miteinbeziehen, indem Sie es als *ambiguous* oder *unclear* bezeichnen.

3. Schritt: Stellungnahme zur Bildaussage. Bringen Sie die Hauptaussage der Bildvorlage auf den Punkt und/oder beziehen Sie Stellung, indem Sie z. B. die Wirkung des Bildes auf den Betrachter beurteilen.

4. Schritt: Vergleich der Bildvorlage mit dem Text (wenn die Aufgabenstellung dies erfordert). Gehen Sie zum Text zurück und suchen Sie die Passagen heraus, die im Zusammenhang mit der Bildvorlage von Bedeutung sind. Beurteilen Sie, ob die Bildvorlage mit der Aussage des Textes in Einklang steht oder ihr widerspricht.

1. Beschreibung des Bildes
- *In the foreground/background/centre there is …*
- *The speech bubble* (Sprechblase) */thought bubble* (Denkblase) */*
  caption (Bildunterschrift) */label* (Aufschrift) *says that …*
- *On the left/right you can see …*
- *The scene depicts/shows …*
- *The … looks as if …*
- *The person on the left appears to … / It seems as if the person …*
- *The man/woman is wearing/holding …*

2. Interpretation der Bildaussage
- *The picture /cartoon deals with the recent discussion of …*
- *I think the cartoonist's /artist's / photographer's use of irony / exaggeration is intended*
  to create … / is aimed at making … / conveys …
- *The person in the centre represents /symbolizes /shows …*
- *This indicates /shows / reveals that …*
- *The cartoonist /artist / photographer criticizes / wants to express the idea that …*
- *Because the foreground / background is …, the impression is given that …*
- *From the way the people are depicted it is obvious that …*
- *The point of the cartoon seems to be that …*

3. Stellungnahme, Beschreibung der Wirkung auf den Betrachter
- *I agree with the cartoonist / artist, but …*
- *Because of …, the picture touches me / leaves me cold.*
- *I think the … is a symbol of …*
- *The … helps to create a(n) … atmosphere, which forces you to / has the effect of …*

4. Vergleich der Bildvorlage mit einem Text
- *While the text says that …, the cartoon / picture shows / makes the point that …*
- *In the text we found out that …*
- *The cartoon / picture illustrates the facts / information in the text in the following way: …*
- *The cartoon / picture gives a completely different impression than the information in*
  the text.

Interpretation von Grafiken, Diagrammen und Tabellen

Wie im Falle von Cartoons ist es auch bei Grafiken, Diagrammen und Tabellen sinnvoll,
einen Grundstock an Formulierungen zur Beschreibung und Interpretation parat zu haben.
Halten Sie die folgenden Schritte ein, um Ihre Antwort sinnvoll zu gliedern:

1. Schritt: Beschreibung der Vorlage. Hier geht es nicht darum, alle Details aufzuzählen,
sondern zu beschreiben, worum es in der Vorlage geht und welche Daten
dargestellt werden.

**2. Schritt: Zusammenfassung der dargestellten Tendenzen, Entwicklungen bzw.
Größen.** Welche Schlussfolgerungen ergeben sich aus den Daten? Kann man
zusammenfassend ein Ergebnis oder Fazit formulieren?

3. Schritt: Vergleich der Vorlage mit dem Text (wenn die Aufgabenstellung dies
erfordert). Gehen Sie zum Text zurück und suchen Sie die Passagen heraus, die
im Zusammenhang mit der Grafik von Bedeutung sind. Beurteilen Sie, ob die
dargestellten Daten mit der Aussage des Textes in Einklang stehen oder ihr
widersprechen.

Typen von Diagrammen

	USA	UK
2005	495	105
2015	718	85

Tabelle *(table)*

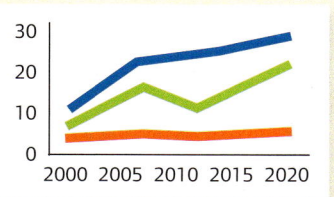
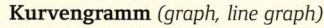

Kurvengramm *(graph, line graph)*

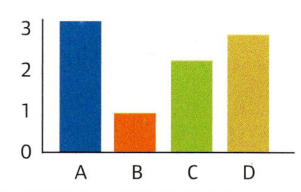

Balkendiagramm *(bar chart)*

Kreis-/Tortendiagramm *(pie chart)*

Sprechen über Zahlen und Mengenangaben (*values, amounts*)
– *more / less than …*
– *no less than …*
– *85 per cent (said that …)*
– *On the other hand, almost …*

Sprechen über Proportionen (*proportions, shares, percentages*)
– *(over) half of …*
– *more/less than one third/quarter of …*
– *the (vast) majority of …*
– *a mere third of …*

Sprechen über Entwicklungen (*developments*) und Tendenzen (*tendencies*)
– *a huge/sharp increase/decrease*
– *a small / slight rise*
– *levels out, remains constant*
– *drastically, gradually, sharply, steadily*
– *rises/increases, hits a maximum*
– *drops/decreases/falls/plunges*
– *over a period of …*
– *between 2005 and 2015*

Vergleich der Informationen aus einer Grafik mit einem Text
– *While the text says that …, the diagram shows that …*
– *The graph illustrates the facts / information in the text in the following way: …*
– *The diagram gives a completely different picture than the information in the text.*

INTERAKTION

Gruppengespräche und Diskussionen führen

Ob es um Gruppengespräche, Diskussionen oder Rollenspiele geht: Machen Sie das meiste daraus, indem Sie die folgenden Punkte beherzigen.

· Lernen Sie die Formulierungen auf der hinteren Umschlagklappe dieses Buches (*Language for Discussion*). Klappen Sie diese während des Unterrichts aus. Die Formulierungen helfen Ihnen, sich klar und logisch auszudrücken.
· Bereiten Sie sich inhaltlich vor, indem Sie sich einzelne Aspekte des Themas nochmal in Stichworten ins Gedächtnis rufen und Schlüsselbegriffe auf Englisch notieren.
· Legen Sie sich, wenn genügend Zeit ist, ein paar Fragen/Antworten zum Thema zurecht.
· Bleiben Sie immer ruhig und denken Sie nach, bevor Sie sprechen.

- Bleiben Sie beim Thema und schweifen Sie nicht ab.
- Gehen Sie auf Ihre Gesprächspartner ein und halten Sie Blickkontakt.
- Beteiligen Sie sich und hören Sie nicht bloß still zu: Gruppenarbeit ist eine hervorragende Gelegenheit zum freien Sprechen.

Melden Sie sich auch immer mal wieder spontan zu Wort und lassen Sie Ausdrücke einfließen, die Interesse, Überraschung, Skepsis usw. äußern – so etwas macht das Gespräch gleich viel lebendiger:

Sich zu Wort melden
– *Can I just say that …*
– *Well, if you ask me …*

Jemand anderen ins Gespräch einbringen
– *What do you think, Sven / Svenja?*

Verständnis, Erstaunen usw. ausdrücken

Ach so. / Ah ja.	*I see. / Right. / Oh, right.*
Oh je!	*Oh dear!*
Echt?	*Really?*
Gut. / Okay.	*Fine.*
Alles klar.	*OK then.*
Das ist doch wohl nicht dein Ernst!	*You're kidding!*

MEDIATION ....

Mediation

Mediation bedeutet das sinngemäße Übertragen von Texten in eine andere Sprache für jemanden, der das Original nicht versteht. Wichtig bei einer Mediation ist immer die Konzentration auf das Wesentliche, im Unterschied zur Übersetzung. Einzelheiten sind bei einer Mediation ebenso zweitrangig wie stilistische Feinheiten.

1. Schritt: Lesen Sie genau, für welche Situation Sie den Text zusammenfassen müssen und für wen. Meist bestimmt die jeweilige Situation, worauf es ankommt.

2. Schritt: Lesen Sie den gesamten Text durch, ohne sich dabei auf Einzelwörter zu konzentrieren. Ignorieren Sie unbekannte Vokabeln wenn möglich, oft sind sie für das Verständnis des Hauptinhalts nicht wesentlich.

3. Schritt: Lesen Sie nochmals, worauf es in der Aufgabenstellung ankommt und in welcher Form die Lösung abgefasst sein soll. Wenn es einzelne Fragen gibt, markieren Sie die für die jeweiligen Fragen wichtigen Textpassagen in unterschiedlichen Farben.

4. Schritt: Fassen Sie die Hauptpunkte des Textes zusammen. Drücken Sie sich klar und verständlich aus; vereinfachen Sie die Sprache des Originals, indem Sie sich darauf konzentrieren, was gesagt wird, nicht wie es gesagt wird.

5. Schritt: Lesen Sie Ihren Text nochmals durch und vergewissern Sie sich, dass der Inhalt des Originals angemessen und verständlich ausgedrückt ist.

EXAM PREPARATION

Was sollte ich jetzt schon über die Abschlussprüfung wissen?

Bis zur Prüfung haben Sie zwar noch ein bisschen Zeit, aber schon im Laufe der 11. Klasse wird sich in den Klassenarbeiten immer mehr widerspiegeln, was Sie später in der Abschlussprüfung wissen und können müssen. Die Abschlussprüfung setzt sich aus den folgenden Einzelprüfungen zusammen:

· Schriftliche Prüfung
· Kommunikationsprüfung
· Zentrale Klassenarbeit Hörverstehen (während des letzten Halbjahrs)
· Präsentationsprüfung (5. Prüfungsfach für Schülerinnen und Schüler, die nicht am schriftlichen Abitur Englisch teilnehmen)

Die folgenden Aufgaben erwarten Sie in der Abschlussprüfung:

SCHRIFTLICHE PRÜFUNG ....

Leseverstehen

Beurteilen von Textaussagen (*True/False statements*)

Für diese Aufgabe werden Sie einen längeren englischen Text (700-800 Wörter) lesen. Ihr Textverständnis wird überprüft, indem Sie zunächst entscheiden, ob die vorgegebenen Aussagen zum Text richtig oder falsch sind, und Ihre Entscheidung auf Deutsch begründen.

1. Schritt: Lesen Sie den Text zuerst einmal schnell durch, um sich einen groben Überblick über das Thema zu verschaffen. Es kommt beim ersten Lesen eines Textes nicht darauf an, jedes Detail zu verstehen.

▶ Skimming, S. 134

2. Schritt: Lesen Sie nun den Text ein zweites Mal und konzentrieren Sie sich darauf, die relevanten Textstellen zu finden. Achten Sie auf Schlüsselbegriffe und markieren Sie die entsprechenden Stellen im Text.

▶ Scanning, S. 134 – 135

3. Schritt Schreiben Sie Ihre Antworten auf Deutsch. Fangen Sie mit ‚true' oder ‚false' an. Danach schreiben Sie die Begründung für Ihre Entscheidung, indem Sie die relevanten Textteile auf Deutsch zitieren.

Informationen auf Deutsch auflisten

In einer zweiten Aufgabe sollen Sie ca. fünf Punkte (z. B. Gründe, Argumente, Beispiele) zu einem bestimmten Aspekt im Text suchen und auf Deutsch auflisten. Dabei ist es wichtig, immer vollständige Sätze zu schreiben. Achten Sie beim Lesen auf Schlüsselwörter, um die gewünschten Informationen schnell zu finden.

1. Schritt Lesen Sie die Aufgabe sorgfältig durch und vergewissern Sie sich, dass Sie sie richtig verstanden haben.

2 Schritt Lesen Sie den Text einmal schnell durch.

3. Schritt Lesen Sie den Text noch einmal und markieren Sie die relevanten Teile des Texts.

4. Schritt Notieren Sie die Punkte, dann schreiben Sie eine Liste in vollständigen Sätzen auf Deutsch.

Textproduktion

In diesem Teil der schriftlichen Prüfung geht es darum, zwei Aufsätze zu schreiben. Ein guter Aufsatz ist klar strukturiert und enthält logische, nachvollziehbare Argumente. Es reicht nicht, die Argumente aufzulisten. Sie sollen in gut strukturierten, grammatikalisch richtigen Sätzen eingebettet sein. Sie sollten in Ihrem Text so viele Argumente wie möglich klar ausführen. Dafür benötigen Sie einen breiten Themenwortschatz, gute Kenntnisse der sprachlichen Mittel (Grammatik) sowie gutes Hintergrundwissen in den Themen, die Sie im Unterricht behandeln. Sie finden nützliche Phrasen auf der hinteren Umschlagklappe (*Language for Writing*).

Textbezogener Aufsatz

Die erste Aufgabe ist mit dem Thema des Lesetextes aus Teil I verbunden. Es wird gutes Hintergrundwissen zum jeweiligen Lehrplanthema vorausgesetzt. Sie können sich auf den Text beziehen, aber Ihre Argumentation sollte auch über diesen Text hinausgehen.

Themenbezogener Aufsatz

Bei der zweiten Aufgabe stehen zwei Themen zur Auswahl, die über den Lesetext hinausgehen. In der Regel sind die zwei Alternativen eng mit den Lehrplanthemen aus Kursstufe 1 und 2 verbunden. Am besten können Sie sich vorbereiten, indem Sie kontinuierlich den Themenwortschatz aufarbeiten, der Ihnen in der Arbeit mit *Crossover* begegnet. Je mehr Begriffe Ihnen zu einem Thema einfallen, umso sicherer werden Sie sich beim Schreiben fühlen. Oft ist es hilfreich, vor dem Schreiben ein Brainstorming zu machen und sich (z. B. in Form einer Liste, Tabelle oder Mind Map) Notizen zu machen, in denen Sie alle wichtigen Begriffe festhalten.

KOMMUNIKATIONSPRÜFUNG

Die Kommunikationsprüfung beginnt immer mit einem kurzen Vortrag (ca. 5 Minuten), in dem Sie nach einer Vorbereitungszeit über vorgegebene Impulsmaterialien sprechen, z. B. Fotos, Cartoons, Grafik oder einen kurzen Text. Im Anschluss daran diskutieren Sie allein oder zu zweit mit der Fachlehrerin / dem Fachlehrer über die Materialien und weitergehende Fragen. Dabei hilft ein breiter Wortschatz und gutes Hintergrundwissen zu den Lehrplanthemen. Bei mündlichen Aufgaben sollten Sie immer den Wortschatz auf der hinteren Umschlagklappe vor sich haben (*Language for Discussion*). In der Prüfungssituation ist es von großem Vorteil, wenn Sie Wendungen parat haben, mit denen Sie z. B. das Gespräch eröffnen, einen Moment Zeit zum Nachdenken gewinnen oder ein Argument erwidern können.

ZENTRALE KLASSENARBEIT HÖRVERSTEHEN

Das Hörverstehen wird innerhalb der Jahrgangsstufe 13 zu einem gesonderten Zeitpunkt verpflichtend geprüft. Dazu gibt es eine zentral gestellte Klausur, die ein paar Wochen vor dem schriftlichen Abitur stattfindet. Sie ist nicht Teil der Abiturprüfung, sondern wird wie eine Klassenarbeit bewertet.

Hörverstehen kann ganz unterschiedlich abgefragt werden. Folgende Aufgabentypen sind möglich: Satzergänzung, Fragen zum Text, Raster ausfüllen. Die Hörtexte sind auf Englisch und die Antworten auf Deutsch.

PRÄSENTATIONSPRÜFUNG

Die Präsentationsprüfung machen diejenigen Schülerinnen und Schüler, die nicht am schriftlichen Abitur Englisch teilnehmen. Die Prüfung findet mit den anderen mündlichen Prüfungen nach dem schriftlichen Abitur statt. Sie werden eine Woche Zeit haben, Ihre Präsentation vorzubereiten. Auf die Präsentation selbst folgt dann noch ein Prüfungsgespräch.

Wichtig für Ihren Erfolg sind insbesondere freies Sprechen, guter sprachlicher Ausdruck, fundierte Sachkenntnisse und die geeignete Medienwahl. Hier kommen z. B. Poster, computergestützte Präsentation, OHP, Flipchart in Frage. Es ist wichtig, einige Wendungen für den Anfang und den Abschluss der Präsentation parat zu haben, z. B. *My presentation is about …, Finally, it can be said …*

▶ Die Arbeitsergebnisse präsentieren, S. 144–145

GRAMMAR SUMMARY

The simple present

1 I **go** to the disco once a week.
2 We **live** in Bavaria.
3 Mr Brown **teaches** us English every day.
4 **I don't like** chocolate.
5 **Does** he **like** chocolate?

· Man gebraucht das **simple present** für regelmäßige, sich wiederholende Ereignisse oder Handlungen (1, 3) und für Dauerzustände (2, 4, 5).
· Mit Ausnahme der 3. Person Singular (*he, she, it*) hat das **simple present** dieselbe Form wie der Infinitiv (1, 2).
⚠ Die **3. Person Singular** endet auf *-(e)s* (3).
· Ist **kein Hilfsverb** im Satz vorhanden, werden **Verneinung** und **Fragen** mit der entsprechenden Form von *to do* gebildet (4, 5).

Das *simple present* wird häufig mit den folgenden Zeitangaben benutzt:

– *always, never, often, rarely, seldom, sometimes*
– *generally, mostly, normally, regularly, usually*
– *every day/week/month/..., every morning/afternoon/...*
– *on Mondays/Tuesdays/..., on weekdays*
– *in (the) summer/winter/...*
– *at Christmas/Easter, at weekends*

The present progressive

1 I**'m calling** to say that Ben's ill.
2 He**'s staying** in bed today.
3 The computer **isn't working**.
4 **Are** you **sleeping**?

· Man benutzt das **present progressive** (auch **present continuous** genannt) für Vorgänge oder Handlungen, die im Moment des Sprechens oder Schreibens passieren und noch nicht abgeschlossen sind (1, 3, 4).
· Es wird auch für vorübergehende Situationen gebraucht (2).
· Das **present progressive** wird mit dem Präsens von *to be* und der *-ing*-Form des Vollverbs gebildet.

- Da beim **present progressive** immer ein Hilfsverb vorhanden ist, wird die **Verneinung** mit *not/n't* gebildet (3).
- Fragen werden durch Umstellung gebildet (4).

Das **present progressive** wird oft mit den folgenden **Zeitangaben** benutzt:

> *at the moment, at present, now, this week/month*

⚠ Diese Verben bilden normalerweise keine **progressive-Form**:

> *be, believe, doubt, feel* (meinen), *hate, hear, imagine, know, like/dislike, love, mean, notice, prefer, realize, recognize, remember, see* (begreifen), *seem, suppose, think* (meinen), *understand, want, wish*

The simple past

1 We **wanted** to go to the USA last year.
2 She **went** on a school trip to London.
3 Jasmin **did not enjoy** her holiday in Rimini last summer.
4 Where **did** you **go** last year?

- Man benutzt das **simple past**, um über Vergangenes zu berichten.
- Das **simple past** wird auch gebraucht, wenn man sagen will, **wann** etwas geschehen ist (1, 3, 4).
- Bei **regelmäßigen** Verben wird das **simple past** durch das Anhängen von *-ed* an den Infinitiv gebildet (1).
  ⚠ Die unregelmäßigen Verben haben eine Sonderform (2), die man sich merken – auswendig lernen! – muss.
- Ist **kein Hilfsverb** im Satz vorhanden, bildet man die **Verneinung** und **Fragen** mit *did/didn't* (3, 4).

▶ Irregular verbs, S. 190

Das **simple past** wird häufig mit den folgenden **Zeitangaben** benutzt:

> – *yesterday, the day before yesterday, the week/month/… before last*
> – *last night/week/month/summer/December/Easter/…*
> – *two/three/… hours/days/years/… ago*
> – *in 2015 / in the 20th century …*
> – *at that time, in those days*

The past progressive

1 The teacher **was talking** to Heather **during the break**.
2 The tourists **were taking** photos when a lion (suddenly) **sprang** towards them.
3 I **wasn't doing** anything particular when he **came** round.
4 **Were** you **having** breakfast when I **phoned**?

- Wenn man ausdrücken möchte, dass eine Handlung zu einem bestimmten Zeitpunkt oder während eines bestimmten Zeitraumes in der Vergangenheit **im Gange** war, benutzt man das **past progressive** (auch **past continuous** genannt) (1).
- Das **past progressive** wird auch benutzt, um zu verdeutlichen, dass eine Handlung im Gange war, als ein neues Ereignis (plötzlich) eintrat (2, 3, 4).
- Man bildet das **past progressive** mit *was/were* und der *-ing*-Form des Vollverbs (1–4).
- Die **Verneinung** wird mit *was not / wasn't* bzw. *were not / weren't* gebildet (3).
- **Fragen** bildet man durch Umstellung (4).
  ⚠ Einige Verben haben **keine progressive-Form** (siehe die Liste unter **present progressive**).

▶ The present progressive, S. 152

The present perfect

1 I**'ve bought** a new car.
2 I **haven't seen** the new film yet.
3 How long **have** you **had** it?
4 We**'ve had** snow **for** two weeks.
5 She**'s had** a cold **since** December.

- Wenn man ausdrücken will, dass etwas geschehen ist, ohne dass „der genaue Zeitpunkt des Ereignisses wichtig ist, wird das **present perfect** benutzt (1, 2)."
- Man gebraucht das **present perfect** auch, um zu sagen, seit wann oder wie lange ein Zustand oder eine Handlung schon andauert (3–5). Dafür wird sehr oft *for* bzw. *since* verwendet. (Im Deutschen steht dafür „seit" plus Gegenwart.)
- Das **present perfect** wird mit *have/has* und der 3. Form des Vollverbs gebildet (1–5).
- Die **Verneinung** wird durch das Einfügen von *not/n't* unmittelbar nach *have/has* gebildet (2).
- **Fragen** bildet man durch Umstellung (3).

Das **present perfect** wird oft mit den folgenden Zeitangaben benutzt:

- *already, still (not), (not) yet*
- *(not) ever, just, lately, never, recently*
- *so far this week/month/…, till/until now*

The present perfect progressive

1 I**'ve been learning** English since I was 10.
2 They**'ve not been speaking** to each other lately.
3 **Has** he **been singing** in the choir for long?

- Das **present perfect progressive** (auch **present perfect continuous** genannt) benutzt man für Handlungen und Vorgänge, die in der Vergangenheit begonnen haben und zum Zeitpunkt des Sprechens bzw. Schreibens noch nicht beendet sind.
- Das **present perfect progressive** wird mit *have/has been* und der *-ing*-Form des Vollverbs gebildet (1).
- Die **Verneinung** bildet man durch das Einfügen von *not/n't* unmittelbar nach *have/has* (2).
- **Fragen** werden durch Umstellung gebildet (3).
  ⚠ Einige Verben haben normalerweise **keine progressive-Form**. (siehe die Liste unter **present progressive**)

▶ The present progressive, S. 152 – 153

The past perfect

1 Laura couldn't pay. She **had forgotten** her purse.
2 Nina **had** already **left** the coffee bar by the time I arrived.
3 When I visited John in hospital, he **had been** there for ten days.

- Mit Hilfe des **past perfect** drückt man aus, dass zwei Handlungen oder Vorgänge in der Vergangenheit aufeinander folgten (1, 2). Die Handlung, die zeitlich voranging, steht im **past perfect**.
- Das **past perfect** wird auch verwendet, um auszudrücken, dass ein Zustand vor einem Zeitpunkt der Vergangenheit begann und zu diesem Zeitpunkt noch andauerte (3).
  ⚠ Wenn zwei oder mehrere kurze Handlungen in der Vergangenheit direkt aufeinander folgen, wird für alle Handlungen das **simple past** verwendet: *The cat **ran** out when Joanne **opened** the door.*

The past perfect progressive

1 Rod **had been travelling** for three months when he ran out of money.
2 When I found Mary, I could see that she **had been crying**.

· Das **past perfect progressive** wird verwendet, wenn man ausdrücken will, dass eine Handlung oder ein Vorgang vor einem Zeitpunkt in der Vergangenheit begonnen hatte und bis (oder fast bis) zu diesem Zeitpunkt andauerte.

The future

A will

1 In the future people **will use** public transport more often.
2 We can only hope that everyone **will accept** this shift in attitudes.
3 You've forgotten your purse? Don't worry. I**'ll lend** you some money.
4 Ms Smith **will not be** at the meeting this afternoon.
5 I **won't come** either.
6 **Will** he **get** the job?

· Das **will-future** benutzt man, um Vorhersagen zu machen (1) oder Hoffnungen bzw,. Vermutungen über die Zukunft zu äußern (2).
· Man benutzt es auch, wenn man sich spontan zu etwas entschließt, Angebote oder Versprechen macht (3).
· Das **will-future** wird mit *will* + Infinitiv des Vollverbs gebildet. Es hat für alle Personen die gleiche Form (1 – 4, 6).
· Die **Verneinung** bildet man durch das Einfügen von *not* unmittelbar nach *will*. Im gesprochenen Englisch sagt man häufig *won't* (4, 5).
· **Fragen** werden durch Umstellung gebildet (6).

Das **will-future** kommt häufig mit den folgenden einleitenden Verben und Ausdrücken vor:

- *believe, expect, forecast, hope, imagine, suppose, think*
- *It's clear/obvious that ..., There's no doubt that ...*

B going to

1 Look at these clouds. It**'s going to rain** soon.
2 This time **I'm going to get** good marks in the class test.
3 Tom **isn't going to work** at the club any more.
4 When **are** you **going to sit** your driving test?

· Das **going to-future** benutzt man für Ereignisse und Situationen, die nach Meinung des Sprechers bald eintreten werden (weil es bereits Anzeichen dafür gibt) (1).
· Es wird auch für Pläne und Absichten gebraucht (2).
· Das **going to future** wird mit *am/is/are* + *going to* + Infinitiv gebildet (1-4).
· Die **Verneinung** bildet man durch das Einfügen von *not/n't* unmittelbar nach *am/is/are* (3).
· **Fragen** werden durch Umstellung gebildet (4).
  ⚠ Der **Gebrauch des Futurs** hängt in gewissem Maße von der Absicht oder Sichtweise des Sprechers ab. Dies gilt insbesondere für das **going to future** und für zukünftige Ereignisse.

C The present progressive / the simple present

1 We**'re leaving** the house at 10.30.
2 The bus **goes** at 11 o'clock.

- Man kann das **present progressive** auch **mit einer Zeitbestimmung der Zukunft** (*at 10.30, this afternoon, on Sunday*) für bereits feststehende Pläne und Verabredungen verwenden (1).
- Genau wie im Deutschen wird auch im Englischen das **simple present mit einer Zeitangabe** benutzt, um fest terminierte Vorgänge (Fahrpläne, Stundenpläne, Programme usw.) anzugeben (2).

⚠ Nach den temporalen Bindewörtern (*after, as soon as, before, until, when*) steht present oder present perfect, obwohl man über die Zukunft spricht.
– *It will probably be late **when I check** into the hotel this evening.*
– *I'll stop working **as soon as I have finished** this report.*

Modal auxiliary verbs

1 He **can speak** several languages.
2 You **must accept** your new situation.
3 We **needn't go** to work today.
4 **May** I **interrupt** you?

- Um zu sagen, was geschehen kann, muss, darf, soll usw., benutzt man ein modales Hilfsverb in Verbindung mit einem Vollverb (1–4).

  ⚠ Im Englischen steht ein Hilfsverb – anders als im Deutschen – nie ohne Vollverb: Lena kann Spanisch. → *Lena can speak Spanish.* NICHT: ~~can Spanish~~

- Modale Hilfsverben – nicht jedoch die Ersatzverben (siehe unten) – haben bei allen Personen immer die gleiche Form, einschließlich der 3. Person Singular (keine -*s*-Endung) (1).
- Die **Verneinung** wird durch das Einfügen von *not/n't* unmittelbar nach dem Hilfsverb gebildet (3).
- **Fragen** bildet man durch Umstellung (4).
- Abgesehen von *could* (wenn es für eine Fähigkeit gebraucht wird) kann man modale Hilfsverben nur im Präsens und – mit einer geeigneten Zeitangabe – mit zukünftiger Bedeutung benutzen, zum Beispiel:
  – *You **can go** home now.* (Präsens)
  – *You **can go** home an hour early tomorrow.* (Futur)
  – *I **must write** these letters now.* (Präsens)
  – *I **must write** a long report next week.* (Futur)

⚠ Um ein modales Hilfsverb z. B. in der Vergangenheit zu verwenden, muss ein geeignetes Ersatzverb gebraucht werden:
must *The provider **had to block** access to the internet last December.*
can *I **couldn't start** the car yesterday.* (Fähigkeit)
*We **weren't allowed to go** home early last Friday.* (Erlaubnis)

Übersicht der modalen Hilfsverben nach Funktion		
Funktion	**Modale(s) Hilfsverb(en)**	
Fähigkeit	He **can** speak several languages. The first satellites **could** only transmit sound.	
Möglichkeit	With your qualifications you **could** work abroad. The boss **may** come in at any moment. He **might** ask you what you are doing.	
Bitte	**Can** I have a word with Ms Sims, please? **Could** I speak to Ms Sims, please? **May** I interrupt you? **Might** I ask you a personal question?	(neutral) (höflich) (betont höflich) (äußerst höflich)
Erlaubnis	You **can** go in now. The boss is free. You **may** go in now.	(neutral) (gefällig)
Verbot	We **mustn't** be late for work tomorrow.	
Pflicht	You **must** wear a hard hat in the factory.	
Wahl	Most shop workers **needn't** work on Sundays.	
Empfehlung	You **should** get better qualifications. You **ought to** get better qualifications. You **must** get better qualifications.	(neutral) (betont) (streng)

The definite article

1 **Sociologists** say that **violence** is increasing among young people.
2 Is **the current trend** partly caused by **the violent films** they watch?
3 **Most sentences** are not tough enough.
4 Nearly **half the prisoners** in **British prisons** are under 25.
5 **Spring** is my favourite season, but **the spring** we're having this year is more like **winter**.
6 We had **breakfast** late this morning, so we came to school **by car** instead of **by bus**.
7 They are thinking of legalizing soft drugs in **the Netherlands**.

- Hat ein Substantiv eine allgemeine, uneingeschränkte Bedeutung – also „alle ohne Ausnahme" – dann steht es ohne Artikel (1).
- Ist die Bedeutung eines Substantives auf bestimmte Fälle eingeschränkt, benutzt man den Artikel (2, 5).
- Ferner wird der Artikel in den folgenden Fällen und Wendungen im Englischen – z. T. anders als im Deutschen – nicht gebraucht:
  - bei *most* in der Bedeutung „die meisten" (3),
  - bei öffentlichen Gebäuden im allgemeinen Sinn (4),
  - bei Mahlzeiten (6),
  - bei Verkehrsmitteln (6),
  - bei Straßennamen,
  - bei Tageszeiten, Wochentagen, Monaten und Jahreszeiten im allgemeinen Sinn (5).
- Der Artikel wird verwendet nach *all* und *half* (4) und mit den Pluralnamen von Staaten (7).

Reported speech

A Aussagesätze

1 Some people **claim** that 'servant' robots **are putting** people out of work.
2 The speaker **reminded** his audience that there **were** some jobs robots **couldn't do**.

- Wenn man einem Dritten berichten möchte, was während eines Gespräches gesagt wurde, benutzt man die **indirekte Rede**.
- Bei Verwendung der indirekten Rede benutzt man ein einleitendes Verb wie *claim, say, remind, answer, think, mention* usw., um zu verdeutlichen, dass eine Äußerung wiedergegeben wird.
- Steht das einleitende Verb in der Vergangenheit – also *said, answered, mentioned* usw. –, dann verschieben sich die Zeiten wie folgt:

direkte Rede		indirekte Rede
simple present *she works hard*	⇒	simple past *she worked hard*
present progressive *she is working hard*	⇒	past progressive *she was working hard*
simple past *she worked hard*	⇒	past perfect *she had worked hard*
past progressive *she was working hard*	⇒	past perfect progressive *she had been working hard*
present perfect *she has worked hard*	⇒	past perfect *she had worked hard*
present perfect progressive *she has been working hard*	⇒	past perfect progressive *she had been working hard*
past perfect *she had worked hard*	⇒	(keine Verschiebung) –
past perfect progressive *she had been working hard*	⇒	(keine Verschiebung) –
will *she will work hard*	⇒	would *she would work hard*
am/is/are going to *she is going to work hard*	⇒	was/were going to *she was going to work hard*
would/might, etc. *she would work hard*	⇒	(keine Verschiebung) –
would have/might have, etc. *she had been working hard*	⇒	(keine Verschiebung) –

⚠ Die modalen Hilfsverben werden folgendermaßen verschoben:

Modalverb	Bedeutung	indirekte Rede
can	Fähigkeit	*could, was/were able to*
can	Erlaubnis	*was/were allowed to*
may	Möglichkeit	*might*
may	Erlaubnis	*was/were allowed to*
must	Pflicht	*had to*
mustn't	Verbot	*was/were not allowed to*
needn't	freie Wahl	*did not/didn't have to*

- Außer wenn man über ein Gespräch, das am selben Tag stattgefunden hat, berichtet, müssen fast alle **Zeit-** und einige **Ortsangaben** entsprechend der folgenden Tabelle geändert werden. (Angaben, die nicht aufgeführt sind, bleiben unverändert.)

direkte Rede	indirekte Rede
today	*(on) that day*
tomorrow	*the next day*
yesterday	*the day before*
the day after tomorrow	*two days later*
the day before yesterday	*two days before*
next day/Friday/week/Christmas/…	*the following day/Friday/week/Christmas/…*
last Friday/week/summer/…	*the Friday/week/summer/… before*
two years/months/weeks/…ago	*two years/months/weeks/… before*
now, at present	*then*
at the moment	*at that moment*
at this time	*at that time*
here	*there*
in this place	*at that place*
this	*that*
these	*those*

B Fragesätze

1 A member of the audience **asked what had led** to the widespread use of robots in factories.
2 She **wanted to know if/whether** her job **was endangered**.

- Bei indirekten **Fragen** unterscheidet man zwischen Fragen mit Fragewort (1) und Fragen ohne Fragewort (2).
- Bei Fragen **mit Fragewort** wird das Fragewort übernommen (1).
- Bei Fragen **ohne Fragewort** benutzt man *if* bzw. *whether* (= ob), um zu verdeutlichen, dass es sich um eine Frage handelt (2).
- Alle anderen Änderungen erfolgen wie bei den Aussagesätzen (siehe **Aussagesätze** oben).

C Bitten, Aufforderungen und Befehle

1 Lucy **asked the engineer to show her** the robot.
2 He **told her not to go** too close to it.

- **Bitten** werden meist durch *asked* (= bitten) (1), **Aufforderungen** und **Befehle** durch *told* (= sagen) (2) eingeleitet.
- Bei **positiven Sätzen** erscheint das Verb als *to* + Infinitiv (1).
- Bei **negativen Sätzen** setzen wir *not* unmittelbar vor *to* (2).

> ⚠ Die beiden Verben *to tell* und *to ask* stehen immer mit einem Objekt, das die ange- sprochene Person erwähnt (1, 2). Ist dies vom Kontext her nicht erkennbar, wird einfach ein passender Begriff eingesetzt:
> – *Jack said, 'Ann, can you tell Carol to give me a ring, please?'*
> – *Jack **asked Ann** to tell Carol to give him a ring.*
> – *Ben said, 'Don't enter the studio when the red light is on.'*
> – *Ben **told everybody** not to enter the studio when the red light was on.*

The passive

1 Measures **are being introduced** to reduce traffic pollution.
2 Pollution **is caused by** some thoughtless people.

- Ist der Verursacher einer Handlung unbekannt oder zweitrangig, benutzt man das Passiv. Im Vordergrund steht also das Ergebnis des Vorgangs (1).
- Möchte man den Verursacher doch angeben, benutzt man einen *by-agent* (2).
  > ⚠ Der Verursacher wird mit *by* – auf keinen mit Fall *from*! – eingeleitet.
- Das Passiv wird mit einer Zeitform von *to be* und der 3. Form des Vollverbs gebildet:

Zeit	Zeitform von *be*	3. Form
simple present	*am/is/are*	*caused*
present progressive	*am/is/are being*	*introduced*
simple past	*was/were*	*buried*
past progressive	*was/were being*	*built*
present perfect	*has/have been*	*installed*
will-future	*will be*	*blocked*
going to-future	*am/is/are going to be*	*sacked*

- Beim Gebrauch von modalen Hilfsverben wird nach folgendem Muster verfahren:

bei Aussagen	Hilfsverb + *be* + 3. Form	*must be displayed*
bei Fragen	Hilfsverb + Subjekt + *be* + 3. Form	*Can ... be persuaded?*

⚠ Das Verb *be* bleibt im Infinitiv immer unverändert.

The impersonal passive

1 **It is said that** petrol should cost more.
2 He **is thought** to have gone to hospital.

- Das **impersonal passive** wird vor allem dann benutzt, wenn man sich objektiv bzw. unbeteiligt ausdrücken möchte. Daher kommt diese Struktur oft in Polizeiberichten, seriösen Zeitungsartikeln usw. vor.
- Bei Verben des Berichtens, Denkens usw. benutzt man häufig das Satzmuster:
  – *It is/was/...* + 3. Form des einleitenden Verbs + *that*-Satz (1).

  Hier sind weitere Beispiele dieses Musters:
  Aktiv Some **say** that companies which cause pollution should be heavily fined.
  Passiv **It is said that** companies which cause pollution should be heavily fined.
  Aktiv Experts **recommended** that more be spent on public transport.
  Passiv **It was recommended** that more be spent on public transport.

- Um das Subjekt des *that*-Satzes zu betonen, kann man folgendes Muster benutzen:
  – Subjekt + *is/was/...* + 3. Form + andere Satzteile (2):
  Aktiv Many **believe** that the minister is thinking of raising fuel taxes.
  Passiv The minister **is believed** to be thinking of raising fuel taxes.

  ⚠ Der *by*-agent wird in solchen Passivsätzen folgendermaßen verwendet:
  Aktiv The speaker felt that the idea was too radical.
  Passiv The idea was felt to be too radical **by** the speaker.

Conditionals

1 If we **invest** in new technology, a lot of people **will lose** their jobs.
2 If more people **took part** in retraining schemes, they **wouldn't have to worry** about finding new employment.
3 We **won't have** political censorship if we **don't start** to censor the internet.
4 **Will** we soon **have** political censorship if we **start** to censor the internet?

- Ein **Konditionalsatz** besteht aus zwei Teilen: dem ***if*-Teil** und dem **Hauptteil**.
  Der ***if*-Teil** drückt eine **Bedingung** aus, der Hauptteil eine **Folge**.
- Bei **Konditionalsätzen** kommen folgende **Zeitmuster** am häufigsten vor:

Typ I	*If + simple* present	+	*will*-future
Typ II	*If + simple* past	+	*would* + Infinitiv
Typ III	*If + past* perfect	+	*would have* + 3. Form des Verbs

- Je nach Sinn kann der *if*-Teil, der Hauptteil oder beide Teile des Satzes **verneint** werden (2, 3).
- Bei **Fragen** kann nur der **Hauptteil** zu einer Frage geformt werden. Dann steht dieser Teil **an erster Stelle** (4).
- *if*-Sätze werden gemäß der **Wahrscheinlichkeit** der zu erwartenden Folge eingesetzt:

  Typ I: Folge (fast) sicher.
  *If we **invest in** new technology, a lot of people **will lose** their jobs.*
  D.h. viele Leute werden (vermutlich) ihre Stellen verlieren, da wir (sehr wahrscheinlich) in die neue Technologie investieren werden.

  Typ II: Folge theoretisch möglich, aber kaum wahrscheinlich.
  *If we **invested in** new technology, a lot of people **would lose** their jobs.*
  D.h. es ist kaum zu erwarten, dass viele Leute ihre Stellen verlieren werden, da wir (wahrscheinlich) nicht in die neue Technologie investieren werden.

Typ III: Folge unmöglich, da die Bedingung nicht erfüllt wurde und bereits in der Vergangenheit liegt.
*If we **had invested in** new technology, a lot of people **would have lost** their jobs.*
D. h. der Sprecher weiß schon, dass keiner den Job verloren hat, da wir in die neue Technologie nicht investiert haben.

Gerund/Infinitive

1 Max **enjoys playing** football.
2 Can you **afford to buy** that DVD collection?
3 Cem and Julie **continued to meet** even though they had spilt up.
4 Cem and Julie **continued meeting** even though they had split up.
5 Alison **normally likes going** to parties, but **today** she would **prefer to stay** at home.

- Nach einigen Verben folgt immer die *-ing*-Form (**gerund**) (1). Am wichtigsten sind:

admit, avoid, consider, deny, enjoy, finish, imagine, mention, mind (etwas dagegen haben)*, miss, practise, risk, suggest*

- **Nach einigen Verben** folgt immer der Infinitiv (**infinitive**) (2). Die **wichtigsten** Verben dieser Gruppe sind:

afford, choose, decide, expect, hope, mean, promise, refuse, want

⚠ Nach den Verben *begin, continue, intend* und *start* können der **Infinitiv** oder die *-ing*-**Form beliebig benutzt werden** (3, 4).

begin, continue, intend, start

- Einige Verben werden **je nach Bedeutung** entweder mit dem **Infinitiv** oder mit der *-ing*-**Form** benutzt. Die **wichtigsten** Verben dieser Gruppe sind:

like, dislike, love, hate, prefer

- Wenn von einer **allgemeingültigen Situation** die Rede ist, folgt auf diese Verben die *-ing*-**Form**. Handelt es sich aber um eine **Ausnahmesituation**, dann verwendet man den **Infinitiv** (5).

advise, allow, encourage, forbid, permit, recommend
Handelt es sich um einen **konkreten Einzelfall**, wird mit diesen Verben ein **Objekt + Infinitiv** verwendet.
*- I strongly **advise you to** be more polite to people.*
Wenn es sich aber um eine **allgemeine Situation** handelt, dann steht das nachfolgende Verb in der *-ing*-**Form**.
*- Most firms don't **allow smoking** in their offices.*

forget/remember
Die Struktur **forget/remember + -ing-Form** bezieht sich auf die Vergangenheit. Sie drückt etwa die Idee „Ich werde nie vergessen …" aus.
⚠ ‚Vergangenheit', bezieht sich hier nicht auf *forget/remember*, sondern auf das nachfolgende Verb.
*- I still **remember getting** my first bicycle.*
*- I'll never **forget going** to the Rock Against Hunger concert last year.*

Die Struktur **forget/remember + Infinitiv** dagegen bezieht sich auf die Zukunft.

⚠️ ‚Zukunft' hier bezieht sich auf das nachfolgende Verb. Sie drückt etwa die Idee aus „Ich darf nicht vergessen, etwas zu tun" bzw. „Ich habe noch etwas zu tun, weil ich es bis jetzt vergessen habe".

- Dad, please **remember / don't forget to pick me up** *from the station.*
- Oh dear. I **forgot / didn't remember to pick Sally up** *from the station.*

regret

Die Struktur **regret + -ing-Form** drückt Bedauern über eine vergangene Situation bzw. einen vergangenen Vorfall aus. Häufig geht es dabei um verpasste Chancen.

- I really **regret leaving** *school without qualifications.*
- I know they will **regret buying** *such a big, expensive car.*

Die Struktur **regret + Infinitiv** – fast immer mit einem Verb des Mitteilens wie *inform*, *say*, *tell* kombiniert – drückt eine schlechte Nachricht aus.

- I **regret to say** *that I can't attend the meeting tomorrow.*
- We **regret to inform** *you that the vacancy has now been filled.*

stop

Bedeutet stop „aufhören, etwas zu tun", steht das nachfolgende Verb in der **-ing-Form**. Bedeutet aber stop „kurz anhalten, um etwas anderes zu tun", folgt ein Verb im **Infinitiv**.

- For heaven's sake **stop shouting** *at me.*
- I'm a little late because I **stopped to give** *somebody a lift.*

try

Bedeutet *try* „etwas ausprobieren", steht das nachfolgende Verb in der **-ing-Form**. Bedeutet aber *try* „sich anstrengen, etwas zu tun", folgt ein Verb im **Infinitiv**.

- I **tried phoning** *Ellie, but she wasn't at home.*
- We**'ll try to repair** *your computer by the weekend.*

Used to do

1. I **used to do** a lot of sport, but I haven't got time now.
2. I **didn't use to drink** coffee, but I do now because I enjoy it.
3. **Did** you **use to watch** a lot of TV when you were a kid?
4. **Didn't** you **use to live** in London?
   - Yes, I did. But now I live in Stuttgart.

- *Used to* + infinitive wird verwendet, um Handlungen, Zustände oder Gewohnheiten, die in der Vergangenheit bestanden haben, zu beschreiben. (1–4) Im Deutschen werden dafür oft Wörter wie *früher oder damals* verwendet.
- Verneinung und Fragen werden mit *did/didn't* gebildet. (2–4)

Adjectives and adverbs

1. John has a **new** DVD player.
2. He always buys **expensive** equipment.
3. My computer has become **very slow**.
4. That CD sounds **terrible**.
5. We can make printouts **quickly** and **cheaply**.

- Um **Personen** oder **Sachen** näher zu beschreiben, benutzt man **Adjektive** (1–4).
- Adjektive stehen **unmittelbar** vor Substantiven oder **unmittelbar nach** einer Form von *be* (bzw. *become* oder *seem*, die *be* ersetzen können) (3).
- **Adjektive** können mit Verben wie *feel, look* (aussehen), *sound, smell* und *taste* eine **sinnliche Wahrnehmung** ausdrücken (4).

163

► Word order, S. 164

- Um ein **Tätigkeitsverb** näher zu beschreiben, setzt man ein Adverb **unmittelbar hinter das Verb** bzw. Verb + Objekt (5).
  ⚠ Im Englischen können ein Verb und sein Objekt – anders als im Deutschen – nicht durch ein Adverb getrennt werden. Also NICHT: We can make quickly printouts.
- Adverbien werden auch benutzt, um **Adjektive**, **andere Adverbien** und **ganze Sätze** näher zu bestimmen:
- *MP3 players have become **surprisingly cheap**.* (Adverb + Adjektiv) *My fax machine prints out **terribly slowly**.* (Adverb + Adverb) ***Luckily** Gerd left a message on my mailbox.* (Satzadverb)
- Die meisten Adverbien werden durch Anhängen von *-ly* an das Adjektiv gebildet (5). Eine kleine Anzahl von Adverbien haben dieselbe Form wie Adjektive; die häufigsten sind *fast, hard, early, late, long, daily*.

Comparison of adjectives and adverbs

1 A hundred years ago life was **slower** and people may have been **happier**.
2 Which technological innovation is the **most/least important**?
3 Today you can copy data **more easily than** ever before.

- **Einsilbige** und **zweisilbige Adjektive**, die auf *-y* enden – zum Beispiel *easy, happy* und *lucky* –, werden mit *-(i)er/-(i)est* gesteigert (1).
- **Mehrsilbige Adjektive** und **Adverbien**, die auf *-ly* enden, werden mit *more/most* gesteigert (2, 3).
  ⚠ Die Adverbien, die dieselbe Form wie das entsprechende Adjektiv haben (*fast, hard, early* usw.), werden mit *-er/-est* gesteigert.
- Um Personen oder Sachen im Satz miteinander zu vergleichen, gibt es folgende Möglichkeiten:

– Kein Unterschied	**as** *good* **as**	genau so gut wie
– Unterschied	**not as** *good* **as**	nicht so gut wie
– Unterschied	*better* **than**	besser als

Word order – positions of adverbs of time, place and frequency

1 She goes shopping **every week**.
2 They play in a club **in Doherty Street**.
3 **Last year** we went to India for our holidays.
4 Paul and Emily went to **the USA last year**.
5 She **always finishes** school early on Fridays.
6 He **is never** at home when I call.
7 I like to stay at home **now and then**.
8 Gina acted **strangely at the party last night**.

- Zeitangaben (Wann?) und Ortsangaben (Wo?, Wohin?) stehen in der Regel am Satzende (1, 2).
- Um die Zeit eines bestimmten Ereignisses hervorzuheben, kann man die Zeitangabe an die erste Stelle setzen (3).
- Stehen eine Zeitangabe und eine Ortsangabe zusammen am Satzende, dann gilt die Reihenfolge Ort vor Zeit (alphabetisch merken: O vor Z!) (4).
- Besteht eine Häufigkeitsangabe aus einem Wort, z.B. *always, often, sometimes*, steht sie unmittelbar vor dem Vollverb (5).
- Lautet das Vollverb *to be*, steht das Häufigkeitsadverb **direkt dahinter** (6).

- Besteht die Häufigkeitsangabe aus mehreren Wörtern, z.B. *every day, now and then*, steht sie wie eine Zeitangabe am Satzende (7).
- Adverbien der Art und Weise stehen in der Regel am Satzende. Kommen noch Zeit- oder Ortsadverbien hinzu, lautet die Reihenfolge: Art und Weise – Ort – Zeit (AOZ) (8).

Relative clauses and contact clauses

1 Car manufacturers are designing cars **which/that** can use hydrogen fuel cells.
2 Wildernesses are being spoiled by tourists **who/that** want to go to 'unspoiled' places.
3 Tony filled in a Dateline questionnaire **(which/that)** he found on the Internet.
4 Fred Foley is a paparazzo **whose** photos sell for huge sums of money.
5 Call centre employees, most of **whom** come from India, work long hours.
6 Some non-GM crops are attacked by pests **against which** they have no resistance.

- Relativsätze werden benutzt, um den Hauptsatz durch zusätzliche Informationen genauer zu bestimmen.
- Für **Sachen** benutzt man das Relativpronomen *which* bzw. *that* (1) und für Personen *who* bzw. *that* (2).
- Steht das Relativpronomen für das **Objekt des Hauptsatzes**, dann kann man es weglassen (3). Solche Relativsätze heißen **contact clauses**.
- Um **Besitz** bzw. **Zugehörigkeit** anzuzeigen, gebraucht man *whose* unmittelbar vor dem **Substantiv** bei Personen und Sachen (4).
- Steht eine **Präposition** vor dem **Relativpronomen**, wird *whom* für Personen und *which* für Sachen benutzt (5, 6). In solchen Fällen ist der Gebrauch von *that* nicht möglich.

Defining and non-defining relative clauses

1 The first Europeans **who** settled in Australia came from Britain.
2 Sydney, **which** is famous for its unusually designed opera house, is situated on the south-eastern coast of Australia.

- Im **ersten Beispielsatz** ist der Sinn des Hauptsatzes *The first Europeans came from Britain* ohne den Relativsatz *who settled in Australia* offensichtlich falsch bzw. unvollständig. Relativsätze dieser Art – die wesentlich für das Verständnis des gesamten Satzes sind – nennt man **defining relative clauses** (notwendige oder bestimmende Relativsätze).
- Im **zweiten Beispielsatz** ist die Aussage des Hauptsatzes *Sydney is situated on the south-eastern coast of Australia* ohne den Relativsatz völlig verständlich, weil der Relativsatz *which is famous for its unusually designed opera house* eine zusätzliche, also nebensächliche, Information enhält. Daher werden solche Relativsätze **non-defining relative clauses** (nicht notwendige oder nicht bestimmende Relativsätze) genannt.
  ⚠ Notwendige Relativsätze werden immer **ohne** trennende **Kommas** benutzt. Dies signalisiert, dass sie fester Bestandteil der Hauptaussage sind.

Participle constructions

1 Malaria, preventable with treatment **costing** less than one pound per bed, is endemic.
2 Many men believe that any work **involved** with cooking is a woman's chore.
3 **Losing** more and more people to AIDS, Africa now needs effective help more urgently than ever before.
4 **Burdened** with declining life-expectancy, large parts of Africa are caught in a poverty trap.
5 **Having fetched** water from a river for many years, some women in developing countries are now happy to have modern systems.
6 **Despite facing** extreme destitution, many residents haven't given up hope.

7 Donors should invest in projects that help local inhabitants become self-supporting, **thereby making** sure that the money isn't wasted.

8 Poor infrastructure is a key barrier to economic growth in Nepal, **thus causing** huge additional costs to the transport of commercial goods.

9 Life is becoming hard in the developing countries, **with** many small farmers **going** out of business.

10 AIDS represents a major challenge to sub-Saharan Africa, currently **killing** more than two million people every year.

Die englische Sprache ist geprägt durch die häufige Verwendung von Partizipialkonstruktionen. Diese ermöglichen einen eleganteren Sprachfluss. Partizipialkonstruktionen verkürzen

- Relativsätze; dabei kann entweder das **present participle** (1) oder das **past participle** (2) verwendet werden.
- Adverbiale Nebensätze; in diesen Fällen unterscheidet man zwischen Partizipialkonstruktionen ohne Konjunktion (3–5) und solchen mit Konjunktion (6–9).
- In Sätzen ohne Konjunktion ist der Inhalt des Satzes auch ohne eine solche klar. Dagegen sind Konjunktionen nötig, um zu verhindern, dass der logische Zusammenhang des Satzes verloren geht. Zum Beispiel wird der Inhalt von Satz 6 unklar, wenn die Konjunktion *despite* ausgelassen wird.
- Wie bei der Verkürzung von Relativsätzen kommen auch bei der Verkürzung von adverbialen Nebensätzen das **present participle** (3, 6–9) und das **past participle** (4) zur Anwendung. Darüber hinaus wird hier auch noch das **perfect participle** verwendet (5), und zwar um die Vorzeitigkeit der Handlung im Nebensatz auszudrücken. *(Nachdem sie jahrelang Wasser aus dem Fluss geholt hatten, …)*
- Schließlich verknüpft man mit einer Partizipialkonstruktion zwei Hauptsätze zu einem einzigen Satz, und zwar ausnahmslos mittels **present participle** (10).

Countable and uncountable nouns

1 Visit our website for more **information** on our firm.   NICHT ~~informations~~

2 Have you read the paper today? The political **news** is interesting.   NICHT ~~news are~~

3 Where can I get some **advice**?   NICHT ~~an advice~~

- Einige wichtige **Substantive** sind **zählbar im Deutschen, nicht jedoch im Englischen**. Diese Substantive können also nicht ohne weiteres mit dem unbestimmten Artikel *a/an* oder mit einem Zahlwort benutzt werden.

Hier ist eine Liste solcher Wörter, die Sie auswendig lernen sollten:

advice, baggage, damage, data, equipment, evidence, furniture, garbage (Abfall), information, knowledge, luck, luggage, machinery, news, progress, research, rubbish, work (housework, homework)

- Um diese Substantive im Plural zu verwenden, muss *some, a bit of* bzw. *a piece of* hinzugefügt werden (3).

   ⚠ Auf einigen Substantiven wie *news* (s. o.), *politics, economics* folgt immer ein Verb im Singular.
   - *Economics is a popular subject.*
   - *Politics doesn't interest me.*
   Auf einigen Substantiven wie *media, police, scissors* folgt immer ein Verb im Plural.
   - *The media have a lot of influence.*
   - *The police are looking for the murderer.*
   - *The scissors need sharpening.*

UNIT WORD LIST

Dieses Wörterverzeichnis enthält alle Wörter in der Reihenfolge ihres Erscheinens (Seitenzahlen sind angegeben). Nicht aufgeführt sind Wörter, die nicht unbedingt zum aktiven Wortschatz gehören müssen. Daher eignet diese Liste hervorragend für die Vorbereitung auf die Abiturprüfung(en). Wörter aus den Hörverständnisübungen sind gelb markiert

Abkürzungen:

AE = amerikanisches Englisch	jdm = jemandem	pl = plural
BE = britisches Englisch	jdn = jemanden	sb = somebody
etw = etwas	jds = jemandes	sth = something

TOPIC 1 Young people in Britain and America

TEXT 1 What teens worry about

to **worry** ['wʌri]	to feel troubled about problems	*sich Sorgen/Gedanken machen*	**page 6**
to **compare** [kəm'peə]	to notice what is the same and what is different	*vergleichen*	
to **skim** [skɪm]	to read sth quickly to get the important points	*(Text) überfliegen*	
adolescent [ˌædə'lesnt]	a young person in his/her teenage years	*Jugendliche/r, Heranwachsende/r*	
carefree ['keəfriː]	having no troubles or responsibility	*sorglos, sorgenfrei*	
to **support sb** [sə'pɔːt]	to take care of sb	*jdn ernähren, jdn versorgen*	
adolescence [ˌædə'lesns]	puberty, teenage years	*Pubertät*	
anxious ['æŋkʃəs]	full of worries	*verunsichernd, sorgenvoll*	
demand [dɪ'mɑːnd]	sth you ask for strongly	*Anforderung*	
depressed [dɪ'prest]	(feeling) sad and hopeless	*deprimiert*	
bullying ['bʊliɪŋ]	agressive actions that hurt sb	*Mobbing*	
to **avoid sb** [ə'vɔɪd]	to stay away from sb	*jdm aus dem Weg gehen*	
strength [streŋθ]	sth you are good at doing	*Stärke*	
weakness ['wiːknəs]	sth you are not good at doing	*Schwäche*	
issue ['ɪʃuː]	a problem or difficult situation	*Problem, Streitfrage, Thema*	
independence [ˌɪndɪ'pendəns]	freedom from control	*Unabhängigkeit*	
to **break up with sb** [ˌbreɪk 'ʌp wɪð]	to end a relationship	*sich von jdm trennen*	
peer [pɪə]	sb of the same age	*Gleichaltrige/r*	**page 7**
pressure ['preʃə]	force	*Druck*	
in terms of [ɪn 'tɜːmz əv]	regarding sth	*hinsichtlich, bezüglich*	
achievement [ə'tʃiːvmənt]	a good result from hard work	*Leistung(en)*	
to **conform** [kən'fɔːm]	to do what other people do	*sich anpassen*	
influence ['ɪnfluəns]	power to change sb or sth	*Einfluss*	
expectation [ˌekspek'teɪʃn]	the idea that sth will happen	*Erwartung*	
to **live up to sth** [ˌlɪv 'ʌp tə]	to be good enough	*einer Sache gerecht werden*	
inadequate [ɪn'ædɪkwət]	not enough, or not good enough	*unzulänglich*	
dissatisfaction [ˌdɪsˌsætɪs'fækʃn]	unhappiness	*Unzufriedenheit*	
eating disorder [ˌiːtɪŋ dɪs'ɔːdə]	health problems related to sb's eating habits	*Essstörung*	
relationship [rɪ'leɪʃnʃɪp]	people or things that are connected with each other	*Beziehung, Verhältnis*	
especially [ɪ'speʃəli]	particularly	*besonders*	
concern [kən'sɜːn]	worry, trouble	*Sorge, Anliegen*	
to **deal with sth** ['diːl wɪð]	to take action	*mit etw umgehen*	
to **be dependent on sb/sth** [bi dɪ'pendənt ɒn]	to need sb/sth	*von jdm/etw abhängig sein*	
additional [ə'dɪʃənl]	extra	*zusätzlich*	
to **avoid sb/sth** [ə'vɔɪd]	to stay away from sb/sth	*jdn/etw vermeiden, meiden*	
unachievable [ʌnə'tʃiːvəbl]	impossible to do or reach	*unerreichbar*	
prefix ['priːfɪks]	letters added to the beginning of a word that change the meaning	*Vorsilbe, Präfix*	**page 8**

	suffix ['sʌfɪks]	letters added to the end of a word that change the meaning	*Nachsilbe, Suffix*
page 9	to **suffer from sth** ['sʌfə frəm]	to experience sth unpleasant	*an/unter etw leiden*
	unfortunately [ʌn'fɔːtʃənətli]	sadly, unluckily	*leider*
	abbreviation [ə,briːvi'eɪʃn]	a shortened word or phrase	*Abkürzung*
	to **concern sb** [kən'sɜːn]	to be a special theme for sb	*jdn betreffen, jdn angehen, jdn kümmern*
	to **interfere with sth** [,ɪntə'fɪə wɪð]	to have a negative effect on	*etw beeinträchtigen*
	broke [brəʊk]	having no money	*pleite*
	trouble ['trʌbl]	a difficult, unpleasant situation	*Schwierigkeiten, Ärger*
	grade [greɪd]	result at the end of school exams	*(Schul-)Note*
	to **hang out with sb** [,hæŋ 'aʊt wɪð]	to spend time with sb	*mit jdm abhängen*
	to **upset sb** [,ʌp'set]	to do sth to hurt sb or make them angry	*jdn verärgern, jdn aufregen*
	to **settle down** [,setl 'daʊn]	to stay in one place, not move on	*sesshaft werden*
page 10	**privacy** ['prɪvəsi]	freedom from attention	*Privatsphäre*
	to **be addicted to sth** [bi ə'dɪktɪd tə]	needing to have sth regularly, like a drug	*auf/nach etw süchtig sein*
	uninterrupted [,ʌn,ɪntə'rʌptɪd]	without pauses	*ununterbrochen, durchgehend*
page 11	**solution** [sə'luːʃn]	answer to a problem	*Lösung*
	impression [ɪm'preʃn]	the impact sth makes	*Eindruck*
	expenses pl [ɪk'spensɪz]	money that is spent	*Ausgaben*

TEXT 2 Education today in the USA

page 12	**education** [,edʒu'keɪʃn]	learning from a teacher or from experience	*Schulbildung, Bildung*
	public school AE [,pʌblɪk 'skuːl]	a school that anyone can attend for free in the USA	*staatliche Schule (in den USA)*
	source [sɔːs]	where sth comes from	*Quelle*
	property ['prɒpəti]	sth that a person owns, for example a house, land	*Grund und Boden, Immobilie(n), Eigentum*
	tax [tæks]	money paid to the government	*Steuer*
	value ['væljuː]	how much sth is worth	*Wert*
	to **own** [əʊn]	to possess	*besitzen*
	wealthy ['welθi]	having lots of money	*wohlhabend*
	neighbourhood ['neɪbəhʊd]	area where a person lives	*Wohnviertel, Wohngegend*
	to **be available** [bi ə'veɪləbl]	ready to be used or obtained	*zur Verfügung stehen*
	sophisticated [sə'fɪstɪkeɪtɪd]	modern and complex (technology)	*modern, technisch ausgereift*
	equipment [ɪ'kwɪpmənt]	things you need to do sth	*Ausstattung, Geräte*
	to **get on** [,get 'ɒn]	to make progress	*vorwärts kommen, weiterkommen*
	to **apply** [ə'plaɪ]	to be relevant	*gelten*
	survey ['sɜːveɪ]	asking many people questions to get information	*Umfrage, Studie, Erhebung*
	percentage [pə'sentɪdʒ]	parts of 100	*Prozentsatz, Anteil*
	to **drop** [drɒp]	to fall	*sinken, (zurück)fallen*
	to **rank** [ræŋk]	to be on a list from highest to lowest, best to worst, etc	*einen (Ranglisten-)Platz belegen*
page 13	to **be anxious to do sth** [bi 'æŋkʃəs tə]	to feel strongly that you want to do sth	*darauf erpicht sein, etw zu tun*
	to **graduate** ['grædʒueɪt]	to finish school or university	*einen Schulabschluss machen*
	majority [mə'dʒɒrəti]	more than half; most	*Mehrheit*
	access to sth ['ækses]	opportunity or right to use sth	*Zugang zu etw*
	to **attend** [ə'tend]	to go to an event, meeting, class, etc	*(Schule etc.) besuchen*
	to **excel at doing sth** [ɪk'sel ət]	to do something very well	*in etw hervorragend sein*
	to **provide** [prə'vaɪd]	to make sth available	*bieten, zur Verfügung stellen*
	victim ['vɪktɪm]	sb who is hurt by another person	*Opfer*
	evidence ['evɪdəns]	sth that shows sth is true	*Beweis(e), Nachweis(e)*
	gap [gæp]	a space	*Kluft*
	budget ['bʌdʒɪt]	money available to spend	*Etat, Budget, Haushalt*
	suburb ['sʌbɜːb]	a place near a city where people live	*Vorort, Außenbezirk*
	decent ['diːsnt]	polite, honest, good	*ordentlich*
	resource [rɪ'sɔːs]	a supply of money or materials	*Ressource, Geldmittel*
	to **let sb down** [,let 'daʊn]	to disappoint or not support sb	*jdn im Stich lassen*

skilled worker [ˌskɪld ˈwɜːkə]	sb with special skills, training, and knowledge	*Facharbeiter/in*	
equipped [ɪˈkwɪpt]	having the things you need	*ausgestattet*	
skill [skɪl]	a talent or ability	*Fähigkeit, Fertigkeit*	
suitable [ˈsuːtəbl]	correct, appropriate	*passend*	
opportunity [ˌɒpəˈtjuːnəti]	chance, possibility	*Chance, Gelegenheit*	
ranking [ˈræŋkɪŋ]	place on a list of people or things from highest to lowest, best to worst, etc	*(Ranglisten-)Platz*	
recently [ˈriːsntli]	a short time ago	*neulich, jüngst*	page 14
subscription [səbˈskrɪpʃn]	an agreeement to buy sth regularly	*Abonnement*	
job application [ˈdʒɒb æplɪkeɪʃn]	a letter to sb about getting a job	*Stellenbewerbung*	
vinegar [ˈvɪnɪɡə]	a sour, acidic liquid used for cooking and cleaning	*Essig*	
to **improve** [ɪmˈpruːv]	to become better at sth	*verbessern, steigern*	page 15
well-being [ˈwel biːɪŋ]	health and wellness	*Wohlbefinden*	
environmental [ɪnˌvaɪrənˈmentl]	about the world around us	*Umwelt-*	
leisure time [ˈleʒə taɪm]	time to relax and enjoy, with no work	*Freizeit*	
to **publish** [ˈpʌblɪʃ]	to make information available to the public	*veröffentlichen*	
assessment [əˈsesmənt]	evaluation, opinion	*Beurteilung*	
performance [pəˈfɔːməns]	how well you do a task	*Leistung, Abschneiden*	
conclusion [kənˈkluːʒn]	ending	*Schluss*	page 16

TEXT 3 Teens and sleep

school board [ˌskuːl ˈbɔːd]	a group of people who are in charge of a school	*Schulbehörde*	page 17
to **propose** [prəˈpəʊz]	to say an idea or possible plan	*vorhaben, vorschlagen*	
to **switch** [swɪtʃ]	to change	*umstellen*	
outraged [ˈaʊtreɪdʒd]	very angry	*empört*	
to **encourage** [ɪnˈkʌrɪdʒ]	to give sb support	*ermutigen*	
currently [ˈkʌrəntli]	at present	*derzeit*	
growth [ɡrəʊθ]	increase in size, number	*Wachstum*	page 18
drowsy [ˈdraʊzi]	sleepy	*schläfrig*	
schedule [ˈʃedjuːl]	timetable	*Zeitplan*	
brain [breɪn]	organ of the body inside the head	*Gehirn*	
on average [ɒn ˈævərɪdʒ]	taking account of performance over a period	*im Durchschnitt*	
confidence [ˈkɒnfɪdəns]	a feeling or belief that you can do sth	*Selbstvertrauen, Zuversicht*	
rest [rest]	being quiet, not moving	*Ruhe*	
alert [əˈlɜːt]	ready, awake and prepared	*aufmerksam*	
to **process** [ˈprəʊses]	to work through a task or problem	*verarbeiten*	
exhausted [ɪɡˈzɔːstɪd]	extremely tired	*erschöpft*	
to **boost** [buːst]	to raise, increase or improve	*heben, erhöhen*	
mood [muːd]	how you feel	*Stimmung*	
to **lower** [ˈləʊə]	to become less	*senken, reduzieren*	
anxiety [æŋˈzaɪəti]	feeling of nervousness, worry, fear	*Ängste, Angst*	
to **be likely to do sth** [bi ˈlaɪkli tə]	a high probability that sb will do sth	*etw wahrscheinlich tun (werden)*	
instead of [ɪnˈsted əv]	as a replacement	*anstatt*	
classmate [ˈklɑːsmeɪt]	sb in the same class as you at school/college	*Klassenkamerad/in*	
extract [ˈekstrækt]	sth taken from a larger whole	*Auszug, Ausschnitt*	page 19
freshman [ˈfreʃmən]	a student in the first year of college	*Student/in im ersten Studienjahr*	
to **worsen** [ˈwɜːsn]	to become worse	*sich verschlimmern*	
response [rɪˈspɒns]	answer	*Antwort*	page 20
to **stare at sth** [ˈsteər ət]	to look at sth for a long time	*auf etw starren, etw anstarren*	

TEXT 4 Is one language and enough?

effort [ˈefət]	hard work	*Mühe(n), Anstrengung(en)*	page 22
environment [ɪnˈvaɪrənmənt]	the world around us	*Umfeld*	
in addition [ɪn əˈdɪʃn]	as an extra	*außerdem*	

	influential [ˌɪnfluˈenʃl]	having power over other people and things	einflussreich
	to estimate [ˈestɪmeɪt]	to calculate roughly	schätzen
	population [ˌpɒpjuˈleɪʃn]	number of people in a city, country, etc	Bevölkerung
	native speaker [ˌneɪtɪv ˈspiːkə]	sb who speaks a language as a first language, not a foreign language	Muttersprachler/in
page 23	trade [treɪd]	buying and selling	Handel
	inspector [ɪnˈspektə]	sb who observes and examines	Prüfer/in
	primary school [ˈpraɪməri skuːl]	the school children attend when they are 5 - 11 years old	Grundschule
	to improve [ɪmˈpruːv]	to become better at sth	sich bessern, besser werden
	challenge [ˈtʃælɪndʒ]	sth that is difficult to do	(schwere) Aufgabe, Herausforderung
	bilingual [ˌbaɪˈlɪŋgwəl]	speaking two languages perfectly	zweisprachig
	local authority [ˌləʊkl ɔːˈθɒrəti]	government of a small area, for example a town or city	Kommunalbehörde
	to struggle [ˈstrʌgl]	to have great difficulty with	sich schwer tun
	absent [ˈæbsənt]	not present	abwesend
	unique [juˈniːk]	very special or unusual	einzigartig
	arrangement [əˈreɪndʒmənt]	way things are organized	Regelung
	whereby [weəˈbaɪ]	by which	wonach
	head teacher [ˌhed ˈtiːtʃə]	the director of a school	Schuldirektor/in
	diversity [daɪˈvɜːsəti]	variety	Vielfalt
	predominantly [prɪˈdɒmɪnəntli]	in the greatest number	überwiegend
	responsibility [rɪˌspɒnsəˈbɪləti]	sth that is your job or duty to deal with	Verantwortung, Zuständigkeit
	to ensure [ɪnˈʃʊə]	to make certain	gewährleisten, dafür sorgen, dass
	multilingual [ˌmʌltiˈlɪŋgwəl]	speaking several languages	mehrsprachig
	to tend to do sth [ˈtend tə]	to do sth habitually	dazu neigen, etw zu tun
page 24	measure [ˈmeʒə]	action taken to achieve sth	Maßnahme
	background [ˈbækgraʊnd]	origins	Hintergrund, Herkunft
	My goodness. [ˌmaɪ ˈgʊdnəs]	what you say when you are surprised	Du meine Güte!
	to exchange [ɪksˈtʃeɪndʒ]	to give sth and get sth in return	austauschen
	partly [ˈpɑːtli]	not all	teilweise
	dishonest [dɪsˈɒnɪst]	not honest	unaufrichtig, unehrlich
	lack [læk]	not having enough of sth	Mangel, Fehlen
	disrespectful [ˌdɪsrɪˈspektfl]	not polite	respektlos
	independent [ˌɪndɪˈpendənt]	not controlled by sb/sth	unabhängig
	to be used to doing sth [bi ˈjuːst tə]	to be accustomed to doing sth	gewohnt sein, etw zu tun
	to consider sth [kənˈsɪdə]	to take sth into account	etw berücksichtigen
	cheating [ˈtʃiːtɪŋ]	getting the answers to a test/exam dishonestly	(Schule:) Pfuschen, Abgucken
	reward [rɪˈwɔːd]	sth received for good work	Lohn, Gewinn
	progress [ˈprəʊgres]	movement forward, toward sth better	Fortschritt(e)
	to accuse sb of sth [əˈkjuːz əv]	to say that sb did sth wrong, illegal or unkind	jdn einer Sache beschuldigen
	to cheat [tʃiːt]	to get the answers to a test/exam dishonestly	schummeln, betrügen
	countable [ˈkaʊntəbl]	it is possible to state the exact number	zählbar
	pronunciation [prəˌnʌnsiˈeɪʃn]	the way a word is spoken	Aussprache
	context [ˈkɒntekst]	situation in which sth occurs	Zusammenhang, Kontext
page 25	to increase sth [ɪnˈkriːs]	to make something bigger	etw steigern, etw erhöhen
	to memorize [ˈmeməraɪz]	to learn sth so you remember it exactly	auswendig lernen
	to enrich [ɪnˈrɪtʃ]	to make sth better, nicer	bereichern
	variety [vəˈraɪəti]	diversity	Vielfalt, Abwechslung
	to promote [prəˈməʊt]	to encourage, support	fördern
page 26	currency [ˈkʌrənsi]	the money system a country uses	Währung

TEXT 5 Child labour

page 27	labour [ˈleɪbə]	work	Arbeit
	to refer to sth [rɪˈfɜː tə]	to mention sth	sich auf etw beziehen
	to deprive sb of sth [dɪˈpraɪv əv]	to take sth away from sb	jdm etw entziehen, jdm etw vorenthalten
	to oblige sb to do sth [əˈblaɪdʒ]	to make sb do sth	jdn zwingen, etw zu tun

to **be exposed to sth** [bi ɪkˈspəʊzd tə]	to be put into a situation that might be harmful	*einer Sache ausgesetzt sein*	
hazard [ˈhæzəd]	danger	*Gefahr*	
condition [kənˈdɪʃn]	circumstances	*Bedingung, Umstand*	
misery [ˈmɪzəri]	suffering, great discomfort	*Elend*	page 28
to **loosen** [ˈluːsn]	to make sth less strict	*lockern*	
restriction [rɪˈstrɪkʃn]	sth that limits or controls	*Einschränkung*	
minor [ˈmaɪnə]	sb under the age of 18	*Minderjährige/r*	
law [lɔː]	an official rule	*Gesetz, Recht*	
to **impose** [ɪmˈpəʊz]	to put into force	*(Regelung usw.) verhängen, anordnen*	
complaint [kəmˈpleɪnt]	saying you are unhappy with sth	*Beschwerde, Klage*	
strict [strɪkt]	following rules	*streng*	
modest [ˈmɒdɪst]	not expensive, not large	*bescheiden*	
inspection [ɪnˈspekʃn]	looking at sth closely	*Kontrolle, Prüfung*	
to **protect (sb from sth)** [prəˈtekt]	to keep sb safe from sth	*(jdn vor etw) schützen*	
to **exploit** [ɪkˈsplɔɪt]	to treat unfairly	*ausbeuten*	
demand (for sth) [dɪˈmɑːnd]	request, call for sth	*Forderung (nach etw)*	
shift work [ˈʃɪft wɜːk]	to work in time periods through the day or night	*Schichtarbeit*	
to **get away with sth** [ˌget əˈweɪ wɪð]	to do sth bad without being caught or punished	*mit etw davonkommen*	
minimum wage [ˌmɪnɪməm ˈweɪdʒ]	the smallest amount workers must be paid	*Mindestlohn*	
to **afford to do sth** [əˈfɔːd]	to have enough money to do sth	*sich es leisten können, etw zu tun*	
manageable [ˈmanɪdʒəbl]	can be controlled	*beherrschbar, kontrollierbar*	
labor union AE [ˈleɪbə juːniən]	a group that protects the rights of workers	*Gewerkschaft*	
to **claim sth** [kleɪm]	to say sth is true	*behaupten*	
dropout [ˈdrɒpaʊt]	sb who leaves school before graduation	*Schulabbrecher/in*	
aim [eɪm]	target, purpose	*Ziel*	
compound noun [ˌkɒmpaʊnd ˈnaʊn]	two nouns joined together to make one new word	*zusammengesetztes Substantiv, Kompositum*	page 29
hardship [ˈhɑːdʃɪp]	sth difficult or unpleasant you must go through	*Not, Entbehrung(en)*	
flexi-time [ˈfleksitaɪm]	being able to start and finish work when you want	*Gleitzeit*	
senior citizen [ˌsiːniə ˈsɪtɪzn]	a person older than 65	*Senior/in*	
wage [weɪdʒ]	money you get for work, paid by the hour, day, or week	*Lohn*	
underage [ˌʌndərˈeɪdʒ]	younger than 18	*minderjährig*	
to **persuade sb** [pəˈsweɪd]	to make sb do or believe sth	*überzeugen, überreden*	page 30
task [tɑːsk]	a piece of work	*Aufgabe*	

TEXT 6 The boomerang generation

to **found** [faʊnd]	to start sth, e.g. a business	*gründen*	
benefit [ˈbenɪfɪt]	advantage	*Vorteil*	page 31
downside [ˈdaʊnsaɪd]	disadvantage	*Nachteil*	
to **treat sb** [triːt]	to act towards sb in a particular way	*behandeln*	
to **swap sth** [swɒp]	to give sth and get sth in return	*tauschen*	
stage [steɪdʒ]	a platform, usually in a theatre	*Bühne*	
indefinitely [ɪnˈdefɪnətli]	without a time limit	*auf unbestimmte Zeit*	
support [səˈpɔːt]	help or encouragement	*Unterstützung*	
labor market AE [ˈleɪbə mɑːkɪt]	interaction between employers and employees	*Arbeitsmarkt*	
cost of living [ˌkɒst əv ˈlɪvɪŋ]	amount of money needed to pay for food, clothes, rent, etc	*Lebenshaltungskosten*	
significant [sɪgˈnɪfɪkənt]	relatively high	*erheblich*	
debt [det]	money sb owes	*Schulden*	
attitude [ˈætɪtjuːd]	feeling or opinion about sb/sth	*Ansicht, Einstellung*	
unemployment [ˌʌnɪmˈplɔɪmənt]	not having a job	*Arbeitslosigkeit*	
vacant [ˈveɪkənt]	empty, open	*(Stelle:) offen*	

page 32	blame [bleɪm]	saying or thinking sb is responsible for sth bad that has happened	Schuld
	willingness ['wɪlɪŋnəs]	being prepared and ready	Bereitschaft
	location [ləʊ'keɪʃn]	place	Ort, Standort
	to succeed [sək'siːd]	to do what you are trying to do with the result you want	erfolgreich sein, Erfolg haben
	to fail [feɪl]	opposite of succeed	scheitern
	to fund [fʌnd]	to provide money for a project	finanzieren
	to be in charge [bi ɪn 'tʃɑːdʒ]	to be the boss	für etw zuständig/verantwortlich sein
	resourceful [rɪ'sɔːsfl]	able to deal with difficult situations and problems	findig, einfallsreich
	sacrifice ['sækrɪfaɪs]	giving up sth important to help sb else	Opfer
	impact ['ɪmpækt]	the way sth affects sth else	Auswirkung(en)
	considerably [kən'sɪdərəbli]	to a large extent/degree	beträchtlich
	previous ['priːviəs]	before sth else in time	vorig, früher
	to maintain [meɪn'teɪn]	support financially	(finanziell) unterhalten
	grad(uate) ['grædʒuət]	sb who has finished university	Hochschulabsolvent/in
	gently ['dʒentli]	softly, not hard	sanft
page 33	salary ['sæləri]	money you get for doing your job, paid every month	Gehalt
	promotion [prə'məʊʃn]	moving to a higher or more important position	Beförderung
	challenging ['tʃælɪndʒɪŋ]	difficult in an interesting way	anspruchsvoll, reizvoll
	undemanding [ʌndɪ'mɑːndɪŋ]	not needing much thought or hard work	anspruchslos
	annual leave [ˌænjuəl 'liːv]	days of paid holiday given to workers every year	Jahresurlaub
	self-employed [ˌself ɪm'plɔɪd]	working independently, not for a company	selbstständig
page 34	gradual ['grædʒuəl]	slow, bit by bit	allmählich, langsam
	sharp [ʃɑːp]	sudden, steep	steil, stark
	slight [slaɪt]	very small	leicht, schwach
page 35	stepmother ['stepmʌðə]	a woman married to sb's father, but not their biological mother	Stiefmutter
	stepfather ['stepfɑːðə]	a man married to sb's mother, but not their biological father	Stiefvater
	stepchild ['steptʃaɪld]	a child of sb's partner from a previous marriage	Stiefkind
	nuclear family [ˌnjuːkliə 'fæməli]	a family made up of two parents and one or more children	Kernfamilie
	roof [ruːf]	top or cover of a building	Dach
	noisy ['nɔɪzi]	loud	laut, lärmend
	to bug [bʌg]	to annoy sb	nerven
	to mess about with [ˌmes ə'baʊt]	to handle sth without permission	herumfummeln
	major ['meɪdʒə]	big, important	groß, größer
	impressive [ɪm'presɪv]	awesome	beeindruckend

TOPIC 2   Cities and regions in the UK and the US

TEXT 1   Northumberland and the Borderlands

page 36	fate [feɪt]	forces outside your control that make things happen	Schicksal
	valley ['væli]	area of land between hills or mountains	Tal
	to grieve [griːv]	to feel sad and unhappy after a death or loss	trauern
	to gamble on sth ['gæmbl ɒn]	to risk losing money in a game of chance	auf etw wetten, auf etw setzen
page 38	county ['kaʊnti]	a political division within a country	Grafschaft
	invader [ɪn'veɪdə]	sb who enters a country by force	Endringling, Invasor
	incredible [ɪn'kredəbl]	difficult or impossible to believe	unglaublich
	site [saɪt]	place where sth is or was situated	Stätte
	collapse [kə'læps]	breaking apart	Zusammenbruch, Zerfall
	enrichment [ɪn'rɪtʃmnt]	improvement in the quality of sth	Bereicherung

decade ['dekeɪd]	10 years	*Jahrzehnt*	
monastery ['mɒnəstri]	a religious house where monks live and work together	*Kloster*	
treasure ['treʒə]	sth valuable	*Schatz*	
to conquer ['kɒŋkə]	to take control of (a country)	*erobern*	
inaccurately [ɪn'ækjərətli]	not correctly	*ungenau*	
to portray [pɔː'treɪ]	to show in a book, film, painting	*darstellen, porträtieren*	
to commit [kə'mɪt]	to do (crime, etc)	*(Tat usw.) begehen*	
arson ['ɑːsn]	crime of starting a fire	*Brandstiftung*	
aristocratic [ˌærɪstə'krætɪk]	from a family with a high social rank	*adlig*	
average ['ævərɪdʒ]	what is usual most of the time	*Durchschnitt, durchschnittlich*	
destination [ˌdestɪ'neɪʃn]	place planned for the end of a journey	*Reiseziel*	**page 39**
portrayal [pɔː'treɪəl]	the way sth is shown in a book, film, painting	*Darstellung, Porträt*	

TEXT 2 Northern Ireland's peace walls

violent ['vaɪələnt]	using force to hurt others	*gewalttätig*	**page 41**
civil rights pl [ˌsɪvl 'raɪts]	rights of people to freedom and equality	*Bürgerrechte*	
violence ['vaɪələns]	the use of physical force to hurt sb/sth	*Gewalt*	
minority [maɪ'nɒrəti]	a smaller number of sth; less than half	*Minderheit*	
occupation [ˌɒkju'peɪʃn]	living in or having possession of sth e.g. a building or country	*Besetzung*	
unification [ˌjuːnɪfɪ'keɪʃn]	bringing things or people together	*Vereinigung*	
withdrawal [wɪð'drɔːəl]	removal	*Rückzug*	
to restore [rɪ'stɔː]	to return sth/sb to an earlier state	*wiederherstellen*	
urban ['ɜːbən]	in a town or city	*städtisch, Stadt-*	**page 42**
to divide [dɪ'vaɪd]	cut into parts	*teilen*	
reconciliation [ˌrekənˌsɪli'eɪʃn]	when enemies agree to be friends	*Versöhnung*	
safety ['seɪfti]	freedom from danger	*Sicherheit*	
to prevent sb from doing sth [prɪ'vent frəm]	to stop sb doing sth	*jdn daran hindern, etw zu tun*	
community [kə'mjuːnəti]	a group of people with a common interest	*Gemeinde*	
limited ['lɪmɪtɪd]	restricted,	*beschränkt*	
to restrict [rɪ'strɪkt]	to set limits	*begrenzen, beschränken*	
agreement [ə'griːmənt]	a decision reached by both sides	*Vereinbarung, Abkommen*	
reshaping [ˌriː'ʃeɪpɪŋ]	organizing sth in a new way	*Umgestaltung, Neugestaltung*	
to release [rɪ'liːs]	to let go	*freilassen*	
sustainability [səˌsteɪnə'bɪləti]	ability to continue over a long time period	*Nachhaltigkeit*	
safe [seɪf]	free from danger	*sicher*	
secure [sɪ'kjʊə]	protected	*sicher, gesichert*	
common ['kɒmən]	usual, often	*häufig*	
city council ['sɪti kaʊnsl]	people who manage a city/local government	*Stadtrat, Stadtverwaltung*	**page 43**
large-scale ['lɑːdʒskeɪl]	done in a big or grand way	*in großem Umfang*	
to prevent [prɪ'vent]	to stop sth	*verhindern*	
process ['prəʊses]	a way of working through a problem or task	*Vorgang*	
event [ɪ'vent]	sth that happens, usually sth special	*Ereignis*	
suspicion [sə'spɪʃn]	the feeling that sb is guilty of doing sth wrong	*Misstrauen, Argwohn*	**page 44**
target ['tɑːgɪt]	goal, what you want to achieve	*Ziel*	
to be scared of sb [bi 'skeəd əv]	to fear sb	*vor jdm Angst haben*	
tension ['tenʃn]	feeling of nervousness	*Spannung(en)*	
slight [slaɪt]	very small	*gering, klein*	
horror ['hɒrə]	fear, shock, disgust	*Schrecken*	

TEXT 3 Living in a bankrupt city

| fuel ['fjuːəl] | sth to burn to get heat or power | *Brennstoff, Kraftstoff* | **page 46** |

173

	to **be in demand** [dɪˈmɑːnd]	a lot of people want it	Nachfrage
	poverty line [ˈpɒvəti laɪn]	minimum income level	Armutsgrenze
	racial [ˈreɪʃl]	grouping people by race	Rassen-
	resident [ˈrezɪdənt]	sb who lives in a place	Einwohner/in, Anwohner/in
	injured [ˈɪndʒəd]	hurt	verletzt
	to **be considered to be** [bi kənˈsɪdəd]	to be thought to be	als etw gelten
	to **peak** [piːk]	to reach the highest point	den Höchststand erreichen
	to **decline** [dɪˈklaɪn]	to decrease, go down	sinken, schwinden
	benefits pl [ˈbenɪfɪts]	money paid by the government for pensions, health, unemployment, etc	(Zusatz-)Leistungen
	to **abandon sth** [əˈbændən]	to leave sth and never return to it	etw verlassen, etw aufgeben
	to **target sth** [ˈtɑːgɪt]	to aim at	auf etw abzielen, sich an etw richten
page 47	**off the top of your head** [ɒf ðə ˌtɒp əv jɔː ˈhed]	without thinking much	aus dem Stegreif
	sigh [saɪ]	to breathe out slowly and loudly	Seufzer
	patience [ˈpeɪʃns]	ability to wait or tolerate	Geduld
	downtown [ˈdaʊntaʊn]	centre of a city	Innenstadt
	owner [ˈəʊnə]	person who owns or possesses sth	Besitzer/in
	mortgage [ˈmɔːgɪdʒ]	money you pay to buy a house	Hypothek
	to **revolve around sth** [rɪˈvɒlv əraʊnd]	to move around a central point	sich um etw drehen
	reluctantly [rɪˈlʌktəntli]	unwillingly	widerwillig
	to **tear down** [ˌteə ˈdaʊn]	to destroy (a building)	abreißen
	to **keep my wits about me** [ˌkiːp maɪ ˌwɪts əˈbaʊt miː]	to think and be rational in a certain situation	meine fünf Sinne beisammen halten
	to **associate with sb** [əˈsəʊʃieɪt wɪð]	to spend time in sb's company	mit jdm Umgang haben
	race relations pl [ˌreɪs rɪˈleɪʃnz]	relationship between different ethnic groups	Beziehungen zwischen ethnischen Gruppen
page 48	to **get sth together** [ˌget təˈgeðə]	to get organized	mit etw die Kurve kriegen
	guess [ges]	opinion or judgement	Mutmaßung
	neglected [nɪˈglektɪd]	without enough care or attention	vernachlässigt
	heritage [ˈherɪtɪdʒ]	culture and traditions of a country	Kulturerbe
page 50	**sound** [saʊnd]	character of the music	Klang
	record label [ˈrekɔːd leɪbl]	a company that makes and sells music	Plattenfirma
	regardless of [rɪˈgɑːdləs]	without thinking or caring about	ungeachtet
	venue [ˈvenjuː]	where sth takes place, e.g. concert, conference	Veranstaltungsort
	contribution [ˌkɒntrɪˈbjuːʃn]	sth given, e.g. money, help, advice	Beitrag
	competition [ˌkɒmpəˈtɪʃn]	contest in which people compete	Wettbewerb
page 51	to **smash** [smæʃ]	to break sth into pieces	kaputt schlagen
	grocery store [ˈgrəʊsəri stɔː]	shop that sells food and drinks	Lebensmittelladen
	disappointment [ˌdɪsəˈpɔɪntmənt]	feeling of unhappiness when sth doesn't happen	Enttäuschung
	ugly [ˈʌgli]	opposite of beautiful	hässlich
	rowdy [ˈraʊdi]	noisy, maybe violent	rauflustig
	sidewalk AE [ˈsaɪdwɔːk]	path at the side of a road for pedestrians	Bürgersteig
	gasoline AE [ˈgæsəliːn]	fuel for cars (USA)	Benzin
	to **pour** [pɔː]	to let a liquid flow	gießen, schütten
	urgent [ˈɜːdʒənt]	very important and immediate	dringend
	joy [dʒɔɪ]	happiness	Freude
	touched [tʌtʃt]	feeling emotional	berührt
	petrol BE [ˈpetrəl]	fuel for cars (UK)	Benzin
page 52	**belongings** pl [bɪˈlɒŋɪŋz]	things that are yours	Habseligkeiten

TEXT 4 London's East End

page 53	to **cope** [kəʊp]	to deal with a situation	zurechtkommen
	tap [tæp]	device that controls the flow of water	Wasserhahn
	rags pl [rægz]	old, worn out clothes	Lumpen
	wits pl [wɪts]	understanding, intelligence	Verstand
	district [ˈdɪstrɪkt]	an area	Bezirk
	docklands pl [ˈdɒkləndz]	place for boats to be loaded and unloaded	Hafenviertel

to **force** [fɔːs]	to compel	*zwingen*	
smelly ['smeli]	stinky	*stinkend, übelriechend*	
reputation [ˌrepjuˈteɪʃn]	the opinion people have about sb/sth	*Ruf*	
notorious [nəʊˈtɔːriəs]	famous for sth bad	*berüchtigt*	
derelict ['derəlɪkt]	empty, no longer cared for	*leer stehend, verlassen*	page 54
to **gain** [geɪn]	to get sth you want	*gewinnen*	page 55
decline [dɪˈklaɪn]	worsening condition	*Verfall*	
affluence ['æfluəns]	having lots of money and a high standard of living	*Wohlstand*	
desirable [dɪˈzaɪərəbl]	worth having	*begehrt*	
to **compete** [kəmˈpiːt]	to try to win sth by defeating others	*konkurrieren*	
venue ['venjuː]	a place where people meet	*Lokal*	
smart [smɑːt]	elegant, chic	*schick*	
sophisticated [səˈfɪstɪkeɪtɪd]	complex, fine	*raffiniert, komplex*	
branch [brɑːntʃ]	a part of a larger organization	*Zweig*	page 57
public transport [ˌpʌblɪk ˈtrænspɔːt]	buses, trains, trams	*öffentliche Verkehrsmittel*	

TOPIC 3 The media today

TEXT 1 Have I got talent?

ambition [æmˈbɪʃn]	a strong wish to get money, power, fame, success, etc	*Ehrgeiz, (ehrgeiziger) Wunsch*	page 58
lyrics pl ['lɪrɪks]	the words of a song	*Liedtext*	page 59
royalty ['rɔɪəlti]	king, queen, prince, princess, etc	*Mitglied(er) des Königshauses*	
entrepreneur [ˌɒntrəprəˈnɜː]	person who runs his/her own business	*Unternehmer/in*	
chef [ʃef]	professional cook	*Koch/Köchin, Küchenchef/in*	
vet [vet]	doctor for animals	*Tierarzt/-ärztin*	
beautician [ˌbjuːˈtɪʃn]	sb who works in a salon for cosmetics, manicures, etc	*Kosmetiker/in*	
to **pool** [puːl]	to collect sth to share	*zusammentragen, sammeln*	page 60
preferably ['prefərəbli]	ideally	*möglichst, am liebsten*	
widespread ['waɪdspred]	common	*weit verbreitet*	
ban [bæn]	sth that is forbidden	*Verbot*	
welfare ['welfeə]	being happy and healthy	*Wohlergehen*	
revised [rɪˈvaɪzd]	changed, updated	*überarbeitet, revidiert*	
contestant [kənˈtestənt]	sb who takes part in a competition	*Teilnehmer/in (an einem Wettbewerb)*	
to **accompany** [əˈkʌmpəni]	to go with sb	*begleiten*	
vulnerable ['vʌlnərəbl]	easily hurt	*verletzlich, wehrlos*	
misleading [ˌmɪsˈliːdɪŋ]	giving wrong ideas	*irreführend*	
participant [pɑːˈtɪsɪpənt]	sb who takes part in sth	*Teilnehmer/in*	page 61
shallow ['ʃæləʊ]	without depth, superficial	*oberflächlich*	
to **achieve** [əˈtʃiːv]	to reach with effort	*erlangen, erzielen*	
to **accuse sb of sth** [əˈkjuːz əv]	to say that sb did sth wrong	*jdm etw vorwerfen*	
furthermore [ˌfɜːðəˈmɔː]	in addition	*außerdem, darüber hinaus*	page 62
opposing [əˈpəʊzɪŋ]	contrary, opposite	*konträr, widerstreitend*	page 63
view [vjuː]	opinion	*Ansicht, Meinung*	
nervous breakdown [ˌnɜːvəs ˈbreɪkdaʊn]	an emotional disorder from too much stress	*Nervenzusammenbruch*	
ordeal [ɔːˈdiːəl]	a very difficult or painful experience	*Zerreißprobe*	
let alone ['let əˈləʊn]	never mind, not to mention	*geschweige denn*	
struggle ['strʌgl]	sth that takes a lot of effort	*Kampf*	
favour ['feɪvə]	an act of kindness	*Gefallen*	
to **materialize** [məˈtɪəriəlaɪz]	to become real	*in Erfüllung gehen*	
to **let sb down** [ˌlet ˈdaʊn]	to disappoint sb	*jdn enttäuschen*	
rejection [rɪˈdʒekʃn]	opposite of 'acceptance'	*Zurückweisung, Ablehnung*	
pushy ['pʊʃi]	aggressive, ambitious	*aggressiv, aufdringlich*	
limelight ['laɪmlaɪt]	focus of attention	*Rampenlicht*	
intriguing [ɪnˈtriːgɪŋ]	fascinating, interesting	*faszinierend, interessant*	
on the whole [ɒn ðə ˈhəʊl]	considering everything	*im Großen und Ganzen*	

TEXT 2 Life as a celebrity

page 64	**divorce** [dɪˈvɔːs]	legal ending of a marriage	*Scheidung*
	embarrassing [ɪmˈbærəsɪŋ]	making sb feel embarrassed, ashamed	*peinlich*
	rumour [ˈruːmə]	information passed around that might not be true	*Gerücht*
page 65	**gap year** [ˈɡæp jɪə]	year between school and university (often spent travelling or working)	*Jahr zwischen Schulabschluss und Studienbeginn*
	fuss [fʌs]	unnecessary excitement	*großes Aufsehen*
	to **trust** [trʌst]	to believe in the truth or ability of sb/sth	*vertrauen*
	to **invent** [ɪnˈvent]	to make sth that has never been made before	*erfinden*
	serviceman [ˈsɜːvɪsmən]	a man who serves in the armed forces	*Soldat*
	servicewoman [ˈsɜːvɪswʊmən]	a woman who serves in the armed forces	*Soldatin*
	armed forces pl [ˌɑːmd ˈfɔːsɪz]	the army/navy/airforce	*Streitkräfte*
	disadvantaged [ˌdɪsədˈvɑːntɪdʒd]	sb who doesn't have the things you need for a normal life	*benachteiligt*
	to **inherit** [ɪnˈherɪt]	to get money or things from sb when they die	*erben*
	ordinary [ˈɔːdnri]	normal, usual, everyday	*normal, gewöhnlich*
	to **praise** [preɪz]	to say or write good things about sb/sth	*loben*
page 66	**surname** [ˈsɜːneɪm]	last name; family name	*Nachname*
	supporter [səˈpɔːtə]	sb who wants success for a person/team/organization	*Anhänger/in, Befürworter/in*
page 67	**pay rise** [ˈpeɪ raɪz]	increase in wage or salary	*Gehaltserhöhung*
page 68	to **constitute sth** [ˈkɒnstɪtjuːt]	to make up or form sth	*etw ausmachen, etw bilden*
	device [dɪˈvaɪs]	a thing made for a special use	*Gerät*
	range [reɪndʒ]	variety	*Umfang, Spektrum*
	hesitation [ˌhezɪˈteɪʃn]	pausing, stumbling	*Zögern*

TEXT 3 Celebrities and their charities

page 70	to **mention** [ˈmenʃn]	to speak or write about briefly	*erwähnen, nennen*
	to **benefit** [ˈbenɪfɪt]	to gain advantage	*profitieren*
	rarely [ˈreəli]	seldom	*selten*
	aid agency [ˈeɪd eɪdʒənsi]	an organization that gives help to people who need it	*Hilfsorganisation*
	cause [kɔːz]	a movement, idea, principle	*Sache, Anliegen*
	according to [əˈkɔːdɪŋ tə]	as stated by	*laut, gemäß, zufolge*
	NGO = non-governmental organization	a group or organization, without state ties	*regierungsunabhängige Organisation*
	involvement [ɪnˈvɒlvmənt]	being actively part of sth	*Beteiligung, Engagement*
	cynical [ˈsɪnɪkl]	not trusting ideas or motives	*zynisch*
	to **support** [səˈpɔːt]	to help or encourage	*unterstützen*
	connection [kəˈnekʃn]	a link or relationship	*Verbindung, Beziehung*
page 71	to **admit** [ədˈmɪt]	to say (unwillingly) that sth is true	*zugeben, eingestehen*
	donation [dəʊˈneɪʃn]	money or things given to help other people	*Spende*
	to **donate** [dəʊˈneɪt]	to give money or things to help other people	*spenden*
page 72	to **change one's mind** [ˌtʃeɪndʒ wʌnz ˈmaɪnd]	to make a new decision or have a new opinion	*seine Meinung ändern*
	to **paraphrase** [ˈpærəfreɪz]	to say sth in a different way	*umschreiben*
	brand [brænd]	a particular make of goods	*Marke*
	word of mouth [ˌwɜːd əv ˈmaʊθ]	information passed on by speaking	*Mundpropaganda*
	launch [lɔːntʃ]	putting a new product on the market	*Markteinführung, Start*
page 73	**stray** [streɪ]	having no home or owner	*streunend, herrenlos*
	vocational training [vəʊˌkeɪʃənl ˈtreɪnɪŋ]	learning to do a job	*Berufsausbildung*
	to **establish** [ɪˈstæblɪʃ]	to start sth, e.g. a business	*gründen, aufbauen*
	orphan [ˈɔːfn]	a child with no parents	*Waise, Waisenkind*

earthquake [ˈɜːθkweɪk]	vibrations caused by movement of the Earth's crust	*Erdbeben*	
to **launch** [lɔːntʃ]	to introduce a new product	*starten, (Produkt) einführen, vorstellen*	**page 74**
profit [ˈprɒfɪt]	the money you have when income is higher than costs	*Gewinn*	
in need [ɪn ˈniːd]	not having the things that are necessary for life	*in Not*	
to **impress** [ɪmˈpres]	to make sb feel admiration and respect	*beeindrucken*	
organic [ɔːˈɡænɪk]	produced naturally, without chemicals	*Bio-*	
fulfilment [fʊlˈfɪlmənt]	carrying out, completion, realization	*Erfüllung, Einlösung (eines Versprechens)*	
on behalf of sb [ɒn bɪˈhɑːf əv]	for sb	*für jdn*	
developing country [dɪˌveləpɪŋ ˈkʌntri]	a poor country that wants to become economically more advanced	*Entwicklungsland*	

TEXT 4 It's a digital world

alien [ˈeɪliən]	strange, foreign	*fremd*	**page 75**
slave [sleɪv]	sb who is owned by and forced to work for another person	*Sklave/Sklavin*	
to **glance at sth** [ˈɡlɑːns ət]	to look at sth quickly	*einen (schnellen) Blick auf etw werfen*	
addictive behaviour [əˌdɪktɪv bɪˈheɪvjə]	doing something harmful again and again	*Suchtverhalten*	
to **imagine** [ɪˈmædʒɪn]	to form a picture in your mind	*sich (etw) vorstellen*	
reckless [ˈrekləs]	not thinking or caring about the consequences	*leichtsinnig, unbesonnen*	
reliance on sth [rɪˈlaɪəns ɒn]	dependence on sth	*Abhängigkeit von etw, Angewiesensein auf etw*	
scary [ˈskeəri]	shocking, frightening	*beängstigend*	**page 76**
distracted [dɪˈstræktɪd]	unable to pay attention	*abgelenkt*	
human [ˈhjuːmən]	the nature of people	*menschlich*	
persuasive [pəˈsweɪsɪv]	able to make sb think or believe sth	*überzeugend*	
to **comprise** [kəmˈpraɪz]	to include, cover	*umfassen*	
convenient [kənˈviːniənt]	practical	*praktisch, bequem*	**page 77**
possessions pl [pəˈzeʃnz]	things you own	*Besitz(tümer), Hab und Gut*	**page 78**
to **confess** [kənˈfes]	to say that you did sth wrong or illegal	*gestehen*	
superfluous [suːˈpɜːfluəs]	no longer needed or wanted	*überflüssig*	
signature [ˈsɪɡnətʃə]	sb's name written in his/her handwriting	*Unterschrift*	**page 79**
inequality [ɪnɪˈkwɒləti]	the state of not being equal	*Ungleichheit, Unterschied(e)*	**page 80**
to **bridge** [brɪdʒ]	to make a connection between things	*überbrücken, (Kluft) überwinden*	
essential [ɪˈsenʃl]	absolutely necessary	*unentbehrlich, notwendig*	

TEXT 5 Time for a digital detox

anxious [ˈæŋkʃəs]	afraid, nervous	*besorgt, ängstlich*	**page 81**
recent [ˈriːsnt]	not long ago	*aktuell, aus jüngster Zeit*	
frequent [ˈfriːkwənt]	often happening	*häufig*	
screen [skriːn]	flat surface on a TV, phone or computer for viewing	*Bildschirm, Display*	
to **enrol in sth** [ɪnˈrəʊl ɪn]	to register	*sich für etw anmelden*	
reluctance [rɪˈlʌktəns]	unwillingness	*Widerwillen*	**page 82**
to **lose track of time** [luːz ˌtræk əv ˈtaɪm]	have no idea what time it is	*das Zeitgefühl verlieren*	
to **complain** [kəmˈpleɪn]	to say you are not happy about sth	*sich beklagen, sich beschweren*	
to **neglect** [nɪˈɡlekt]	to not care or pay attention to sb/sth	*vernachlässigen*	
session [ˈseʃn]	a period of time for an activity	*Sitzung*	
to **disturb** [dɪˈstɜːb]	to interrupt, bother	*stören*	
occasional [əˈkeɪʒənl]	not very often	*gelegentlich*	
urgently [ˈɜːdʒəntli]	very important and immediate	*dringend*	
economics [ˌiːkəˈnɒmɪks]	the study of economic principles	*Wirtschaftswissenschaft(en)*	**page 84**
obviously [ˈɒbviəsli]	clearly	*natürlich, offensichtlich*	
initial [ɪˈnɪʃl]	first	*erste/r/s, anfänglich*	
to **fiddle** [ˈfɪdl]	to play around with	*herumspielen*	

distraction [dɪ'strækʃn]	sth that makes it difficult to think or pay attention	Ablenkung
knitting ['nɪtɪŋ]	using wool and two needles to make clothing	Stricken
pattern ['pætn]	instruction you follow to make sth	Muster
for real [fə 'rɪəl]	true, a fact	wirklich, tatsächlich
to flick through ['flɪk θruː]	to look quickly through a book or magazine	durchblättern
time-consuming ['taɪmkənsjuːmɪŋ]	taking up a lot of time to do	zeitraubend
reliable [rɪ'laɪəbl]	dependable	zuverlässig
to subscribe to sth [səb'skraɪb tə]	to pay for sth you get regularly e.g. newspaper, app	etw abonnieren

TEXT 6 Television then and now

page 86	social ['səʊʃl]	part of a group or society	gesellig, sozial
	on demand [ɒn dɪ'mɑːnd]	available when you want it	auf Abruf, auf Nachfrage
	anti-social [ˌæntɪ'səʊʃl]	avoiding the company of others	ungesellig, unsozial
page 87	to waste [weɪst]	to use without a meaningful result	verschwenden
	habit ['hæbɪt]	sth you do every day	Gewohnheit
	to rule sth out [ˌruːl 'aʊt]	to exclude (the possibility of) sth	etw ausschließen
page 89	invention [ɪn'venʃn]	sth that has never been made before	Erfindung
	chewing gum ['tʃuːɪŋ gʌm]	soft candy to chew	Kaugummi
	to distinguish [dɪ'stɪŋgwɪʃ]	to see a difference between people or things	unterscheiden
	hero ['hɪərəʊ]	a person who has done sth brave	Held
	role model ['rəʊl mɒdl]	sb whose behaviour or success can be set as an example	Vorbild
	likelihood ['laɪklɪhʊd]	probability	Wahrscheinlichkeit

TOPIC 4   The state where in – the USA and the UK

TEXT 1 The UK Parliament

page 90	civil war [ˌsɪvl 'wɔː]	war between people in the same country	Bürgerkrieg
	authority [ɔː'θɒrəti]	body with the power to give orders or take action	Behörde
	to betray sb/sth [bɪ'treɪ]	to give information about sb/sth to an enemy	jdn/etw verraten
page 91	election [ɪ'lekʃn]	selecting a person for public office	Wahl
	eventually [ɪ'ventʃuəli]	in the end	schließlich
	guilty ['gɪlti]	to be responsible for a crime	schuldig
	treason ['triːzn]	betraying your country	Hochverrat
	representative [ˌreprɪ'zentətɪv]	sb who acts on behalf of others	Abgeordnete/r
	to dissolve [dɪ'zɒlv]	to cancel, terminate	auflösen
	to execute ['eksɪkjuːt]	to kill as a legal punishment	hinrichten
	to abolish [ə'bɒlɪʃ]	to officially end or stop sth	abschaffen
page 92	to restore [rɪ'stɔː]	to bring back to its former position	wieder einsetzen
	resistance [rɪ'zɪstəns]	the use of force to oppose sth	Widerstand
	to turn up [ˌtɜːn 'ʌp]	to appear, arrive	erscheinen
	devolution [ˌdiːvə'luːʃn]	the transfer of power from a central to a regional government	Dezentralisierung
page 95	needs pl [niːdz]	basic requirements	Bedürfnisse
	constituency [kən'stɪtjuənsi]	a number of voters living in a certain district	Wahlkreis
	mature [mə'tʃʊə]	fully developed	reif, erwachsen
	disgrace [dɪs'greɪs]	sth shameful	Schande
	abolition [æbə'lɪʃn]	official end of sth	Abschaffung
	fee [fiː]	money paid for service, advice, education	Gebühr
	poverty ['pɒvəti]	being poor	Armut

leisure facilities pl [ˌleʒə fə'sɪlətiz]	public buildings for sports, meeting halls, cafes, etc	*Freizeiteinrichtungen*	

TEXT 2 Living and dying on Death Row

to **stare** [steə]	to look at sth for a long time	*starren*	page 97
soul [səʊl]	spiritual part of a person	*Seele*	
opponent [ə'pəʊnənt]	sb who is against sth, believes it is wrong	*Gegner/in*	
suicide ['suːɪsaɪd]	killing yourself	*Selbstmord*	
sentencing ['sentənsɪŋ]	deciding which punishment a criminal will get	*Strafmaßverkündung*	
trial ['traɪəl]	examination of evidence in a law court	*Gerichtsverfahren, Prozess*	
regret [rɪ'gret]	annoyance, disappointment	*Bedauern*	
to **sentence** ['sentəns]	to state that sb is to have a certain punishment	*verurteilen*	
cop [kɒp]	police officer	*Polizist/in*	page 98
sentence ['sentəns]	punishment given by a law court	*Strafe*	
parole [pə'rəʊl]	permission for a prisoner to leave prison earlier than planned	*bedingte Haftaussetzung, Bewährung*	
to **triple** ['trɪpl]	increase by three times more	*(sich) verdreifachen*	
death penalty ['deθ penlti]	when a criminal is put to death for murder, etc	*Todesstrafe*	
preferable ['prefərəbl]	more desireable	*vorzuziehen, besser*	
to **condemn** [kən'dem]	to sentence	*verurteilen*	
to **legislate** ['ledʒɪsleɪt]	to make a law	*(ein Gesetz) erlassen*	
harsh [hɑːʃ]	hard, severe	*hart, scharf*	
to **convict sb of sth** [kən'vɪkt əv]	to find sb guilty of a crime in a court of law	*jdn wegen etw verurteilen*	
circumstances pl ['sɜːkəmstənsɪz]	details surrounding a situation	*Umstände*	
to **degrade** [dɪ'greɪd]	to treat sb/sth badly and without respect	*zersetzen, abbauen*	
sanity ['sænəti]	good mental health	*geistige Gesundheit*	
shame [ʃeɪm]	a bad feeling when you know you have done sth wrong	*Schande, Jammer*	
state-sponsored ['steɪt spɒnzəd]	paid for by the government	*staatlich gefördert*	
malfunctioning [ˌmæl'fʌŋkʃnɪŋ]	not working correctly	*Versagen, Störung*	page 99
to **refrain from sth** [rɪ'freɪn frəm]	to not do sth	*etw unterlassen*	
convenience store [kən'viːnɪəns stɔː]	a shop that is open late and sells food, drinks, and other essential items	*Eckladen, Spätkauf*	
prior to ['praɪə tə]	before	*vor*	
ultimate ['ʌltɪmət]	most extreme	*stärkste/r/s, schlimmste/r/s*	
denial [dɪ'naɪəl]	refusal to give	*Verweigerung, Verleugnung*	
to **deter** [dɪ'tɜː]	to make sb decide not to do sth	*abschrecken*	
passion ['pæʃn]	strong or powerful emotion	*Leidenschaft*	
unlikely [ʌn'laɪkli]	probably won't happen	*unwahrscheinlich*	
blackmail ['blækmeɪl]	demanding money by threatening to reveal harmful information	*Erpressung*	page 100
burglary ['bɜːgləri]	breaking into a building and stealing things	*Einbruchdiebstahl*	
rape [reɪp]	forced sex without consent	*Vergewaltigung*	
shoplifting ['ʃɒplɪftɪŋ]	taking things from a shop without paying	*Ladendiebstahl*	
offender [ə'fendə]	a person who commits a crime	*Straftäter/in*	

TEXT 3 Immigration

refugee [ˌrefju'dʒiː]	sb who has fled from a country to escape from war, political problems, etc	*Flüchtling*	page 102
asylum seeker [ə'saɪləm siːkə]	sb who has left danger in his/her country and is looking for safety in another country	*Asylsuchende/r, Asylbewerber/in*	
decency ['diːsnsi]	good and polite behaviour	*Anstand*	page 103

	desert ['dezət]	an area with no water, often covered in sand	Wüste
	to disguise [dɪs'gaɪz]	to make sth/sb unrecognisable	verkleiden, tarnen
	to trap [træp]	to catch sth so it cannot escape	festhalten, einschließen
	to leap sth [li:p]	to jump over sth	etw überspringen
	guard [gɑːd]	sb who protects a building, person, etc	Wache
page 104	to disobey [dɪsə'beɪ]	to not do sth you are told to do	nicht gehorchen
	ID = identity card [ˌaɪ 'diː, aɪ'dentəti kɑːd]	document that proves who you are	Personalausweis
	to rule [ruːl]	to be in charge of a country	regieren, herrschen
	desirable [dɪ'zaɪərəbl]	worth having	wünschenswert
	detention centre [dɪ'tenʃn sentə]	a place where persons (i.e. asylum seekers) must stay and cannot leave	Internierungslager
page 105	pregnant ['pregnənt]	having a baby inside your body	schwanger
	dietary ['daɪətri]	food-related	Ernährungs-
	to insist [ɪn'sɪst]	to demand strongly	darauf bestehen
	vital ['vaɪtl]	extremely important	unverzichtbar
page 106	innocent ['ɪnəsnt]	sb who has done nth wrong	Unschuldige/r
	sweat [swet]	perspiration	Schweiß
	intention [ɪn'tenʃn]	a thing you plan to do or achieve	Absicht
	faith [feɪθ]	trust, belief	Vertrauen, Glaube
	sin [sɪn]	breaking a religious or moral law	Sünde
page 108	small change [ˌsmɔːl 'tʃeɪndʒ]	coins (5c, 10c, etc)	Kleingeld
	to beg [beg]	to ask for money, food, etc on the street	betteln
	valid ['vælɪd]	justified	berechtigt
	slice [slaɪs]	a piece of sth	Scheibe, Stück
	shortage ['ʃɔːtɪdʒ]	not enough of sth	Mangel
	breaking point ['breɪkɪŋ pɔɪnt]	the moment when sb loses control	Belastungsgrenze
	affluent ['æfluənt]	having lots of money and things	wohlhabend
	birth rate ['bɜːθ reɪt]	number of births in a certain period of time	Geburtenrate
	benefits pl ['benɪfɪts]	money paid by the government to support sb who cannot work	Sozialleistungen
	ambitious [æm'bɪʃəs]	wanting success, money and power	ehrgeizig
	utter ['ʌtə]	complete, total	völlige/r/s

TEXT 4 Young people and politics

page 109	mid-term election [mɪd ˌtɜːm ɪ'lekʃn]	an election in a year when there is no presidential election	Zwischenwahl
	turnout ['tɜːnaʊt]	the number of people who vote	Wahlbeteiligung
	particularly [pə'tɪkjələli]	especially	besonders
	participation [pɑːˌtɪsɪ'peɪʃn]	taking part in	Teilnahme, Teilhabe
	apathetic [æpə'θetɪk]	lacking interest or enthusiasm	teilnahmslos, apathisch
	cosmopolitan [ˌkɒzmə'pɒlɪtən]	having wide experience of the world	kosmopolitisch
	volunteer [ˌvɒlən'tɪə]	sb who works for no money	ehrenamtlich
	tuition fees pl [tju'ɪʃn fiːz]	money paid for university education	Studiengebühren
page 110	to tell sth apart [tel ə'pɑːt]	to see that sth is different from sth else	etwas auseinanderhalten
	reluctance [rɪ'lʌktəns]	unwillingness	Abneigung, Unlust
	perception [pə'sepʃn]	the way sb sees and understands sth	Wahrnehmung
	current ['kʌrənt]	present	aktuelle/er/es
page 112	to excuse sb from sth [ɪk'skjuːz frəm]	to set sb free from a duty	jdn von etw befreien
	jury ['dʒʊəri]	members of the public who listen to a case in court and decide whether or not sb is guilty of a crime	Geschworene
	variety [və'raɪəti]	range of different things or people	Vielzahl
	wisdom ['wɪzdəm]	knowledge sb has from their life experience	Weisheit
	to raise children [ˌreɪz 'tʃɪldrən]	to bring up children	Kinder großziehen
	care [keə]	worry	Sorge
page 113	edition [ɪ'dɪʃn]	one programme in a series	Ausgabe
	amendment [ə'mendmənt]	a formal or offical change to a document	Zusatzartikel (zu einem Gesetz)

achievement [əˈtʃiːvmənt]	a good result from hard work	Leistung, Errungenschaft	page 114
to **centre around** sth [ˈsentə əraʊnd]	to make sth the focus of attention or interest	sich um etw drehen	
equal [ˈiːkwəl]	being exactly the same, or on the same level	gleich	
pay [peɪ]	money for work	Bezahlung, Lohn	
increasingly [ɪnˈkriːsɪŋli]	more and more	zunehmend	
workforce [ˈwɜːfɔːs]	all the people who are working	arbeitende Bevölkerung	
property [ˈprɒpəti]	sth that a person owns, for example a house, a car	Eigentum	

TEXT 5 Elitist education in the UK

superior to sth [suːˈpɪəriə tə]	better than sth else	einer Sache überlegen	page 115
regulation [ˌregjuˈleɪʃn]	a rule or law	Vorschrift	
public school BE [ˌpʌblɪk ˈskuːl]	a school you must pay to attend (UK)	Privatschule	
chairman [ˈtʃeəmən]	person in charge of a meeting, company or event	Vorsitzender	page 116
to **matter** [ˈmætə]	to be important	wichtig sein	
credible [ˈkredəbl]	believable	glaubwürdig	
to **lock** sb **out** [ˌlɒk ˈaʊt]	to stop sb getting in	jdn aussperren	
judge [dʒʌdʒ]	a person who makes the final decision in a court of law	Richter	
civil servant [ˌsɪvl ˈsɜːvənt]	person employed in a government department	Beamter/in	
unreasonable [ʌnˈriːznəbl]	not appropriate	unangemessen	
to **underestimate** [ˌʌndərˈestɪmeɪt]	to undervalue sb	unterschätzen	
consequence [ˈkɒnsɪkwəns]	sth that happens as a result of sth	Folge, Konsequenz	page 117
despite [dɪˈspaɪt]	sth happens, when sth else could have stopped it	trotz	
moreover [mɔːrˈəʊvə]	in addition	außerdem, darüber hinaus	
superiority [suːˌpɪəriˈɒrəti]	feeling more important than sb else	Überlegenheit	page 118
inferiority [ɪnˌfɪəriˈɒrəti]	feeling less important than sb else	Unterlegenheit, Minderwertigkeit	
disability [ˌdɪsəˈbɪləti]	a physical or mental problem that limits what sb can do	Behinderung	page 119
on the contrary [ɒn ðə ˈkɒntrəri]	the opposite is true	im Gegenteil	

TEXT 6 The American Dream

to **include** sth [ɪnˈkluːd]	to make sth part of sth	etw einschließen, etw beinhalten	page 121
prosperity [prɒˈsperəti]	affluence and a good life	Wohlstand	
root [ruːt]	basis, source	Wurzel	
liberty [ˈlɪbəti]	freedom	Freiheit	
pursuit [pəˈsjuːt]	trying to get sth	Streben	
according to [əˈkɔːdɪŋ tə]	depending on	je nach	
ability [əˈbɪləti]	capacity or power to do sth	Fähigkeit	
regardless of [rɪˈgɑːdləs əv]	independent of	unabhängig von	
to **persist** [pəˈsɪst]	to continue	fortbestehen	
limitless [ˈlɪmɪtləs]	without limits for borders	grenzenlos	page 122
to **pursue** [pəˈsjuː]	to try to get sth	verfolgen	
to **focus on** sth [ˈfəʊkəs ɒn]	to give a lot of attention to sth	sich auf etw konzentrieren	
food for thought [ˌfʊd fə ˈθɔːt]	sth to think about	Stoff zum Nachdenken	
honesty [ˈɒnəsti]	integrity, telling the truth	Ehrlichkeit	
curiosity [ˌkjʊəriˈɒsəti]	wanting to know or learn about sth	Neugier	
loyalty [ˈlɔɪəlti]	being true or faithful	Loyalität	
force [fɔːs]	strength, power	Kraft	
faith [feɪθ]	belief	Glaube	
nightmare [ˈnaɪtmeə]	a bad dream	Albtraum	
consumer [kənˈsjuːmə]	sb who buys and uses things	Verbraucher/in	page 123
recovery [rɪˈkʌvəri]	return to a normal state	Erholung	
award [əˈwɔːd]	prize	Preis, Auszeichnung	page 125

A–Z WORD LIST

Dieses Worterverzeichnis enthält alle in *Crossover 1* Ausgabe Baden-Württemberg eingeführten in den Texten angegebenen Vokabeln in alphabetischer Reihenfolge.

Abkürzugnen:

AE = amerikanisches Englisch	jdm = jemandem	pl = plural
BE = britisches Englisch	jdn = jemanden	sb = somebody
etw = etwas	jds = jemandes	sth = something

A

A-level 115 *Abitur*

to **abandon sth** 46 *etw verlassen, etw aufgeben*

abbreviation 9 *Abkürzung*

ability 121 *Fähigkeit*

to **abolish** 91 *abschaffen*

abolition 95 *Abschaffung*

absent 23 *abwesend*

access to sth 13 *Zugang zu etw*

to **accompany** 60 *begleiten*

according to 70 *laut, gemäß, zufolge;* 121 *je nach*

to **accuse sb of sth** 24 *jdn einer Sache beschuldigen;* 61 *jdm etw vorwerfen*

to **achieve** 61 *erlangen, erzielen*

achievement 7 *Leistung(en);* 114T *Errungenschaft*

to **acknowledge** 65 *anerkennen;* 127 *eingestehen*

addicted, to be ~ to sth 10 *auf/nach etw süchtig sein*

addiction, Internet A~ Disorder (IAD) 81 *Internetabhängigkeitssyndrom (IAS)*

addictive behaviour 75 *Suchtverhalten*

addition, in ~ 22 *außerdem*

additional 7 *zusätzlich*

address, inaugural ~ 122 *Antrittsrede*

to **admit** 71 *zugeben, eingestehen*

adolescence 6 *Pubertät*

adolescent 6 *Jugendliche/r, Heranwachsende/r*

to **advocate** 98 *befürworten*

affluence 55 *Wohlstand*

affluent 108T *wohlhabend*

to **afford to do sth** 28 *sich es leisten können, etw zu tun*

to **agonize over sth** 119 *sich über etw den Kopf zerbrechen*

agreement 42 *Vereinbarung, Abkommen*

aid agency 70 *Hilfsorganisation*

aim 28 *Ziel*

alert 18 *aufmerksam*

alien 75 *fremd*

alley 36 *Gasse*

to **alter** 75 *verändern*

ambition 58 *Ehrgeiz, (ehrgeiziger) Wunsch*

ambitious 108T *ehrgeizig*

amendment 113 *Zusatzartikel (zu einem Gesetz)*

to **annex** 91 *annektieren*

annual leave 33 *Jahresurlaub*

anti-social 86 *ungesellig, unsozial*

anxiety 18 *Ängste, Angst*

anxious 6 *verunsichernd, sorgenvoll;* 81 *besorgt, ängstlich;* to **be ~ to do sth** 13 *darauf erpicht sein, etw zu tun*

apathetic 109 *teilnahmslos, apathisch*

apparently 60 *anscheinend*

appeal 97 *Berufung*

application, job ~ 14 *Stellenbewerbung*

to **apply** 12 *gelten*

aristocratic 38 *adlig*

armed 18 *bewaffnet;* ~ **forces** pl 65 *Streitkräfte*

arrangement 23 *Regelung*

arson 38 *Brandstiftung*

arty 58 *pseudokünstlerisch*

aspiration 59 *Ziel, Bestrebung*

to **assert** 6 *geltend machen, durchsetzen*

assessment 15 *Beurteilung*

asset 129 *Pluspunkt*

to **associate with sb** 47 *mit jdm Umgang haben*

asylum seeker 102 *Asylsuchende/r, Asylbewerber/in*

to **attend** 13 *(Schule etc.) besuchen*

attention, sustained ~ 76 *anhaltende Aufmerksamkeit, Daueraufmerksamkeit*

attitude 31 *Ansicht, Einstellung*

to **attribute sth to sth** 127 *etw einer Sache zuschreiben*

authority 90 *Behörde;* **local ~** 23 *Kommunalbehörde*

available, to be ~ 12 *zur Verfügung stehen*

average 38 *Durchschnitt, durchschnittlich;* **on ~** 18 *im Durchschnitt*

to **avoid** 7 *vermeiden, meiden;* ~ **sb** 6 *jdm aus dem Weg gehen*

award 125 *Preis, Auszeichnung*

B

background 24T *Hintergrund, Herkunft*

backing 70 *Befürwortung, Unterstützung*

ballot 110 *Stimmzettel*

ban 60 *Verbot*

barely 60 *kaum*

barmy 53 *verrückt, plemplem*

bars pl 97 *Gitter*

beautician 59 *Kosmetiker/in*

bedding 51 *Bettzeug*

to **beg** 108T *betteln*

behalf, on ~ of sb 74T *für jdn*

behavioral AE 28 *Verhaltens-*

behaviour, addictive ~ 75 *Suchtverhalten*

belongings pl 52 *Habseligkeiten*

beneficiary 70 *Nutznießer/in*

to **benefit** 70 *profitieren*

benefit 31 *Vorteil*

benefits pl 46 *(Zusatz-)Leistungen;* 108T *Sozialleistungen*

to **betray sb/sth** 90 *jdn/etw verraten*

bidding, to do sb's ~ 91 *tun, was jd will*

bilingual 23 *zweisprachig*

birth rate 108T *Geburtenrate*

to **bitch** 58 *lästern*

blackmail 100 *Erpressung*

blame 31 *Schuld*

to **blare** 50 *heulen, plärren*

bleary-eyed 19 *übernächtigt*

bloke 65 *Kerl*

bloodshed 38 *Blutvergießen*

board, school ~ 17 *Schulbehörde*

boarder 115 *Internatsschüler/in*

to **boost** 18 *heben, erhöhen*

borough 54 *Stadtbezirk*

borstal 53 *Jugendstrafanstalt*

bound, to be ~ to do sth 36 *dazu bestimmt sein, etw zu tun*

to **brag** 19 *angeben, prahlen*

brain 18 *Gehirn*

branch 57 *Zweig*

brand 72 *Marke*

to **break up with sb** 6 *sich von jdm trennen*

breakdown, nervous ~ 63T *Nervenzusammenbruch*

breaking point 108T
Belastungsgrenze
to **bridge 80** *überbrücken, (Kluft)*
überwinden
broke 9T *pleite*
broker 54 *Börsenmakler/in;*
insurance ~ 81 *Versicherungs-*
makler/in
buddy 23 *Kamerad, Kumpel*
budget 13 *Etat, Budget, Haushalt*
to **bug 35T** *nerven*
bullying 6 *Mobbing*
burglary 100 *Einbruchdiebstahl*
to **buzz 20** *brummen*

C

cage 97 *Käfig*
capital punishment 97 *Todesstrafe*
to **capitalize on sth 81** *aus etw*
Kapital schlagen
care 112 *Sorge*
carefree 6 *sorglos, sorgenfrei*
caregiver 31 *Bezugsperson*
to **carve sth out 32** *sich etw aufbauen*
to **catch up on sth 87** *etw*
(Versäumtes) nachholen
cattle 65 *Rinder*
cause 70 *Sache, Anliegen*
ceasefire 41 *Waffenstillstand*
celebratory, to be ~ about sth 23
etw feiern
to **centre around sth 114T** *sich um*
etw drehen
chairman 116 *Vorsitzender*
challenge 23 *(schwere) Aufgabe,*
Herausforderung
challenging 33 *anspruchsvoll, reizvoll*
to **change one's mind 72** *seine*
Meinung ändern
charge 97 *Anklage;* to **be in ~ of sth**
32 *für etw zuständig/verantwortlich*
sein
to **cheat 24** *schummeln, betrügen*
cheating 24T *(Schule:) Pfuschen,*
Abgucken
cheerily 23 *fröhlich*
chef 59 *Koch/Köchin, Küchenchef/in*
chewing gum 89 *Kaugummi*
to **chop off 75** *abhacken*
circumstances pl 98 *Umstände*
to **cite 129** *zitieren*
city council 43 *Stadtrat,*
Stadtverwaltung
civil: ~ rights pl 41 *Bürgerrechte; ~*
servant 116 *Beamter/in; ~* **war 90**
Bürgerkrieg
to **claim 28** *behaupten*
claim to fame 38 *Besonderheit,*
Ruhmestitel
classmate 18 *Klassenkamerad/in*
codify 98 *kodifizieren, festlegen*
coffin 64 *Sarg*
to **coin 121** *prägen*

collapse 38 *Zusammenbruch, Zerfall*
to **commit 38** *(Tat usw.) begehen*
common 42 *häufig*
commonplace 41 *alltäglich*
community 42 *Gemeinde;* **inter-~ 43**
zwischen den Gemeinden
to **compare 6** *vergleichen*
to **compete 55** *konkurrieren*
competition 50 *Wettbewerb*
to **complain 82** *sich beklagen, sich*
beschweren
complaint 28 *Beschwerde, Klage*
compound noun 29 *zusammen-*
gesetztes Substantiv, Kompositum
to **comprise 76** *umfassen*
concern 7 *Sorge, Anliegen*
to **concern sb 9** *jdn betreffen, jdn*
angehen, jdn kümmern
conclusion 16 *Schluss*
concrete 97 *Beton*
to **condemn 98** *verurteilen*
condition 27 *Bedingung, Umstand*
to **conduct sth 76** *etw durchführen*
to **confess 78** *gestehen*
confession 64 *Beichte*
confidence 18 *Selbstvertrauen,*
Zuversicht
confinement, solitary ~ 97
Einzelhaft, Isolationshaft
to **conform 7** *sich anpassen*
connection 70 *Verbindung, Beziehung*
to **conquer 38** *erobern*
conquest 38 *Eroberung*
consent 42 *Zustimmung*
consequence 117 *Folge, Konsequenz*
to **consider sth 24T** *etw*
berücksichtigen
considerably 32 *beträchtlich*
considered, to be ~ sth 46 *als etw*
gelten
constituency 95 *Wahlkreis*
constituent 95 *Wähler/in (eines*
Wahlkreises)
to **constitute sth 68** *etw ausmachen,*
etw bilden
consultant 129 *Berater/in*
consumer 123 *Verbraucher/in*
contestant 60 *Teilnehmer/in (an*
einem Wettbewerb)
context 24 *Zusammenhang, Kontext*
contrary, on the ~ 119 *im Gegenteil*
contributing factor 31 *Zusatzfaktor*
contribution 50T *Beitrag*
convenience store 99T *Eckladen,*
Spätkauf
convenient 77 *praktisch, bequem;*
super-~ 87 *mega-bequem*
to **converse 47** *sich unterhalten*
to **convict sb of sth 98** *jdn wegen etw*
verurteilen
convincingly 18 *überzeugend*
cop 98 *Polizist/in*
to **cope 53** *zurechtkommen*

corpulent 91 *beleibt*
cosmopolitan 109 *kosmopolitisch*
cost of living 31
Lebenshaltungskosten
cosy 116 *gemütlich*
council, city ~ 43 *Stadtrat, Stadt-*
verwaltung
counselling service 127
Beratungsstelle
countable 24 *zählbar*
county 38 *Grafschaft*
to **course 18** *strömen*
crap vulg 53 *Unsinn*
credible 116 *glaubwürdig*
cruise 49 *Fahrt*
to **crush 92** *zerschlagen*
curb 51 *Bordstein*
curiosity 122 *Neugier*
currency 26 *Währung*
current 110 *aktuelle / -er / es*
currently 17 *derzeit*
CV = curriculum vitae 129
Lebenslauf
cynical 70 *zynisch*

D

damn 36 *verdammt*
dare, How ~ you! 104 *Was erlauben*
Sie sich!
to **deal with sth 7** *mit etw umgehen*
death penalty 98 *Todesstrafe*
debt 31 *Schulden*
decade 38 *Jahrzehnt*
decay 49 *Verfall*
decency 103 *Anstand*
decent 13 *ordentlich*
Declaration of Independence 121
Unabhängigkeitserklärung
to **decline 46** *sinken, schwinden*
decline 55 *Verfall*
to **decree 98** *anordnen*
to **degrade 98** *zersetzen, abbauen*
to **delay 32** *verzögern, hinauszögern*
demand 6 *Anforderung;* **46**
Nachfrage; ~ **for sth 28** *Forderung*
nach etw; **on ~ 86** *auf Abruf, auf*
Nachfrage
to **demolish 49** *abreißen*
denial 99T *Verweigerung*
dependent, to be ~ on sb/sth 7 *von*
jdm/etw abhängig sein
depressed 6 *deprimiert*
to **deprive sb of sth 27** *jdm etw*
entziehen, jdm etw vorenthalten
deputy, sheriff's ~ 97 *Hilfssheriff*
derelict 54 *leer stehend, verlassen*
desert 103 *Wüste*
desirable 55 *begehrt;* **104**
wünschenswert
desperately 13 *dringend*
to **despise 124** *verachten*
despite 117 *trotz*
destination 39 *Reiseziel*

gently 32 *sanft*

gentrification 54 *Gentrifizierung*

Geordie 36 *Spitzname für jdn aus Tyneside*

to get: ~ to sb 19 *jdm an die Nieren gehen;* **~ away with sth** 28 *mit etw davonkommen;* **~ on** 12 *vorwärts kommen, weiterkommen;* **~ sth together** 48 *mit etw die Kurve kriegen*

to glance at sth 75 *einen (schnellen) Blick auf etw werfen*

glued, to be ~ to sth 75 *an etw kleben*

godforsaken 36 *gottverlassen*

goodness, My ~. 24T *Du meine Güte!*

government-funded 95 *staatlich finanziert*

grad(uate) 32 *Hochschulabsolvent/in*

grade 9T *(Schul-)Note*

to grade 23 *benoten*

gradual 34 *allmählich, langsam*

to graduate 13 *einen Schulabschluss machen*

graffitied 42 *mit Graffiti bemalt*

to grant 112 *gewähren*

to grieve 36 *trauern*

grind 19 *Plackerei*

grip 122 *Griff*

grocery store 51 *Lebensmittelladen*

growth 18 *Wachstum*

guard 103 *Wache*

guardian 60 *Erziehungsberechtigte/r*

guess 48 *Mutmaßung*

guilty 91 *schuldig*

H

habit 87 *Gewohnheit*

to hang: ~ sb 91 *jdn hängen;* **~ out with sb** 9T *mit jdm abhängen*

hardship 29 *Not, Entbehrung(en)*

hardwired 18 *programmiert, veranlagt*

harsh 98 *hart, scharf*

hazard 27 *Gefahr*

head 116 *Schulleiter/in;* **~ teacher** 23 *Schuldirektor/in;* **off the top of your ~** 47 *aus dem Stegreif*

health care 112 *Gesundheitswesen*

heritage 49 *Kulturerbe*

hero 89 *Held*

hesitation 68 *Zögern*

hike 81 *Wanderung*

to hire sb 12 *jdn einstellen*

historian 121 *Historiker/in*

home ownership 109 *eigenes Haus, eigene Wohnung*

honesty 122 *Ehrlichkeit*

horror 44T *Schrecken*

hub 49 *Drehkreuz*

human 76 *menschlich*

I

ID = identity card 104 *Personalausweis*

to imagine 75 *sich (etw) vorstellen*

impact 32 *Auswirkung(en);* 128 *Wirkung*

to implore 81 *anflehen*

to impose 28 *(Regelung usw.) verhängen, anordnen*

to impress 74T *beeindrucken*

impression 11 *Eindruck*

impressionable 75 *beeinflussbar*

impressive 35T *beeindruckend*

to improve 15 *verbessern, steigern;* 23 *sich bessern, besser werden*

inaccurately 38 *ungenau*

inadequate 7 *unzulänglich;* 23 *ungenügend*

inaugural address 122 *Antrittsrede*

to include sth 121 *etw einschließen, etw beinhalten*

to increase sth 25 *etw steigern, etw erhöhen*

increasingly 114T *zunehmend*

incredible 38 *unglaublich*

indeed 115 *in der Tat*

indefinitely 31 *auf unbestimmte Zeit*

independence 6 *Unabhängigkeit;* **Declaration of I~** 121 *Unabhängigkeitserklärung*

independent 24T *unabhängig;* **~ school** 115 *Privatschule*

to indicate 109 *erkennen lassen, zeigen*

inequality 80 *Ungleichheit, Unterschied(e)*

inferiority 118 *Unterlegenheit, Minderwertigkeit*

influence 7 *Einfluss*

influential 22 *einflussreich*

to inherit 65 *erben*

initial 84T *erste/r/s, anfänglich*

injured 46 *verletzt*

inmate 97 *Häftling, Insasse/Insassin*

inner-city 13 *in der Innenstadt*

innocent 106 *Unschuldige/r*

to insist 105 *darauf bestehen*

inspection 28 *Kontrolle, Prüfung*

inspector 23 *Prüfer/in*

instead of 18 *anstatt*

insurance broker 81 *Versicherungsmakler/in*

intention 106 *Absicht*

inter-community 43 *zwischen den Gemeinden*

to interfere with sth 9T *etw beeinträchtigen*

Internet Addiction Disorder (IAD) 81 *Internet-Abhängigkeitssyndrom (IAS)*

intimidating 129 *einschüchternd*

intriguing 63 *faszinierend, interessant*

invader 38 *Endringling, Invasor*

to invent 65 *erfinden*

invention 89 *Erfindung*

involvement 70 *Beteiligung, Engagement*

issue 6 *Problem, Streitfrage, Thema*

J

job application 14 *Stellenbewerbung*

joy 51 *Freude*

judge 116 *Richter*

jug 53 *Krug*

jury 112 *Geschworene*

K

to kick in 18 *anfangen zu wirken*

to kid 20 *scherzen*

kit 53 *Klamotten, Sachen*

knight 91 *Ritter*

knitting 84T *Stricken*

L

labor AE: **~ market** 31 *Arbeitsmarkt;* **~ union** 28 *Gewerkschaft*

labour 27 *Arbeit*

lack 24T *Mangel, Fehlen*

to lack sth 13 *etw nicht haben*

landline 86 *Festnetz(anschluss)*

lap 31 *Schoß*

large-scale 43 *in großem Umfang*

launch 72 *Markteinführung, Start*

to launch 74T *starten, (Produkt) einführen, vorstellen;* **~ sb** 32 *jdn in die Welt schicken*

law 28 *Gesetz, Recht*

to leap sth 103 *etw überspringen*

leave, annual ~ 33 *Jahresurlaub*

to legislate 98 *(ein Gesetz) erlassen*

leisure: ~ facilities pl 95 *Freizeiteinrichtungen;* **~ time** 15 *Freizeit*

let alone 63T *geschweige denn*

to let sb down 13 *jdn im Stich lassen;* 63T *jdn enttäuschen*

level playing field 129 *Chancengleichheit*

to liaise 23 *als Verbindungsperson fungieren*

liberty 121 *Freiheit*

lifer 98 *Lebenslängliche/r*

like 112 *(Slang:) irgendwie*

likelihood 89 *Wahrscheinlichkeit*

likely, to be ~ to do sth 18 *etw wahrscheinlich tun (werden)*

limelight 63T *Rampenlicht*

limited 42 *beschränkt*

limitless 122 *grenzenlos*

to link 70 *in Verbindung bringen*

link, to forge ~s 23 *Brücken schlagen*

literacy 119 *Lese- und Schreibfähigkeit*

to live up to sth 7 *einer Sache gerecht werden*

livestock 38 *Vieh*

living, cost of ~ 31

Lebenshaltungskosten
local authority 23 *Kommunalbehörde*
location 31 *Ort, Standort*
to **lock sb out** 116 *jdn aussperren*
to **long** 36 *sich sehnen*
to **loosen** 28 *lockern*
to **lose track of time** 82 *das Zeitgefühl verlieren*
to **lower** 18 *senken, reduzieren*
loyalty 122 *Loyalität*
lyrics pl 59 *Liedtext*

M

to **maintain** 32 *(finanziell) unterhalten*
major 35T *groß, größer*
majority 13 *Mehrheit*
to **make way for sth** 55 *einer Sache weichen*
malfunctioning 99T *Versagen, Störung*
manageable 28 *beherrschbar, kontrollierbar*
to **maraud** 38 *plündern*
mark 75 *Spur(en)*
to **materialize** 63T *in Erfüllung gehen*
to **matter** 116 *wichtig sein*
mature 95 *reif, erwachsen*
measure 24 *Maßnahme*
to **measure up to sb** 7 *jdm gewachsen sein, mit jdm mithalten (können)*
to **memorize** 25 *auswendig lernen*
memory 97 *Erinnerung*
to **mention** 70 *erwähnen, nennen*
to **mess about** 35T *herumfummeln*
mid-term election 109 *Zwischenwahl*
to **mill around** 51 *umherlaufen*
millennial generation 31 *Personen, die zwischen 1980 und 2000 geboren sind*
mind, to **change one's ~** 72 *seine Meinung ändern*
mindful 82 *achtsam*
minimum wage 28 *Mindestlohn*
minor 28 *Minderjährige/r*
minority 41 *Minderheit*
misery 28 *Elend*
misleading 60 *irreführend*
mismatch 31 *Diskrepanz*
modest 28 *bescheiden*
monastery 38 *Kloster*
mood 18 *Stimmung*
moor 38 *Moor*
moreover 117 *außerdem, darüber hinaus*
mortgage 47 *Hypothek*
to **mourn** 64 *trauern*
mouth, word of ~ 72 *Mundpropaganda*
multilingual 23 *mehrsprachig*
to **muster** 81 *aufbringen*

N

to **nag** 6 *meckern, nörgeln*
narrowly 122 *eng*

native speaker 22 *Muttersprachler/in*
need, in ~ 74T *in Not*
needs pl 95 *Bedürfnisse*
to **neglect** 82 *vernachlässigen*
neglected 49 *vernachlässigt*
neighbourhood 12 *Wohnviertel, Wohngegend*
nervous breakdown 63T *Nervenzusammenbruch*
NGO = non-governmental organization 70 *regierungsunabhängige Organisation*
nightmare 122 *Albtraum*
noisy 35T *laut, lärmend*
notorious 53 *berüchtigt*
nuclear family 35T *Kernfamilie*
to **nudge** 32 *den Anstoß geben*

O

to **oblige sb to do sth** 27 *jdn zwingen, etw zu tun*
obliged 90 *verpflichtet*
obviously 84T *natürlich, offensichtlich*
occasional 82 *gelegentlich*
occupation 41 *Besetzung*
odd, to **be the ~ out** 23 *aus der Reihe fallen*
offender 100 *Straftäter/in*
opponent 97 *Gegner/in*
opportunity 13 *Chance, Gelegenheit*
opposing 63 *konträr, widerstreitend*
to **opt for sth** 109 *sich für etw/dafür entscheiden*
ordeal 63T *Zerreißprobe*
ordinary 65 *normal, gewöhnlich*
organic 74T *Bio-*
to **originate** 95 *stammen*
orphan 73 *Waise, Waisenkind*
outcome 70 *Ergebnis, Resultat*
outraged 17 *empört*
overreliance on sth 76 *übermäßige Abhängigkeit von etw*
to **own** 12 *besitzen*
owner 47 *Besitzer/in*
ownership, home ~ 109 *eigenes Haus, eigene Wohnung*

P

pace, to **keep ~ with sth** 129 *mit etw Schritt halten*
to **pair sb up with sb** 23 *jdn mit jdm zusammenbringen*
to **paraphrase** 72 *umschreiben*
parole 98 *Bewährung*
participant 61 *Teilnehmer/in*
participation 109 *Teilnahme, Teilhabe*
particularly 109 *besonders*
partly 24T *teilweise*
passion 99T *Leidenschaft*
patience 47 *Geduld*
pattern 84T *Muster*
paved 106 *gepflastert*
pay 114T *Bezahlung, Lohn;* **~ rise** 67

Gehaltserhöhung
to **pay off** 18 *sich lohnen*
to **peak** 46 *den Höchststand erreichen*
peculiar 92 *eigenartig, merkwürdig*
peer 7 *Gleichaltrige/r*
pen 98 *Gehege*
penalty, death ~ 98 *Todesstrafe*
percentage 12 *Prozentsatz, Anteil*
perception 110 *Wahrnehmung*
performance 15 *Leistung, Abschneiden*
permanent secretary 116 *Staatssekretär*
perplexed 86 *verdutzt*
to **persist** 121 *fortbestehen*
to **persuade** 30 *überzeugen, überreden*
persuasive 76 *überzeugend*
petrol BE 51 *Benzin*
picket fence 124 *Lattenzaun*
to **plaster** 17 *kleben, kleistern*
playing field, level ~ 130 *Chancengleichheit*
to **pool** 60 *zusammentragen, sammeln*
population 22 *Bevölkerung*
porch 47 *Veranda*
to **portray** 38 *darstellen, porträtieren*
portrayal 39 *Darstellung, Porträt*
possessions pl 78 *Besitz(tümer), Hab und Gut*
potentially 75 *möglicherweise*
to **pour** 51 *gießen, schütten*
poverty 95 *Armut;* **~ line** 46 *Armutsgrenze*
to **praise** 65 *loben*
prayer 106 *Gebet*
predominantly 23 *überwiegend*
preferable 98 *vorzuziehen, besser*
preferably 60 *möglichst, am liebsten*
prefix 8 *Vorsilbe, Präfix*
pregnant 105 *schwanger*
preoccupation with sth 122 *ständige (gedankliche) Beschäftigung mit etw*
to **preside** 97 *vorsitzen*
pressure 7 *Druck*
pretender 58 *Blender, Angeber*
to **prevent** 43 *verhindern;* **~ sb from doing sth** 42 *jdn daran hindern, etw zu tun*
previous 32 *vorig, früher*
primary school 23 *Grundschule*
prior to 99T *vor*
privacy 10 *Privatsphäre*
to **process** 18 *verarbeiten*
process 43 *Vorgang*
profit 74T *Gewinn*
progress 24T *Fortschritt(e)*
to **promote** 25 *fördern*
promotion 33 *Beförderung*
to **prompt** 81 *veranlassen*
pronunciation 24 *Aussprache*
property 12 *Grund und Boden, Immobilie(n);* 114T *Eigentum*
proportion 127 *Anteil*
to **propose** 17 *vorhaben, vorschlagen*

prosperity **121** *Wohlstand*

to **protect (sb from sth) 28** *(jdn vor etw) schützen*

to **provide 13** *bieten, zur Verfügung stellen*

public: ~ **school 12** *AE: staatliche Schule (in den USA);* **115** *BE: Privatschule;* ~ **sector 116** *Staatsdienst, öffentlicher Dienst;* ~ **transport 57** *öffentliche Verkehrsmittel*

to **publish 15** *veröffentlichen*

punishment, capital ~ **97** *Todesstrafe*

to **purchase 32** *kaufen*

purely 122 *bloß*

to **pursue 122** *verfolgen*

pursuit 121 *Streben*

to **push back 17** *(nach hinten) verschieben*

pushy 63T *aggressiv, aufdringlich*

to **put sb off 70** *jdn abschrecken*

Q

to **quit 106** *aufhören, aufgeben*

R

race relations *pl* **47** *Beziehungen zwischen ethnischen Gruppen*

racial 46 *Rassen-*

to **rage 38** *wüten*

rags *pl* **53** *Lumpen*

raid 38 *Überfall*

to **raise children 112** *Kinder großziehen*

to **ramble 36** *umherstreifen*

rampart 38 *Schutzwall*

range 68 *Umfang, Spektrum;* **116** *Bandbreite*

to **rank 12** *einen (Ranglisten-)Platz belegen*

ranking 13 *(Ranglisten-)Platz*

rape 100 *Vergewaltigung*

rarely 70 *selten*

rate, birth ~ **108T** *Geburtenrate;* **at a startling** ~ **55** *in erstaunlichem Tempo*

razor wire 97 *Stacheldraht*

real, for ~ **84T** *wirklich, tatsächlich*

recent 81 *aktuell, aus jüngster Zeit*

recently 14 *neulich, jüngst*

reckless 75 *leichtsinnig, unbesonnen*

reconciliation 42 *Versöhnung*

record label 50T *Plattenfirma*

recovery 123 *Erholung*

to **refer to sth 27** *sich auf etw beziehen*

to **refrain from sth 99T** *etw unterlassen*

refugee 102 *Flüchtling*

regardless 50T *ungeachtet;* ~ **of 121** *unabhängig von*

regret 97 *Bedauern*

regulation 115 *Vorschrift*

to **reinvent 75** *neu erfinden*

rejection 63T *Zurückweisung, Ablehnung*

relationship 7 *Beziehung, Verhältnis*

to **release 42** *freilassen*

reliable 84T *zuverlässig*

reliance on sth 75 *Abhängigkeit von etw, Angewiesensein auf etw*

to **relinquish sth 81** *auf etw verzichten*

reluctance 82 *Widerwillen;* **110** *Abneigung, Unlust*

reluctantly 47 *widerwillig*

representative 91 *Abgeordnete/r*

repugnant 129 *abstoßend*

reputation 53 *Ruf*

reshaping 42 *Umgestaltung, Neugestaltung*

resident 46 *Einwohner/in, Anwohner/in*

resistance 92 *Widerstand*

resource 13 *Ressource, Geldmittel*

resourceful 32 *findig, einfallsreich*

response 20 *Antwort*

responsibility 23 *Verantwortung, Zuständigkeit*

rest 18 *Ruhe*

to **restore 41** *wiederherstellen;* **92** *wieder einsetzen*

to **restrict 42** *begrenzen, beschränken*

restriction 28 *Einschränkung*

retailer 112 *Einzelhändler/in*

to **retain 55** *beibehalten*

retribution 38 *Vergeltung*

revised 60 *überarbeitet, revidiert*

to **revitalize 49** *neu beleben*

to **revolve around sth 47** *sich um etw drehen*

reward 24T *Lohn, Gewinn*

rights *pl,* **civil** ~ **41** *Bürgerrechte*

to **roam 36** *herumstreunen*

role model 89 *Vorbild*

roof 35T *Dach*

root 121 *Wurzel*

roundabout 55 *Kreisverkehr*

rowdy 51 *rauflustig*

royalty 59 *Mitglied(er) des Königshauses*

to **rule 104** *regieren, herrschen;* ~ **sth out 87** *etw ausschließen*

rumour 64 *Gerücht*

to **run sth 95** *etw durchführen*

rush 20 *Rausch*

S

sacred 106 *ehrwürdig*

sacrifice 32 *Opfer*

safe 42 *sicher*

safety 42 *Sicherheit*

salary 33 *Gehalt*

sanity 98 *geistige Gesundheit*

scale, large- ~ **43** *in großem Umfang*

scared, to be ~ **of sb 44T** *vor jdm Angst haben*

scary 75 *beängstigend*

sceptre 104 *Zepter*

schedule 18 *Zeitplan*

scholarship 115 *Stipendium*

school, fee-paying ~ **116** *Schule mit Schulgebühren;* **independent** ~ **115** *Privatschule;* **primary** ~ **23** *Grundschule;* **public** ~ **12** *AE: staatliche Schule (in den USA);* **115** *BE: Privatschule;* ~ **board 17** *Schulbehörde*

to **scramble 58** *drängeln*

screen 81 *Bildschirm, Display;* **silver** ~ **58** *Kinoleinwand*

season 87 *(TV-Serie:) Staffel*

secretary, permanent ~ **116** *Staatssekretär*

sectarian 42 *konfessionell*

sector, public ~ **116** *Staatsdienst, öffentlicher Dienst*

secure 42 *sicher, abgesichert*

seed, to sow the ~**s for sth 91** *den Boden für etw bereiten*

self-employed 33 *selbstständig*

senior citizen 29 *Senior/in*

to **sentence 97** *verurteilen*

sentence 98 *Strafe*

sentencing 97 *Strafmaßverkündung*

servant, civil ~ **116** *Beamter/in*

serviceman 65 *Soldat*

servicewoman 65 *Soldatin*

session 82 *Sitzung*

to **settle down 9T** *sesshaft werden;* **109** *einen Haushalt gründen*

shallow 61 *oberflächlich*

shame 98 *Schade, Jammer*

sharp 34 *steil, stark*

sheriff's deputy 97 *Hilfssheriff*

shift 59 *Wandel, Veränderung;* ~ **work 28** *Schichtarbeit*

shoplifting 100 *Ladendiebstahl*

shore 36 *Küste*

shortage 108T *Mangel*

shriek 51 *durchdringender Schrei*

shrimp 51 *Krabbe(n)*

shutters *pl* **124** *Fensterläden*

sidewalk *AE* **51** *Bürgersteig*

sigh 47 *Seufzer*

signature 79 *Unterschrift*

significant 31 *erheblich*

silver screen 58 *Kinoleinwand*

sin 106 *Sünde*

site 38 *Stätte*

sixth-former 23 *Oberstufenschüler/in*

to **skid 50** *rutschen, schlittern*

skill 13 *Fähigkeit, Fertigkeit*

skilled worker 13 *Facharbeiter/in*

to **skim 6** *(Text) überfliegen*

to **skinny dip 38** *nackt baden*

slave 75 *Sklave/Sklavin*

slice 108T *Scheibe, Stück*

slight 34 *leicht, schwach;* **44T** *gering, klein*

small change 108T *Kleingeld*

smart **55** *schick*

to smash **51** *kaputt schlagen*

smelly **53** *stinkend, übelriechend*

smug **76** *selbstzufrieden*

to snap at sb **18** *jdn anschnauzen*

snappy, Make it ~. **103** *Aber flott!*

snatch off **51** *herunter reißen*

to soar **127** *in die Höhe schnellen, stark ansteigen*

social **86** *gesellig, sozial;* anti-~ **86** *ungesellig, unsozial*

socialite **61** *Salonlöwe/-löwin*

solitary confinement **97** *Einzelhaft, Isolationshaft*

solution **11** *Lösung*

sophisticated **12** *modern, technisch ausgereift;* **55** *raffiniert, komplex*

soul **97** *Seele*

sound **50T** *Klang*

source **12** *Quelle*

to sow the seeds for sth **91** *den Boden für etw bereiten*

spare **87** *übrig geblieben*

spatial **78** *räumlich*

to spin **106** *sich drehen*

to splash sth across the media **64** *über etw groß in den Medien berichten*

to squeeze in **18** *einschieben, hineinzwängen*

stage **31** *Bühne*

to stand for election **95** *kandidieren*

to stare **97** *starren*

stare **47** *Starren*

to stare at sth **20** *auf etw starren, etw anstarren*

startling, at a ~ rate **55** *in erstaunlichem Tempo*

state: ~-sanctioned **98** *staatlich zugelassen;* ~-sponsored **98** *staatlich gefördert*

stepchild **35** *Stiefkind*

stepfather **35** *Stiefvater*

stepmother **35** *Stiefmutter*

strap **53** *Riemen*

stray **73** *streunend, herrenlos*

street-jobber **53** *Straßenhändler*

strength **6** *Stärke*

stretch, at a ~ **75** *ohne Unterbrechung*

strict **28** *streng*

stride, to get into one's ~ **91** *in Schwung kommen*

to strive for sth **121** *etw anstreben*

store, convenience ~ **99T** *Eckladen, Spätkauf;* grocery ~ **51** *Lebensmittelladen*

struggle **63T** *Kampf*

to struggle **23** *sich schwer tun*

to subscribe to sth **84T** *etw abonnieren*

subscription **14** *Abonnement*

suburb **13** *Vorort, Außenbezirk*

to succeed **32** *erfolgreich sein, Erfolg haben*

to suffer from sth **9** *an/unter etw leiden*

suffix **8** *Nachsilbe, Suffix*

to suggest **116** *unterstellen*

suicide **97** *Selbstmord*

suitable **13** *passend*

super-convenient **87** *mega-bequem*

superfluous **78** *überflüssig*

superior to sth **115** *einer Sache überlegen*

superiority **118** *Überlegenheit*

support **31** *Unterstützung*

to support **70** *unterstützen;* ~ sb **6** *jdn ernähren, jdn versorgen*

supporter **66** *Anhänger/in, Befürworter/in*

surname **66** *Nachname*

survey **12** *Umfrage, Studie, Erhebung*

suspicion **44T** *Misstrauen, Argwohn*

sustainability **42** *Nachhaltigkeit*

sustained attention **76** *anhaltende Aufmerksamkeit, Daueraufmerksamkeit*

to swap **31** *tauschen*

swastika **65** *Hakenkreuz*

sweat **106** *Schweiß*

sweep **51** *Schwung*

to switch **17** *umstellen*

synopsis **124** *Zusammenfassung (einer Handlung)*

T

tackle **103** *Angriff, Tackling*

to tackle sth **130** *etw anpacken*

tap **53** *Wasserhahn*

target **44T** *Ziel*

to target sth **46** *auf etw abzielen, sich an etw richten*

task **30** *Aufgabe*

tax **12** *Steuer*

to tear down **47** *abreißen*

telethon **71** *Spendensammelaktion im Fernsehen*

to tell sth apart **110** *etwas auseinanderhalten*

tempting **32** *verlockend*

to tend to do sth **23** *dazu neigen, etw zu tun*

tension **44T** *Spannung(en)*

term, in ~s of **7** *hinsichtlich, bezüglich*

thatch **103** *Strohdach*

thought, food for ~ **122** *Stoff zum Nachdenken*

tie **38** *Bindung*

time-consuming **84T** *zeitraubend*

tissue **18** *Gewebe*

top, off the ~ of your head **47** *aus dem Stegreif*

tormentor **6** *Peiniger*

torture **97** *Folter*

touch, out of ~ **109** *abgehoben*

touched **51** *berührt*

track, to lose ~ of time **82** *das Zeitgefühl verlieren*

trade **22** *Handel*

to trade sth off for sth **31** *etw gegen/für etw eintauschen*

transport, public ~ **57** *öffentliche Verkehrsmittel*

to trap **103** *festhalten, einschließen*

treason **91** *Hochverrat*

treasure **38** *Schatz*

to treat **31** *behandeln*

trial **97** *Gerichtsverfahren, Prozess;* to put sb on ~ **91** *jdn vor Gericht stellen*

to triple **98** *(sich) verdreifachen*

trouble **9T** *Schwierigkeiten, Ärger*

truant, to play ~ **6** *die Schule schwänzen*

trunk **81** *Truhe*

to trust **65** *vertrauen*

tuition fees *pl* **109** *Studiengebühren*

to tumble **106** *taumeln*

turmoil **38** *Unruhe(n)*

to turn: ~ out **109** *zur Wahl gehen;* ~ up **92** *erscheinen*

turnout **109** *Wahlbeteiligung*

turnstile **103** *Drehkreuz*

two-up, two-down **53** *kleines Reihenhaus mit je zwei Zimmern oben und unten*

U

ugly **51** *hässlich*

Ulster **41** *Nordirland*

ultimate **99T** *stärkste/r/s, schlimmste/r/s*

ultimately **116** *letztendlich*

unachieveable **7** *unerreichbar*

unattainable, to be ~ **105** *nicht zu beschaffen sein*

to uncover **38** *entdecken*

undemanding **33** *anspruchslos*

underage **29** *minderjährig*

to underestimate **116** *unterschätzen*

undergo **54** *durchmachen*

unemployment **31** *Arbeitslosigkeit*

unfortunately **9** *leider*

unification **41** *Vereinigung*

uninterrupted **10** *ununterbrochen, durchgehend*

union, labor ~ *AE* **28** *Gewerkschaft*

unique **23** *einzigartig*

unlikely **99T** *unwahrscheinlich*

unreasonable **116** *unangemessen*

unsavoury **129** *unappetitlich*

to upset sb **9T** *jdn verärgern, jdn aufregen*

urban **42** *städtisch, Stadt-*

urchin **53** *Straßenkind, Gassenjunge*

urgent **51** *dringend*

urgently **82** *dringend*

used, to be ~ to doing sth **24T** *gewohnt sein, etw zu tun*

utter **108T** *völlige/r/s*

V

vacant 31 *(Stelle:) offen*
valid 108T *berechtigt*
valley 36 *Tal*
value 12 *Wert*
variety 25 *Vielfalt, Abwechslung;* 112 *Vielzahl*
venue 50T *Veranstaltungsort*
venue 55 *Lokal*
vet 59 *Tierarzt/-ärztin*
vibrant 55 *lebendig, pulsierend*
victim 13 *Opfer*
view 63 *Ansicht, Meinung*
vinegar 14 *Essig*
violence 41 *Gewalt*
violent 41 *gewalttätig*
vital 105 *unverzichtbar*

vocational training 73 *Berufsausbildung*
volunteer 109 *ehrenamtlich*
voracious 65 *unersättlich, gierig*
vulnerable 60 *verletzlich, wehrlos*

W

wage 29 *Lohn;* **minimum ~** 28 *Mindestlohn*
war, civil ~ 90 *Bürgerkrieg*
warrior 38 *Krieger*
to **waste** 87 *verschwenden*
way, to **make ~ for sth** 55 *einer Sache weichen*
weakness 6 *Schwäche*
wealthy 12 *wohlhabend*
welfare 60 *Wohlergehen*
well-being 15 *Wohlbefinden*

whereby 23 *wonach*
whole, as a ~ 116 *insgesamt;* **on the ~** 63 *im Großen und Ganzen*
widespread 60 *weit verbreitet*
willingness 31 *Bereitschaft*
wire, razor ~ 97 *Stacheldraht*
wisdom 112 *Weisheit*
withdrawal 41 *Rückzug;* 81 *Entzug*
wits pl 53 *Verstand;* to **keep my ~ about me** 47 *meine fünf Sinne beisammen halten*
word of mouth 72 *Mundpropaganda*
workforce 114T *arbeitende Bevölkerung*
to **worry** 6 *sich Sorgen/Gedanken machen*
to **worsen** 19 *sich verschlimmern*
wounded 65 *verwundet*

189

IRREGULAR VERBS

be – was/were – been	*sein*
beat – beat – beaten	*schlagen, besiegen*
become – became – become	*werden*
begin – began – begun	*anfangen, beginnen*
behold – beheld – beheld	*erblicken,beobachten, sehen*
bind – bound – bound	*binden*
break – broke – broken	*brechen*
build – built – built	*bauen*
burn – burned/burnt – burned/burnt	*(ver)brennen*
buy – bought – bought	*kaufen*
cast – cast – cast	*(seine Stimme) abgeben; werfen*
catch – caught – caught	*fangen, verstehen*
choose – chose – chosen	*(aus)wählen*
come – came – come	*kommen*
cost – cost – cost	*kosten*
creep – crept – crept	*(ein)schleichen*
cut – cut – cut	*schneiden*
do – did – done	*tun, machen*
deal – dealt – dealt	*sich befassen; handeln; austeilen*
draw – drew – drawn	*zeichnen*
dream – dreamt – dreamt	*träumen*
drink – drank – drunk	*trinken*
drive – drove – driven	*fahren*
eat – ate – eaten	*essen*
fall – fell – fallen	*fallen*
feed – fed – fed	*füttern, ernähren*
feel – felt – felt	*(sich) fühlen, empfinden*
fight – fought – fought	*kämpfen*
find – found – found	*finden*
fit – fit/fitted – fit/fitted	*passen*
fly – flew – flown	*fliegen*
forget – forgot – forgotten	*vergessen*
freeze – froze – frozen	*(ge)frieren*
get – got – got (AE gotten)	*bekommen*
give – gave – given	*geben*
go – went – gone	*gehen, fahren*
grow – grew – grown	*wachsen*
hang – hung – hung	*hängen*
have – had – had	*haben*
hear – heard – heard	*hören*
hide – hid – hidden	*(sich) verstecken*
hit – hit – hit	*schlagen; treffen auf*
hold – held – held	*halten, festhalten*
hurt – hurt – hurt	*verletzen, weh tun*
keep – kept – kept	*behalten*
know – knew – known	*kennen, wissen*
lay – laid – laid	*legen*
lead – led – led	*führen*
learn – learnt/learned – learnt/learned	*lernen*
leave – left – left	*abfahren, verlassen, weggehen*
let – let – let	*lassen*

lie – lay – lain	*liegen*
light – lit – lit	*anzünden, beleuchten*
lose – lost – lost	*verlieren*
make – made – made	*machen*
mean – meant – meant	*meinen, bedeuten*
meet – met – met	*treffen*
pay – paid – paid	*bezahlen*
put – put – put	*setzen, stellen, legen*
quit – quit/quitted – quit/quitted	*verlassen, aufhören*
read – read – read	*lesen*
ride – rode – ridden	*reiten, fahren*
rise – rose – risen	*(an)steigen*
ring – rang – rung	*läuten, klingeln*
run – ran – run	*laufen, rennen*
say – said – said	*sagen*
see – saw – seen	*sehen*
seek –sought – sought	*suchen*
sell – sold – sold	*verkaufen*
send – sent – sent	*senden, schicken*
set – set – set	*setzen, stellen*
shake – shook – shaken	*schütteln*
show – showed – shown	*zeigen*
shut – shut – shut	*schließen*
sing – sang – sung	*singen*
sink – sank/sunk – sunk/sunken	*sinken*
sit – sat – sat	*sitzen*
sleep – slept – slept	*schlafen*
smell – smelt/smelled – smelt/smelled	*riechen*
speak – spoke – spoken	*sprechen*
spell – spelt/spelled – spelt/spelled	*buchstabieren*
spend – spent – spent	*ausgeben, verbringen*
spin – spun – spun	*sich drehen, herumwirbeln*
stand – stood – stood	*stehen*
steal – stole – stolen	*stehlen*
strive – strove/strived – striven/strived	*streben (nach)*
swim – swam – swum	*schwimmen*
take – took – taken	*nehmen*
teach – taught – taught	*unterrichten, beibringen*
tell – told – told	*sagen, erzählen*
think – thought – thought	*denken*
thrive – thrived/throve – thrived/thriven	*florieren*
throw – threw – thrown	*werfen*
understand – understood – understood	*verstehen*
wake – woke/waked – woken/waked	*aufwachen, wecken*
wear – wore – worn	*tragen*
win – won – won	*gewinnen*
write – wrote – written	*schreiben*

QUELLENVERZEICHNIS

Bildquellen:

S. 6: Shutterstock / antoniodiaz; S. 9: Shutterstock / MJTH; S. 10: Cartoonstock / Wilfred Hildonen; S. 12: Shutterstock / Viktorus; S. 15: OECD - Organisation for Economic Co-operation and Development ; S. 17: Alamy Stock Photo / Kuttig - People - 2; S. 18: Image Source / Jonathan Gibson; S. 19: Penguin Random House LLC; S. 20: Alamy Stock Photo / LatinStock Collection; S. 23: Glow Images / Superstock; S. 25/1: Cartoonstock / Kate Taylor; S. 25/2: Cartoonstock / Karsten Schley; S. 25/3: Cartoonstock / Scott Hilburn; S. 26/1: Shutterstock / jdrv; S. 26/2: Shutterstock / StockLite; S. 27/1: akg-images / Science Photo Library; S. 27/2: Shutterstock / Africa Studio; S. 27/3: International Labour Organization – ILO (www.ilo.org); S. 30/1: World Vision Canada; S. 30/2: Corbis / Christopher Morris www.christophermorris.co; S. 31: Shutterstock / YanLev; S. 33/1: Cartoon Stock / Gary Cook; S. 33/2: Cartoon Stock / Grizelda; S. 33/3: Shutterstock / Peshkov; S. 35: Alamy Stock Photo / Cultura Creative (RF); S. 37/1: laif / Sunset Box / Allpix; S. 37/2: Shutterstock / David Evison; S. 37/3: Shutterstock / verityjohnson; S. 37/4: Shutterstock / Khosro; S. 41/1: Cartoonstock / Alan Davies; S. 41/2: Alamy Stock Photo / Dermot Blackburn; S. 42: Alamy Stock Photo / Radharc Images; S. 44: Alamy Stock Photo / Thornton Cohen; S. 45: Cartoonstock / BryanBartholomev; S. 46/1: Shutterstock / Linda Parton; S. 46/2: Shutterstock / Joseph Sohm; S. 47: Shutterstock / ducu59us; S. 49: Shutterstock / Steve Lagreca; S. 50: Alamy Stock Photo / MARKA; S. 52: © Deutsche Welle / Gero Schließ; S. 53: Alamy Stock Photo / Heritage Image Partnership Ltd; S. 54/1: Shutterstock / Mr Pics; S. 54/2: Alamy Stock Photo / M&N; S. 54/3: Alamy Stock Photo / YAY Media AS; S. 54/4: Shutterstock / Sailesh Patel; S. 54/5: Shutterstock / Banana Republic images; S. 56/1: Cartoonstock / Gene Mora; S. 56/2: Cartoonstock / Gene Mora; S. 56/3: Cartoonstock / Gene Mora; S. 56/4: Cartoonstock / Gene Mora; S. 56/5: Cartoonstock / Gene Mora; S. 58: picture alliance / HERBERT P. OC; S. 60: Shutterstock / Val Thoermer; S. 63: Alamy Stock Photo / Robert Gray; S. 64/1: Cartoonstock / Kate Taylor; S. 64/2: Alamy Stock Photo / TC; S. 67: Shutterstock / Ekaterina Kirillina; S. 69: Shutterstock / Thinglass; S. 70: Shutterstock / Featureflash; S. 72: Charitybuzz Inc.; S. 74: action press / REX FEATURES LTD; S. 75/1: Shutterstock / Peshkova; S. 75/2: Shutterstock / Andreas Odersky; S. 78: Shutterstock / Yauhen_D; S. 80: Alamy Stock Photo / stockchildren; S. 81/1: Cartoon Stock / Jeff Stahler; S. 81/2: Shutterstock / Alexander Kockin; S. 85: Corbis / Richard Levine; S. 86/1: Alamy Stock Photo / PhotoAlto sas; S. 86/2: Alamy Stock Photo / Tetra Images; S. 86/3: Shutterstock / Sheftsoff Women Girls; S. 86/4: Shutterstock / Daniel M Ernst; S. 86/5: Shutterstock / Yeko Photo Studio; S. 86/6: Shutterstock / David Gilder; S. 90: Shutterstock / Claudio Divizi; S. 91/1: Shutterstock / David Pereiras; S. 91/2: Shutterstock / jdrv; S. 91/3: Shutterstock / DrimaFilm; S. 91/4: Alamy Stock Photo / Radharc Images; S. 91/5: Alamy Stock Photo / Ivy Close Images; S. 92/1: Alamy Stock Photo / Elena Elenaphotos21; S. 92/2: akg-images / Jan Luyken; S. 92/3: Alamy Stock Photo / Justin Kase zsixz; S. 92/4: akg-images / Sotheby's; S. 95/1: British Youth Council, London; S. 95/2: Shutterstock / Viacheslav Nikolaenko; S. 97: Shutterstock / Nagel Photography; S. 99: Fotolia / DDRockstar; S. 102: Shutterstock / Lucian Coman; S. 103/1: Shutterstock / Rob Wilson; S. 103/2: Alamy Stock Photo / lee avison; S. 104: akg-images / IAM; S. 106: Shutterstock / View Apart; S. 108: Shutterstock / Photographee.eu; S. 109: Shutterstock / Sofi photo; S. 112: Shutterstock / lev radin; S. 114: Cartoonstock / John Power; S. 115/# : Glow Images / Paul Tomlins / Eye Ubiquitous; S. 116: Photoshot / UPPA; S. 119: Alamy / MARKA; S. 121/1: Shutterstock / Fer Gregory; S. 121/2: Alamy Stock Photo / Lev Dolgachov; S. 121/3: Shutterstock / llaszlo; S. 121/4: Alamy / Tony Tallec; S. 121/5: Shutterstock / michaeljung; S. 121/6: Shutterstock / kurhan; S. 121/7: Shutterstock / karen roach; S. 122: Cartoonstock / Rick Enright; S. 123: Shutterstock / Everett Historical; S. 124: action press / Everett Collectio; S. 126: Caitlin Brown ; S. 127/1: Alamy Stock Photo / Vstock; S. 127/2: National Society for the Prevention of Cruelty to Children (NSPCC); S. 129: Alamy Stock Photo / Richard Green; S. 131/1: Cartoonstock/Betsy Streeter; S. 131/2: Cartoonstock/S. Harris; S. 131/3: Cartoonstock/Ron Therien; S. 132/1: Cartoonstock/Marty Bucella; S. 132/2: Cartoonstock/Aaron Bacall; S. 132/4: Cartoonstock/ Wilburn Dawbarn

Textquellen:

S. 17: Jane Bianchi, The Teen Who Woke Up Her School, The Huffington Post, 2014, used by permission; S. 19: Excerpted from Teen Angst? Nah…, by Ned Vizzini, copyright © 2000. Used with permission of Free Spirit Publishing Inc., Minneapolis, MN, 800-735-7323, www.freespirit.com, all rights reserved; S. 23: Patrick Barkham, The school where they speak 20 languages: a day at Gladstone Primary, The Guardian, 2013, used by permission; S. 31: Suzanne McFarlin, We Make It Easy for Our Children to Not Grow Up, The Huffington Post, 2014, used by permission; S. 36: Text: Knopfler, Mark, Copyright: Will D Side Ltd tj musicservice GmbH, Hamburg; S. 38: Gemma Hall, Northumberland: The heritage coast, Britain Magazine, 2013, used by permission; S. 41: Jack Sommers, Why Northern Ireland's 'Peace Walls' Show No Signs Of Following Berlin's , The Huffington Post, 2014, used by permission; S. 47: Aaron Foley, How To Explain Living In A Bankrupt City, 2013, http://detroit.jalopnik.com/how-to-explain-living-in-a-bankrupt-city-1305676331, used by permission; S. 50: Joyce Carol Oates, Copyright © 1988 Ontario Review, Inc. Reprinted by permission of John Hawkins & Associates, Inc.; S. 53: Ron S. King; S. 58: Celebrity, Text: Cooper, Charlotte Louise/ Morgan, Joshua Thomas/Morgan, William John / EMI Music Publishing Ltd., EMI Music Publishing Germany GmbH, Berlin; S. 75: James Delingpole, Is Digital Technology Sending Us Out Of Our Minds?, TIME online, 2014, used by permission; S. 81: Jemima Sissons, Time for a digital detox, BBC/Capitalist, 2014, used by permission; S. 87: Data adapted by WEEKlY REACH; S. 91: Kristiina Cooper, A brief history of the UK Parliament, 2014, used by permission; S. 97: Ronald W. Clark, Florida State Prison, used by permission; S. 97: by James Ridgeway and Jean Casella, adapted from an essay originally published by the Marshall Project, https://www.themarshallproject.org/2014/11/30/what-death-penalty-opponents-don-t-get; S. 103: Chris Cleave, I wish I was a British pound coin, Sceptre 2008, used by permission; S. 106: Text: Earle, Stephen Copyright: Exile on Jones Street, Music: Neue Welt Musikverlag GmbH, Hamburg; S. 112: Don Kaplan © Daily News, L.P. (New York), used with permission; S. 115: Judith Burns, Deeply elitist UK locks out diversity at top, BBC News, 2014, used by permission; S. 127: Sam Thomas, Eating disorders in children are soaring, but is the Internet really to blame?, The Huffington Post, 2014, used by permission; S. 129: Jon Kelly, Should anti-tattoo discrimination be illegal?

EUROPEAN UNION

0 100 200 300 400 500
km

ICELAND

NORWAY

SWEDEN
Stockholm

FINLAND
Helsinki

RUSSIA

ESTONIA
Tallinn

LATVIA
Riga

LITHUANIA
Vilnius

RUSSIA

BELARUS

DENMARK
Copenhagen

UNITED KINGDOM
London

IRELAND
Dublin

NETHER-LANDS
Amsterdam
Utrecht
Antwerp
Brussels

Rostock
Hamburg
Berlin

GERMANY
Cologne
Dresden
Frankfurt

Prague
CZECH REPUBLIC

POLAND
Warsaw

UKRAINE

BELGIUM
Luxembourg
LUXEM-BOURG

Rouen
Paris

Stuttgart
Strasbourg
LIECHTEN-STEIN
Munich
Innsbruck

SLOVAKIA
Bratislava

Vienna
AUSTRIA

Budapest

HUNGARY

MOLDOVA

ROMANIA
Bucharest

FRANCE

SWITZER-LAND

The Alps

SLOVENIA
Ljubljana

Genoa

Zagreb
CROATIA
BOSNIA-HERZE-GOVINA

SERBIA

MONTE-NEGRO
KOSOVO
MACE-DONIA

BULGARIA
Sofia

ANDORRA

SAN MARINO

MONACO

ITALY
Rome

ALBANIA

GREECE
Athens

PORTUGAL
Lisbon

Madrid
SPAIN

MOROCCO

ALGERIA

TUNISIA

Valletta
MALTA

LIBYA

TURKEY

Canary Islands (Spain)

Tenerife

MOROCCO

TURKEY

Nicosia
SYRIA

CYPRUS
LEBANON